First

Person,

First

Peoples

First Person, First Peoples

NATIVE AMERICAN

COLLEGE GRADUATES TELL

THEIR LIFE STORIES

EDITED BY ANDREW GARROD

AND COLLEEN LARIMORE

▼ ▼ ▼

Cornell University Press   Ithaca and London

First published 1997 by Cornell University Press.

First printing, Cornell Paperbacks, 1997.

Printed in the United States of America.

TCF This book is printed on Lyons Falls Turin Book, a paper that is totally chlorine-free and acid-free.

Library of Congress Cataloging-in-Publication Data

First person, first peoples : native American college graduates tell
   their life stories / edited by Andrew Garrod and Colleen Larimore.
       p.   cm.
   Includes bibliographical references.
   ISBN 0-8014-3383-5 (alk. paper). — ISBN 0-8014-8414-6 (pbk. :
alk. paper)
   1. Indians of North America—Education (Higher)—New Hampshire—
Hanover.   2. Indian college students—New Hampshire—Hanover—
Interviews.   3. Minority college graduates—New Hampshire—Hanover—
Interviews.   4. Dartmouth College.   Native American Program.
I. Garrod, Andrew, 1937–   . II. Larimore, Colleen, 1963–   .
E97.65.N4F57   1997
378.1'982997—dc21   96-40397

Cloth printing   10 9 8 7 6 5 4 3 2 1
Paperback printing   10 9 8 7 6 5 4 3 2 1

This book is dedicated first to the students, alumni, faculty, and staff of the Native American community at Dartmouth College, especially to those individuals who were kind and courageous enough to share their stories in this book. Many of the authors, when initially approached with the proposal to put their stories in print, refused because they did not feel their experiences and lives worthy of publication. What finally convinced most of them to undertake this project was their hope, and our hope, that these stories might somehow help others, especially young Native people who are considering pursuing their own goals through higher education.

I would also like to dedicate this book with love to my sisters, Maidie and Jan, and to my brother, Martin.
A. G.

I would like to dedicate this book with love and appreciation to my family: to my brothers and sister for their example, to the memory of my father, who was denied opportunity in his lifetime, and especially to my mother, who has made all things possible in mine.
C. L.

Contents

ix   Foreword by *Louise Erdrich*

xv   Preface

1   Introduction

WHEN WORLDS COLLIDE

23   Refuse to Kneel   *Bill Bray*

43   I Walk in Beauty   *Davina Ruth Begaye Two Bears*

64   A Tlingit Brother of Alpha Chi   *Ricardo Worl*

80   First Morning Light   *Gemma Lockhart*

PLANTED IN THE GROUND

93   My Grandmother and the Snake   *Nicole Adams*

115   I Dance for Me   *Elizabeth Carey*

136   Why Didn't You Teach Me?   *Robert Bennett*

154   The Web of Life   *Marianne Chamberlain*

COMING FULL CIRCLE

171   Coming Home   *Arvo Quoetone Mikkanen*

189   Machiavelli and Me   *Siobhan Wescott*

200   My Grub Box   *Vivian Johnson*

212   Full Circle   *Lori Arviso Alvord*

230   The Good Ol' Days When Times Were Bad   *N. Bruce Duthu*

249   About the Editors and Foreword Writer

251   Photograph Credits

Foreword

▼▼▼▼▼▼▼▼▼▼▼▼▼▼▼▼▼▼▼

LOUISE ERDRICH

        In the fall of 1971, my mother showed me a picture of one of Dartmouth's ice sculptures featured in a *National Geographic* magazine. One year later I entered the college, a bewildered freshperson in red cowboy boots, a member of the first class of women and Native Americans. Four years after, I left wearing a pair of resurrected moccasins, returned with my precious B.A. to North Dakota, ricocheted back and forth to the east coast, worked at urban Indian newspapers, and taught poetry. In 1981 I entered into college life again, married to Michael Dorris, the founder of the Native American Studies department, my former professor, then partner and colleague. How profoundly that picture of my mother's find, the ice sculpture—appropriately enough, the theme was Oz and the sculpture a towered city—affected my life.

This is a book of such stories. Everyone who enters the world of college has one, and many are gripping. But this book is the first to collect the voices of Native students. It is, in fact, a historical collection. One hundred years after the institution of the reservation system, after the predicted disappearance of Native peoples, after the centuries of all-out war and institutional racism, I am tremendously proud to introduce a book about the perseverance of Native life and knowledge.

Every Native American is a survivor, an anomaly, a surprise on earth. We were all slated for extinction before the march of progress. But surprise, we *are* progress. What was apparent to Native people long ago—the interrelatedness of earth and all its species—is slowly and painfully becoming part of world awareness. Collected here are the voices of young and vibrant people who have a deep connection to the older world, often a world of loss and heartache, but also a grounded and rich world based in rooted peace. For every student lucky and brave enough to go to Dartmouth, there are numberless cousins who will suffer hunger, unemployment, poverty, addiction, early death. That is the reality Native students bring to Dartmouth. And although Ivy League privilege and all of the trappings of wealth and class dazzle some, few are seduced into turning their backs on their extended families. One of the most remarkable things about Native students at Dartmouth is how many have returned to work in their communities.

Davina Begaye Two Bears's walk into beauty is a triumph of effort, love, and of course frybread! "Coming Home," by Arvo Quoetone Mikkanen, brings a youth lived in earnest, to benefit other Indian people, to a lovely conclusion in maturity. I am proud to know Arvo, as I am to know so many of the students represented in this collection, and I am moved by their honesty and sense of humor. Lori Alvord's staunch courage, her ability to take risks and her tenacity in seeing them through, give her story of persevering in medical school a weight that hit home for our family—as I write, my sister Angela Erdrich, having graduated from Dartmouth medical school, is finishing her residency and searching for a job in the Indian Health Service. Dr. Alvord's story also reminds me of one of the bravest people I know, Dartmouth graduate Dr. Eva Smith, a Native woman and an example of strength of spirit.

Gemma Lockhart is called to Dartmouth College by woods and streams, and survives there because of a deep response to her surroundings. As is the case with many Native students, she is followed to Dartmouth by a younger sibling—as I was by my sister Heid Erdrich, a writer committed to helping other Native artists and to teaching Native literature in her community. Thanks to the efforts of every single teacher and Native student who has ever been at Dartmouth, there is a growing family of such students, a frybread network of sisters, brothers, cousins, friends, fellow tribal members.

Vivian Johnson's essay, "My Grub Box," introduced one of my favorite metaphors for what we carry along to survive—the basic necessities for living, which vary from person to person, but within these stories are strikingly similar: reliance on community and an appreciation of the blessings of connection. Although each writer's background is vastly different from the next, although included are people of completely different tribal groups, mixed blood, full blood, students who speak their Native language and others who don't, their common ground is a need to integrate, a need to make sense of a world that does not include them, a need to return to places deeply longed for and understood.

Remarkable in a capitalist society, and yet perhaps not amazing given the sources, not a single narrative is about the wish to attain status, the ambition to make large amounts of money, or the desire to become famous. Instead, these students make a circular path, and even wind backwards down the generations, *come home.* They value their own traditions, even while exposed to an intensely attractive and bewildering set of new ideas and seductive materialism. They gain depth through the trials they face, academically and socially, at a demanding school. They long for mothers, fathers, sisters, brothers, and perhaps most of all, their grandparents, whose lives they feel diminishing in vigor as they themselves grow in strength.

Bruce Duthu writes a moving essay about his connection with his grandfather, Pe-pere, whose essential message was, in Bruce's words, "it wasn't a matter of succeeding or failing, but of assuming responsibility for my decisions." Tender and clearsighted, Nicole Adams gives us a picture of her grandmother's strength. She also provides a piercing analysis of family life, and speaks of the value of learning from elders. She calls upon the women she loves as guides all through her life, and confronts the painful reality of alcohol. Her grandmother's success in overcoming addiction changes her, and Adams makes it clear why pressure by college drinking groups, given the anguish alcohol causes in Native homes, is so terribly troubling.

Siobhan Wescott searches out and finds an intellectual community that has always remained important to her, and her heartfelt commemoration of her friend Stacey Coverdale is a testament to closeness and love. Bill Bray's piece is a proud travel narrative, stiff, combative, and poised. Again and again, his escape from overwhelming circumstances is to read, and that is also true of many other students. Ricardo Worl has an ability to bounce back from disappointments, and his positive and cheerful attitude is a joy and an example. Marianne Chamberlain speaks of her longing for the huge skies of her homeland, and relates a story of connection and commitment in spite of the frightening sexual harassment she faced and being at odds with other students over life values. The courage she drew from is the same well of feminine strength that Elizabeth Carey carries with her when she dances her traditional hula, finding in the expression of her cultural heritage great joy, freedom, and the warmth of communication. "If I could somehow express the idea in all of its essence with my motions, then the chant would take shape visually, and would come alive nourished by my heart and soul," Elizabeth Carey writes.

Often, these students are exhausted cultural emissaries, and each deals with stereotypes peculiar not only to Native Americans, but to his or her tribe. Explaining what it is to be Native, is, it seems, one of the tasks one takes on in becoming a Dartmouth student. As Gemma Lockhart points out, however, it is a job that affects the future of many Native people, for Dartmouth educates decision makers, leaders of our country, and the positive ripple effect of one Dartmouth Native explaining to other students what it is to be human is incalculable, and very important.

When Robert Bennett sets out to become a successful human, his values are so tuned to the *wasicu* or non-Indian world that he finds, in his painfully honest essay, that he has to relearn who he is and confront his own stereotypes about Indian people. "Why Didn't You Teach Me?" is one of the most honest accounts I've ever read of a Native person's search for identity, literally chilling, but gentle and rigorous. His loving relationship with his grandmother is life instruction for Bennett, an athlete who places a baseball in his grandmother's grave, sending it with her to the next world. I have thought often of Robert Bennett's loving gesture to his grandmother, for the final image is a beautiful vision of the two of them playing catch across time, space, through life and death, in a game that continues on.

Students often mention Michael Dorris, who founded the Native American Studies department. I cannot help but do the same. He gave himself utterly to the task, and used his tough humor, tenacity, and courage to make sure the program and the department would be of ongoing integrity. So it continues. Without him, there would be no voices to collect. Even in the most difficult of times, he's graced many others with his sharp wit and ability to listen and support. There are so many who made a difference. Colleen Larimore, Greg Prince, and Tony Quimby, financial aid officer, whose kind blue eyes, welcoming presence, and dedicated juggling of loans and bottom lines got so many students through the next and the next month at Dartmouth. John and Jean Kemeny had the courage to make real their vision, the kindness to continue on. They gave tremendous warmth and loving attention to many students, including me. Judy and David McLaughlin and, at present, Jim and Sheba Freedman have supported and cared for the program with graciousness and wisdom.

So many voices are included, so many missing.

My roommate Lydia Begay. Grace Newell, whose energy and purpose always gave heart to those around her and whose teasing reminded us of home. Duane Birdbear, Bruce Oakes, Dr. Cleora Hubbard, and again, Michael Dorris—all of whom were kind to this wide-eyed, chainsmoking, wild-haired, disorganized, red-booted young woman from North Dakota and managed, with their love and examples, to bring me through.

Preface

▼ ▼ ▼ ▼ ▼ ▼ ▼ ▼ ▼ ▼ ▼ ▼ ▼ ▼ ▼ ▼ ▼ ▼ ▼

In selecting contributions to this book, we have sought the life stories of Native American men and women in roughly equal numbers; to provide a cross section of age and experience, we solicited essays from some who were students at the time, others who had recently graduated, and still others who are well established in their careers. After initial discussions of the project and pertinent issues, we invited these friends and former students to write about their lives.

We asked them to reflect on their family and schooling before college, and to identify the factors that had helped or hindered them in the transition from home to college. We encouraged them to think about sources of their deepest joys and greatest fears in the college years, and to discuss profound learning experiences in and out of the classroom, their interactions with mentors, their friendships, and their activities within and outside of the Native American community. We asked them what influence their experiences in higher education had on their self-concept or cultural identity as Native Americans. And those who were a significant number of years beyond their college experience were encouraged to examine their current relationships with their home communities and to describe how higher education may have influenced those connections.

We made no assumptions about exactly where any one story might go; we encouraged our contributors to find their own voices, develop their own themes, and analyze their own experiences in ways that made sense to them. Our primary aim was not to call forth elegant prose, but simply to get the story out. We made no attempt to help the writers revise their work until they considered their stories finished. Our aim was to build up their confidence in the value of their stories and in their capacity to tell them compellingly. The variations in tone, degree of self-analysis, and the style of expression reflect our commitment to respect each writer's story and life. At the end of the process, most manuscripts ranged from forty to sixty pages long. We then discussed with the authors how their essays could be edited to the requisite page length. The entire process was collaborative.

We have, perhaps somewhat arbitrarily, divided the book thematically into three sections. The first part, "When Worlds Collide," touches on the cultural discontinuity many students experienced when they went from their home community to a college community, and how they attempted to reconcile these disparities during their college years. The second section, "Planted in the Ground," explores issues of Native identity and how that identity was challenged, shaped, or reinforced during or after college. Finally, "Coming Full Circle" details the authors' desires to give back to the Native community (whether defined as their own particular tribal group or Native Americans in general) by applying the skills they acquired through higher education. The majority of the essays by older contributors appear in this final section; these are the writers who have had more time to reflect on how the college experience honed their analytic skills, encouraged intellectual confidence, developed skills and traits they can call on to serve their Native communities, and taught them to be, in the words of Gemma Lockhart, "stronger than strong." Not coincidentally, these essays, with their authors' perspectives balanced by time and life experience, also seem to be the most positive about college and the opportunities it afforded. Perhaps Bill Bray explains the phenomenon best with his recognition that time and distance smooth away rough edges and rearrange perspectives; many alumni "remodel Dartmouth in [their] house of memory."

The African American writer James Baldwin speaks to the power of all minority testimonies when he says, "While the tale of how we suffer, and how we are delighted, and how we may triumph is never new, it always must be heard" (*Notes of a Native Son*). These are the kinds of stories for and about Native Americans that are rarely, if ever, recounted. Here they are told.

Any project that is three years in the making is likely to owe significant debts to those who have contributed in multiple ways to its realization. This book is no exception.

Special thanks for moral and administrative support are due to Michael Hanitchak, director of the Native American Program at Dartmouth College; Julie Ratico, the administrative assistant in this program; Linda Welch, the administrative assistant for Native American Studies; and Colin Calloway, Professor of Native American Studies.

Several friends—Karen Maloney, Shelby Grantham, Aassia Haroon, Stephanie Brown, Janet Webster, Jay Davis, Kari McCadam, and Sandra White—generously offered close readings and helpful editorial suggestions at different stages of the manuscript's preparation. My research assistant, Stuart Jordan, ever resourceful and cheerful, checked critical statistics and references and is owed my deep thanks. I thank three other Dartmouth students—Michael Weinberg, Frank Aum, and Kimberly Williams—for their intelligence, sound judgment, and editorial skills, all of which are very much reflected in the book. Their availability, computer dexterity, optimism, friendship, and genuine interest in the stories told in this volume immeasurably lightened the burden of its preparation. They were a joy to work with. I cannot thank Kimberly adequately for all her hard work—especially in refining the manuscript and assembling the book prior to publication submission. She was ably assisted by Kimberly Di Tomasso, Rachel Derkits, and Cabell King.

A. G.

My heartfelt appreciation goes out to Lakota/Gros Ventre elder and trainer Avis Archambault of the Rosebud Sioux Reservation and Scottsdale, Arizona; Dr. Candace Fleming of the Kickapoo and Oneida Nations and the National Center for American Indian and Alaska Native Mental Health Research at the University of Colorado at Denver; and psychologist in private practice Dr. Alethea Young, of the Cherokee Nation of Oklahoma and Hanover, New Hampshire. I owe a debt of gratitude to each of these remarkable individuals for the influence they have had on my life, the contributions they have made to the Native American community at Dartmouth, and the light that each has shed on the issues explored in this book. I also thank my partner, Margaret Worden, for her unwavering support, timely editorial suggestions, and enduring love.

C.L.

Finally, we thank Bernhard Kendler of Cornell University Press for his immediately enthusiastic reception of our book proposal and for his sustained and sustaining encouragement.

Hanover, New Hampshire

First

Person,

First

Peoples

▼ ▼ ▼ ▼ ▼ ▼ ▼ ▼ ▼ ▼ ▼ ▼ ▼ ▼ ▼ ▼ ▼ ▼ ▼

Introduction

First Person, First Peoples: Native American College Graduates Tell Their Life Stories contains stories of Native American college students struggling for survival on several planes—intellectual, emotional, physical, and spiritual—and striving for success on their own terms in a cultural setting not their own. The tie that binds the stories together is not that all the authors attended Dartmouth College or that they all successfully negotiated the way from entering freshman to college graduate. The crucial journey, both literal and figurative, is the one between their home communities and the culture that this predominantly white college represents. It is learning to walk this path in balance without losing oneself in the process that is vital. That each of our authors is now a Dartmouth College graduate is particularly noteworthy because Dartmouth, having been founded to educate Native Americans, had a truly dismal record in doing so for the first two hundred years of its existence. In the last twenty-five years, however, this mainly white Ivy League school has made a dramatic turnaround and now has one of the most successful Native American graduation records in the nation. It therefore stands as an example to other institutions not only of what *not* to do but also of what can be done.

Statistics reveal that for every hundred Native American students entering ninth grade, sixty will graduate from high school, about twenty will enter a postsecondary institution, and perhaps three will receive a four-year college degree (Tierney, 1992). The autobiographies in this book translate such statistics into human dimensions, each story unique and suggestive of a reality that we hope will push readers beyond the realm of their own experience. As a group, however, the Native student population at Dartmouth is representative; it is an accurate reflection of the percentages of Native people who have lived (and are living) lives that reflect the dismal social and economic realities—school attrition and substandard educational opportunities, alcohol abuse and addiction, suicide in adolescence and young adulthood, poverty and unemployment—that middle America has unfortunately come to associate with Native Americans. Statisticians use means and trends to construct a facsimile of an "average Native American college student," eliding the uniqueness that arises from individual variation—a uniqueness that can be captured only by first-person accounts.

Autobiographical narrative is becoming widely recognized as a powerful source of insight into development, and colleges and universities around the country are using narratives as case studies for courses in psychology, sociology, anthropology, ethnic studies, counseling, and human development. As Carol Witherell and Nel Noddings (1991) point out in *Stories Lives Tell: Narrative and Dialogue in Education*, narrative has the power not just to change the teller/writer but to affect the listener/reader as well. While exploring the authentic related experiences of others, we deepen our understanding of our own experience and of the worldviews that this experience helps to construct. This book tells the stories of unique individuals from a broad diversity of backgrounds who have overcome significant obstacles to beat the odds. These are the stories of how Native American students succeed, not how they fail.

The authors of the thirteen essays that appear in this book were selected from a pool of hundreds of students and alumni and are representative of the diversity of cohort, tribal affiliation, geographic location, and experience of Dartmouth's Native American community as a whole. All of the essays were written by Native Americans who were then students at Dartmouth College or had graduated from Dartmouth. Before they began this project, we asked them to consider their lives before college, including their family, community, and previous schooling. As editors, we were particularly interested in how students navigated the transition from home to college, and what factors aided or impeded that transition. One issue we asked all authors to address was the extent to which their years at Dartmouth affected their perceptions of themselves as Native Americans. Finally, we asked those who were out of college to reflect upon their relationships with their home communities and the impact their experience in higher education had on their links to those communities. It was the clash between the home community and the college that provided the starting point for most of these stories.

When Worlds Collide

When academics depict the often difficult experiences of Native American students at institutions of higher learning, many (e.g., Sidel 1994) evoke the image of an individual trying to walk between two worlds. This metaphor implies that in order to survive and participate successfully in mainstream culture, Native American students must learn an alien way to walk, talk, think, and act, behaving as themselves only when they are at home in the Indian world. This expectation places the burden of assimilation squarely on the shoulders of Native American students and can be, as the contributors to this book attest, brutalizing to one's identity and spirituality.

For many Native Americans, personal and cultural identity, as well as spirituality, are inextricably intertwined with connections to family, community, tribe, and homeland. This intricate web of interrelationships and the sustaining power of the values with which our authors were raised pushed them toward higher learning while at the same time pulling them back to their home communities. For some, the desire to pursue a college education came as much from a love of learning imparted to them by childhood role models as from a deep-seated need to disprove racist stereotypes of Native Americans as underachieving, unintelligent, and alcoholic. Common to all our contributors is the wish to use higher education to help their home community and the deeply rooted desire to contribute in some way to its cultural survival.

For Native students raised to think of themselves as parts of an interconnected whole, leaving home to attend college can cause intense feelings of loss and isolation. To separate oneself from this intricate tapestry of interconnections is to leave behind the entire fabric of one's identity. For many such students, college is the first place they have ever lived where being a member of one's particular clan or tribe, or coming from one's particular reservation or region of the country, means little or nothing to anyone else. All of these markers, once so suffused with meaning, are invisible or unintelligible to peers, professors, and deans. All signifiers are gone; so, in a very real sense, is the context of one's identity and place in the world.

Also missing for many Native students entering predominantly white institutions of higher learning is a system of values, beliefs, and expectations held in common with non-Native peers. It is during this time that many Native students begin to realize how divergent their home communities and upbringings are from the American mainstream. College life, like mainstream existence, is fragmented into separate components: academic or professional, personal, and social. What happens in the classroom or at work, on the playing field, in the dormitory, in the fraternity house, and elsewhere on campus is not designed or expected to affect the student's overall development in any important way. Students are expected and—to a large extent—encouraged by the institution and by the larger society to develop separate public and private personae and to pursue individual agendas.

At Dartmouth, as at countless other institutions of higher education, one's home life and upbringing are assumed to complement this particular philosophy of education and life. For many Native students, albeit to varying degrees, the opposite is often true. Native peoples have traditionally viewed health and personal development as inextricable parts of a complex whole; one's physical, intellectual, emotional, and spiritual aspects are seamlessly interwoven, and one can maintain health and well-being only by achieving balance among all of them. To be healthy, one must have access to caretakers (such as medicine men and women, other elders, and members of the immediate and extended family) whose knowledge, training, and life experiences overlap and interact with one another.

In the dominant society and on mainly white college campuses, this type of holistic care is virtually nonexistent. A student who is suffering from a physical ailment, emotional turmoil, or a crisis in faith must seek out a variety of professionals whose training and areas of specialty rarely, if ever, overlap. Similarly, by the standards of the dominant culture, a college that furnishes young people with only intellectual opportunities is assumed to be providing them with an education. In a Native sense, however, providing instruction for growth in one area without attending to the others leaves an individual out of balance. As Elizabeth Carey writes in her essay, many Native students who express dissatisfaction with Dartmouth are often simply asking for the *rest* of their education: those aspects of learning that go beyond intellectual experiences in the classroom to shed light on the interconnection between mind and heart, body and spirit.

The clash in cultural values is also felt inside the classroom and is complicated by rural, reservation, and inner-city backgrounds that leave many Native American students educationally underprepared to compete at selective institutions. Increasingly in this country, the quality of education one receives is determined by where one lives. Public schools are integrated by law, but integration—itself an unrealized dream in many parts of the United States—does not guarantee equality of educational opportunity. Good teachers are hard to recruit and even harder to retain at schools that are underfunded and overcrowded. Developing the learning potential of students all too often takes a backseat to managing classroom behavior, and in such settings the failure of Native American (and other minority) students is not problematic, it is expected.

Even for those relatively few Native students who overcome lowered expectations and a lack of college preparation, the battle is far from over once they enter college. More than one of every three students at Dartmouth has attended a private secondary school.

Obviously, earning stellar grades in reservation and inner-city schools is not the same as earning them at preparatory academies such as Andover and Exeter. As Nicole Adams says, however, many Native students do not discover the difference until they are faced with it in a college classroom. Rote learning, memorization, and regurgitation of facts enabled them to garner top marks in public high school, but in college they find that critical thinking, analytical reading, independent research, and twenty- to thirty-page papers written in formal academic prose are the required minimum. Many Native students must not only learn large amounts of unfamiliar material quickly; they must also acquire a new set of academic skills with which to master new information. They must move, in William Perry's terms (1981), from a dualistic epistemology in which there are right/wrong answers and authority is located outside of the self to a more relativistic way of knowing, where authority resides within the self and knowledge is viewed as personally constructed. Academic success at an institution such as Dartmouth depends on the student's ability to achieve a relativistic way of thinking.

Ironically, class discussion in small groups, one of the hallmarks of a Dartmouth education—and, not coincidentally, of preparatory school education—captures in a nutshell the cultural clash between mainstream and traditional Native values. In these informal settings, the professor often becomes a participant in the discussion rather than its leader, and students are expected to demonstrate knowledge by engaging one another in academic dialogue and even debate. As Lori Arviso Alvord writes, Navajos have social taboos against competing as individuals and attracting undue attention to themselves in a group. This is the way many Native societies try to orient children toward such traditional values as cooperation, harmony, and humility. From this cultural perspective, the competitive behavior encouraged and even required in many college classrooms is immodest, inappropriately aggressive, and even selfish because it works against the group's (versus the individual's) efforts to master new skills.

Native students rarely articulate the clash of cultural values they experience in the classroom, and it is virtually invisible to non-Native peers and professors. Silence on the part of Native students is often misinterpreted as lack of interest or even of intelligence. As Arvo Mikkanen points out, many Native students assume that because white classmates appear more poised and eager to express their opinions in class, they must be brighter. In fact, white students and prep school graduates may simply be culturally conditioned to speak up and display what they know in a classroom (Mehan 1981). Nevertheless, Native students sometimes jump to the conclusion that they are "admissions office mistakes," and many nonminority students surmise that Native Americans (and other minorities) are affirmative action cases. These misperceptions shortchange Native students who have achieved outstanding records, albeit often at subpar high schools, and fail to take into account the other "minorities" who receive special consideration in the admissions process—recruited athletes, musicians, artists, and invisible minorities such as the children of alumni and of potential donors to the institution.

History of Native Americans at Dartmouth College

That so many Native Americans' dreams of pursuing a higher education should lead them to Dartmouth College in the first place is ironic, for until fairly recently the "Indian heritage" most often associated with this institution was largely a misnomer. True, Dartmouth College, like Harvard and Princeton universities and the College of William and Mary, was founded in part to educate Native Americans. According to Dartmouth's charter, granted by King George III of England in 1769, the college was established "for the education and instruction of youth of the Indian tribes in the land in reading, writing and all parts of learning which shall appear necessary and expedient for civilizing and Christianizing children of pagans as well as . . . English youth and any others." It was the belief of Eleazar Wheelock, Dartmouth's founder, that once Native Americans were converted to Christianity and trained as missionaries, they would be much more successful than non-Native missionaries in efforts to Christianize the members of their tribes. It is less well known that Wheelock actually opened two schools in Hanover, New Hampshire, in 1769. As well as founding Dartmouth College, he relocated Moor's Charity School from Lebanon, Connecticut, to the Dartmouth campus. Segregated and unequal, the former Moor's School was for the Indians; otherwise, Dartmouth was reserved for the sons of Englishmen.

Wheelock's first Indian student, Samson Occum, campaigned

throughout Europe to raise the £12,000 with which Wheelock launched his academic endeavor. To Occum's dismay, and without the knowledge of the college's benefactors abroad, Wheelock placed growing emphasis on the education of white students. By 1829, his original commitment to Native American education was completely forgotten (Blodgett 1935). When the true state of affairs at Dartmouth became known, many foreign benefactors withdrew their support, but by that time the college had accumulated an endowment that was more than adequate to ensure its survival. Wheelock and his successors did virtually nothing to honor the founding mission of the college, and by 1969 Dartmouth had graduated just nineteen Native Americans.

It was not until 1970 that a president of Dartmouth, newly inaugurated John Kemeny, reaffirmed the college's commitment to Native American education and pledged to recruit and enroll a significant number of Native students. To carry out that pledge, President Kemeny established the college's Native American Program (NAP) and directed the admissions office to begin actively recruiting Native American students. What the first class of Native students encountered when they entered Dartmouth that fall was an institution that had been insulated from the influence of significant numbers of Native Americans for nearly two centuries.

By 1970, the college and campus culture had mythologized much of its own Indian history and manufactured a variety of so-called Indian traditions. Newly enrolled Native students rightly pointed out that the Indian symbol and mascot, the breaking of "Indian peace pipes" at pregraduation celebrations, and the depiction of drunken and half-naked Indian men and women in the mythical representation of the college's founding in the Humphrey (or Hovey) murals, to name but a few Dartmouth icons, were not derived from any Native cultures; they represented nothing but fantasies. In 1970, however, the campus community was not prepared to heed the protests of its newest students, and it only recently has begun to reexamine and relinquish those traditions that many present-day Native students still find objectionable.

Then, as now, many Native students were struck by the irony in the college's governance: having gone to great effort to recruit them, it was clinging to traditions that fostered a student culture that alienated them. The "Indian" was never adopted as the official symbol of the college. Nevertheless, the Indian symbol and the students and alumni who champion it are still a source of anguish for many Native students at Dartmouth. As Bob Bennett writes in his account, Native students are often made to feel like invited but unwelcome guests of the college. Another contributor sees in the Indian symbol a not so subtle reminder that some students and alumni would rather have the Dartmouth Indian than real Indians on campus.

Many Native Americans are unable to fathom why non-Native people fail to equate the use of Native Americans as mascots with unacceptable bigotry aimed at blacks, Jews, or women. As has been pointed out time and again at Dartmouth and elsewhere, such hypothetical mascots as the "Washington White Trash," "Atlanta Niggers," and "Cleveland Jewboys" would simply not be tolerated today. According to Gemma Lockhart, "Dartmouth Indians" has the same visceral impact as those other epithets would have: it is "a kick to the stomach" to those on the receiving end.

Many non-Native people, for their part, cannot comprehend why Native Americans take offense at being used as mascots by college and professional athletic organizations. As Bruce Duthu points out, the situation at Dartmouth is even more complex, because the Indian symbol has itself become a symbol for many other controversial issues: the admission of minority and female students; the establishment of women's and ethnic studies programs; the more visible and vocal presence of gay, lesbian, and bisexual students on campus; and still others. For people dissatisfied with the changes of the past twenty-five years or so, the controversy surrounding the Indian symbol serves as a marker in time between the "old" and the "new" Dartmouth.

Interestingly, the Indian symbol controversy is a double-edged sword for Native American students. On the one hand, it exponentially complicates for them the process of developing their identities. While they attempt to reconcile the traditional Native values they were raised with and the mainstream values that prevail at Dartmouth, they must reaffirm who they are. And while they rebel against the stereotypical Indian identity imposed on them from the outside, they must affirm who they are *not*. On the other hand, if education can be equated with community discussion about a particular topic, we can presume that much more education about Native Americans takes place at Dartmouth than at any college that is not embroiled in a controversy about an Indian symbol. Education does not come without a cost, however; many Native students become nearly full-time educators as they try to make Dartmouth a more bearable place to live. In doing so, they must grapple with not only garden-variety ignorance but overt racism. As Bill Bray writes, the Indian symbol in itself cannot hurt Native students, because a caricature is not who or what they are. It is the people who persist in supporting the Indian symbol after being told that their actions are hurtful who make Dartmouth "a smaller, darker place for all."

Planted in the Ground

How, then, has Dartmouth, of all places, succeeded where so many other institutions have failed (or failed to try) to redress the historical lack of educational opportunity for Native Americans? Part of the answer is institutional commitment. Dartmouth's admissions office has helped the college achieve a critical mass of 138 Native students on campus in 1996 and more than 300 Native Americans from over 120 tribes in the alumni body. Dartmouth's undergraduate population of over 4,000 is nearly 3.3 percent Native American, whereas only 180 of the country's 3,000 colleges and universities have Native student enrollments of as much as 2 percent, and most of them are two-year and public institutions.

At Dartmouth and around the country, however, retaining Native students remains one of the biggest challenges facing college student support services. According to a report issued by the American Council on Education in 1992, more than half of all Native students who enter college leave after their first year. Retention services are crucial during this period in which old support systems seem far away and ineffectual and new supports are not yet in place. Dartmouth's Native American Program provides academic advice and personal counseling, acts as advocate and teacher to students who are learning for the first time how to navigate a maze of administrative bureaucracy, assists students in organizing events to raise campus consciousness about Native cultures and contemporary issues, and plans intragroup events aimed at sustaining Native students' cultural identity and spirituality.

According to the contributors to this book, of all the services offered by Dartmouth's NAP, perhaps the most vital is the provision of a safe environment in which to wrestle with larger identity issues. Young people of college age face important choices—who they want to be, how to relate to others, and what values should guide them. In Erik Erikson's terms (1950), adolescents have entered a psychological moratorium, a hiatus between childhood security and adult independence, a period when they must undergo crisis in order to define their commitments. This process takes on added significance and involves additional turmoil for members of minority groups (Garrod et al., 1995).

Cultural dissonance, academic setbacks, financial difficulties, and assaults on identity and self-esteem often cause depression in Native students. If no intervention takes place, depression can rapidly lead to a variety of self-defeating behaviors, most commonly alcohol and drug abuse, fighting, rape, suicide, reckless driving, unsafe sexual activity, impulsive theft, and truancy (Fleming 1992). At Dartmouth, because an intervention program is in place to combat the root causes of depression, nearly 75 percent of Native students persist and graduate, as compared with the national average graduation rate for Native American college students of 15 percent (Deskins 1987). At colleges that do not provide such support services, a good many Native students who leave before graduation do not merely receive failing grades or quit; they simply self-destruct.

Many Native students enter college wanting very much to fit in and participate in the larger peer society, but end up straining mightily to resist the dominant culture and its values. For those Native students raised in cultures that stress community, cooperation, patience, and humility as ideals, conformity to a campus culture that stresses looking out for number one, competition, assertiveness, and self-concern does not feel right; but then, neither does sticking out like the proverbial sore thumb. Marianne Chamberlain writes that locking away one's spirituality and heritage to gain a sense of belonging at Dartmouth is like pretending to be something one is not. The strain of putting on such a performance day in and day out exacts a huge toll, for Native students have constantly to guess what others expect them to be.

The less Native students are aware that others around them are playing by a different set of social and moral rules, the more confused, angry, alienated, and off balance (emotionally, physically, and spiritually) they can become. A Native American program must be in place to help these students articulate the values with which they were raised and identify those contradictions that trouble them in the larger campus culture. Students must realize that people of another culture often proceed from vastly different assumptions as to what makes a successful student, a functional community member, and a good and decent human being. Once Native students recognize that a predominantly white college is not run according to a Native American cultural frame of reference, they can begin to use their own upbringing and beliefs as a moral compass with which to navigate a path through school. Native American programs can help by providing students with opportunities to reaffirm their cultural identities. It is also vital that these programs, underfunded and understaffed as many may be, spearhead efforts to change the institutional culture of their campuses so that maintaining cultural integrity and earning a college degree will not be mutually exclusive goals.

Like the Native American Program, the college's Native American Studies (NAS) Program has had a profound impact on the lives, learning, and staying power of Native American students. The creative force behind the development of Dartmouth's fledgling NAS program was Michael Dorris, a Modoc anthropologist, who served as its first chair. Since 1972, NAS has provided undergraduates with a wide array of course offerings, as well as research and internship opportunities designed to expose students to Native history, cultures, and contemporary issues. In the process, it has received national recognition and acclaim as one of the finest programs of its kind.

To most Native students, as well as their non-Native classmates, NAS courses afford a first penetrating look at the 40,000 years of indigenous history that unfolded before the arrival of Columbus, at accounts of first contact between European and Native peoples that diverge from those taught in the vast majority of primary and secondary schools, and at the complexity of the social, political, and economic challenges facing tribes today. The irony of having to learn Native American history and contemporary social problems from a Native perspective in college courses taught largely by non-Native American professors is not lost on these students. Not surprisingly, NAS courses awaken intense dissatisfaction in many Native students. Part of their anger is aimed at the schools they attended earlier: why did they never teach these things? As Bob Bennett writes in his essay, however, some students aim their frustration at the families and communities that were equally silent about the things they are learning only now. Both sources of frustration lead many Native students to return home armed with newly articulated questions about their own tribal histories, cultures, and families.

For most Native students NAS courses also represent the first time that any teacher has considered Native American studies to be a serious academic subject worthy of consideration by non-Native students as well as by scholars. This is the first opportunity many Native students have had to share their own cultures with other students in an academic setting. It is also the first time most of them have looked at Native cultures and contemporary issues through the lens of academic inquiry. Intentional or not, this affirming combination of firsts helps many Native students attach meaning to their education at Dartmouth and exposes them to a multitude of possible choices for career through which they can contribute to their home communities.

Institutional commitment aside, the other reason why Dartmouth has met with success in Native American education has to do with the character and resolve of its Native students. Without exception, the authors of this book identify the source of their inner strength as the love and support of their families and communities. Lessons learned as they were growing up proved to be the most sustaining when they faced the challenges they describe in this book. Native students at predominantly white colleges do not have the luxury of an unexamined life, a luxury that is afforded to most of their non-Native classmates. Those Native Americans who choose schools such as Dartmouth are challenged at every turn by the probing questions of others, as well as by their own need to know more about their tribal cultures. For these authors, public scrutiny and private introspection ultimately reinforced rather than weakened their cultural values. The role models they chose in college were those who resonated most with the people they knew in childhood, as witness Gemma Lockhart's tribute to the professors and mentors who valued aspects of life she had been taught to appreciate as she was growing up in South Dakota. The students adapted the survival skills they learned at home—their "grub boxes," to borrow a phrase from Vivian Johnson's narrative—to fit a new situation, and so were able to persist at Dartmouth and succeed according to their own values.

One of the most powerful of those survival skills is an ability to create community. As Siobhan Wescott writes, most Native students quickly realize that it is the strength of their families that has gotten them to college in the first place, so they seek a substitute for that support system in Native American student organizations. Native Americans at Dartmouth (NAD) provides many, but not all, with relief from the alienation they experience in the larger student community. Together, students from numerous tribal nations, from reservation, rural, urban, and suburban backgrounds, learn the art of compromise. Such compromise occurs each year at Dartmouth, when students, some as culturally different from one another as Swedes and Zulus, collaborate to organize a pow wow; they learn to value one another's differences and strengths and come to recognize these differences as a vital part of their education. At their best, these students are masters at creating community out of diversity—a skill that college campuses, as well as the nation as a whole, would do well to learn.

NAD provides some Native students with a refuge from the ignorance and intolerance sometimes found in the larger college community. As Marianne Chamberlain and others point out, however, it is not immune to many of the same flaws and failings. Within the Native student community, too, there is racism, as light-skinned Native students with some white ancestry can attest. Ethnocentrism is evident among peoples of different tribes or groups (American Indians and Native Hawaiians, for example). Some Native men display sexism, denigrating Native women in positions of leadership as "nontraditional." And students who are openly gay, lesbian, or bisexual are sometimes subjected to homophobia. In this regard, NAD is but a microcosm of larger Native communities (and society as a whole). Students bring with them from home a wide variety of strengths and weaknesses; they hold values that sustain and unite as well as attitudes that denigrate and divide.

According to Lakota/Gros Ventre elder and trainer Avis Archambault (1992), the flip side of the racism to which Native people are subjected is the internalized oppression that Native Americans inflict on themselves and on one another. Internalized oppression occurs on an individual level when Native students incorporate negative beliefs about Native Americans into their own self-image, thereby holding themselves back with self-defeating attitudes and behaviors. It also occurs when Native students incorporate these negative beliefs into an image of Native Americans as a group, then use that distorted image to oppress other members of the group. While it is relatively easy to identify the racist stereotypes of Native Americans held by people of other races, it is exceedingly difficult for Native students to admit, even to themselves, that these stereotypical images of Native Americans as unmotivated, unintelligent, alcoholic, and dependent have also helped to shape their attitudes toward themselves and their own people.

Native students who direct internalized oppression at their peers often do so in an attempt to uphold cultural integrity or to preserve group unity. In other words, a Native student should not be highly motivated to study and earn high grades at Dartmouth because it is a "white college." A Native student should party hard and drink with other Native Americans to show solidarity with the Native community. Native students should socialize only with other Native Americans, or run the risk of being perceived as "acting white" or as thinking that they are too good for their own people. Native students who feel compelled to administer or pass the test of who is or is not a "real Indian" often succeed only in turning the negative stereotypes of Native Americans into self-fulfilling prophecies.

Whether it is aimed at oneself or at others, internalized oppression is a significant obstacle to retaining individual Native students in college and to sustaining community among groups of Native Americans. On a personal level, as Davina Begaye Two Bears and other authors attest, oppression or rejection experienced at the hands of other Native people is by far the most devastating, because many Native students view the Native student community as their best or last hope for attaining a sense of belonging at college. At a community level, this type of oppression is enormously destructive because it suggests that the dominant campus culture is not the only thing that holds Native student communities back; to a significant degree, they may be doing it to themselves.

Coming Full Circle

According to many of our authors, the wish to contribute to their home communities is what inspired them to attend college in the first place. However, when faced with the prospect of a four-year education that seemed to have little immediate relevance to their lives and cultures, some lost this sense of purpose. As Ricardo Worl writes, the individualistic goal of earning a degree to acquire job skills and a lucrative position after graduation is not enough to sustain many Native students. This attitude is especially prevalent when Native students equate a college education with assimilation into the dominant culture. As dropout statistics attest (Tierney, 1993), most vote with their feet and leave school rather than compromise their cultural identities. Many of the authors talk about a specific turning point when they realized that, though they had little control over the form and content of their college education, they could decide what significance it was going to hold for them and their communities. For these young people, education no longer represented a one-for-one replacement of tribal identity with mainstream identity, but rather an opportunity to gather and sharpen tools to ensure Native American cultural survival.

Native peoples have survived since ancient times not by staying the same but by adapting their cultures to suit their changing circumstances. The only difference between the adaptations that took place in the first forty-odd millennia and those that have taken place in the last five centuries is that before contact with Europeans Native peoples decided for themselves which elements of their cultures would be saved and which would be changed or discontinued. The power to decide, or self-determination, is the fine line that separates cultural adaptation from cultural assimilation. Young Native American professionals are using Western economics, politics, law, medicine, anthropology, and even education to try to regain this basic right of self-determination for their tribes. The ways in which they were able to reframe their educational experience and rediscover their sense of purpose hold much significance for Native American college students struggling with the same issues today.

The voices of the Native people in this book are unique, because they portray unique individuals; but they are also representative, touching on themes common to Native American college students across the country. The conclusion the authors draw about their educational experiences have direct implications for Native students, their families, and their communities, as well as for the colleges they attend. The premise behind the popular image of Native college students trying to walk between two worlds—Indian and white—in their efforts to succeed in higher education must be reexamined. Colleges that expect Native students to drop seventeen or eighteen years of cultural identity formation and moral development at the doorstep in order to receive the benefits of a formal education are doomed to failure. Statistics clearly show that the overwhelming majority of Native students would rather sacrifice their educational goals than abandon their cultural identities and values (Tierney 1993). The onus, then, is on educational institutions to learn the hard lessons of the past few centuries and respond appropriately.

Through changes in classroom instruction and pedagogy, administrative practice and policy, colleges and universities must show Native students that what they have been taught in their tribal cultures and what they bring with them to the educational process are useful and worthy of keeping and developing. It is not enough to use institutional power to keep a relatively few Native students from falling through the cracks. Power must be shared with Native students, their families, and their communities, as well as with Native faculty, administrators, and alumni. Colleges and universities cannot take the attitude of "What can we do for you?" because, to paraphrase the sociologist Charles Willie (1987), dominant-culture schools cannot do for Native people what they must do for themselves. Native Americans must be the ones to decide which features of the tribal and dominant cultures can coexist and which ones must be recast and adapted. Once admitted into the decision-making process, Native people will seek to change, or indigenize, those institutions of which they become a part.

The dramatic turnaround at Dartmouth College is not due solely to the benevolence of an educational institution that has rededicated itself to its founding mission. Dartmouth has succeeded in Native American education to the extent that it has allowed itself to be changed by Native Americans. Slowly but surely, with each new generation of students Dartmouth seems to be learning that it is not enough simply to open its door in the expectation that the Native Americans who enter will abandon their cultural identities like unwanted baggage. The college has demonstrated its institutional commitment by inviting Native students, alumni, faculty, and staff, albeit at times begrudgingly, to shape as well as partake in the educational process. And in doing so the college has revitalized itself and made its campus better suited for a student body that will become ever more culturally diverse in the new millennium.

Many Native American families and communities fear that when their children go away to predominantly white colleges, they will lose their cultural identity. Colleges such as Dartmouth, however, actually lead Native students to want and need to know more, not less, about their tribal heritage. At college, their identities and values are challenged and questioned in ways they once could not have imagined. The contributors to this book discovered that much of what they needed to know to stay in college could be found in the lessons learned and values instilled in them during childhood. In a very real sense, knowing who one is can afford the greatest capacity for resilience and resourcefulness, and only Native American families and communities can provide students with this unmatched asset.

These thirteen narratives afford us a glimpse of a new way in which Native students may negotiate the difficult journey between home and college, tribal culture and dominant culture. Walking between two worlds is a balancing act better suited to a circus aerialist performing on a high-wire than to a young Native American trying to survive at a predominantly white college. Through their eyes and in their words, the authors help us begin to see that maybe there is but one world after all, and that Native American cultural identity has endured for a reason. Native American students must trust that the identities they inherit, the values they are taught, and the spirits they are born with will serve them well no matter where life's journey may take them—whether at home, in ceremony, at school, or on the job. And it is only by reaffirming their sense of self and place in this world and in history that Native American families and communities can help their young people learn to find their way in this life.

REFERENCES

Archambault, A. "Racism and Internalized Oppression." Unpublished manuscript. Scottsdale, Ariz., 1992.

Baldwin, J. *Notes of a Native Son.* Boston: Beacon, 1953.

Blodgett, H. *Samson Occum,* p. 135. Brattleboro, Vt.: Stephen Daye Press, 1935.

Deskins, D. *Minority Recruitment Data.* Totowa, N.J.: Rowman & Allenheld, 1987.

Erikson, E. *Childhood and Society.* New York: Norton, 1950.

Fleming, C. "American Indian and Alaska Native Students at Dartmouth College—Mental Health and Substance Abuse Needs." Report to the Native American Program at Dartmouth College, 1992.

Garrod, A., L. Smulyan, S. Powers, and R. Kilkenny. *Adolescent Portraits: Identity, Relationships, and Challenges.* 2nd ed. Boston: Allyn & Bacon, 1995.

Mehan, H. "Ethnography of Bilingual Education." In *Culture and the Bilingual Classroom*, ed. H. Trueba, G. Guthrie, and K. Au. Rowley, Mass.: Newbury House, 1981.

Perry, W. "Cognitive and Ethical Growth: The Making of Meaning." Chickering, A., ed. *The Modern American College.* San Francisco: Jossey-Bass, 1981.

Sidel, R. *Battling Bias.* New York: Penguin, 1994.

Tierney, W. G. *Official Encouragement, Institutional Discouragement: Minorities in Academe—The Native American Experience.* Norwood, N.J.: Ablex, 1992.

——. "College Experience of Native Americans: A Critical Analysis." In *Beyond Silenced Voices: Class, Race, and Gender in United States Schools*, ed. L. Weis and M. Fine. Albany: SUNY Press, 1993.

Willie, C. V. *Effective Education: A Minority Policy Perspective.* Westport, Conn.: Greenwood Press, 1987.

Witherell, C., and N. Noddings, eds. *Stories Lives Tell: Narrative and Dialogue in Education.* New York: Teachers College Press, 1991.

When Worlds Collide

▼▼▼▼▼▼▼▼▼▼

BILL BRAY

Refuse to Kneel

          I am supposed to acquaint you with the Indian experience. I will apologize right now. There is no Indian experience with which to acquaint you. This is my experience and I happen to be Creek Indian. The two things are not interchangeable and not equal. The best I can hope for is to give you an experience that is slightly off the beaten track.

          I am from Oklahoma. It is not at all the part of the country that you probably think of when the "Sooner State" crosses your mind, if it ever does. You are, no doubt, thinking of west Texas. My Oklahoma is a land of softly rolling hills and rich farmland. In my backyard, I have grown tomatoes as big as your cantaloupes and sweetcorn that bursts in your mouth. I have eaten as many as twenty ears at a sitting. We have peach trees and apple trees, mulberries and persimmons. But most remarkable, perhaps, is that we have locust trees.

These trees are part of the odd family of temporarily glorious trees. For most of the year, they look like a pile of overgrown shrapnel: dark and thorny with small oblong leaves, the size of a dime, growing in clusters. But in the spring, they bloom. Millions of tiny white flowers with a fragrance that would kill a rose with envy. Locust trees surrounded our house, bringing shade and protecting us from the brutal northern wind and the searing Oklahoma sun. And Mama hated them.

My mother hated many things for many reasons, but her hate of the locust trees was one of the most strange. She hated them for their beauty. She hated the blossoms and said that the flowers were cheap and small, but most of all, she hated the fragrance. "It makes me sick," she used to say. Mama had a problem with cheap things, my father included. Mama fought a war against the locust trees. It was a war that she was destined to lose for one very important reason: I was a subversive firmly in the camp of the locust trees.

Locust trees were a good ally for me to choose. They are vibrantly alive and reproduce in rapid secrecy. They send runners underground and can spring up in clusters in a week. Mama bought a heavy lawnmower and would send me out to mow them down. I would mow some of them, but I would always manage to leave three or four under the fence line or next to rocks. I could always claim that I couldn't get close enough. In a month, they would grow enough so that no mower would be able to chop them down.

I realize that I may have made my mother sound harsh and brutal, but that is only occasionally true. That is a one-dimensional view of her, and if anything can be said about my mother, it is that she is multifaceted. Mama has been married three times to three different men. Now this is an important distinction to be made, because in my part of Oklahoma people like to get married and will often marry and divorce the same person over and over just to alleviate boredom. In a good year, I have known the same couple to get divorced and remarried three or four times. My stepmother once pondered the idea of giving everyone gift certificates for a free divorce for Christmas. But, I was talking about Mama—

my stepmother, Billye, is too complex a person to be taken on in passing.

Mama's first marriage was to my father. It was not a wonderful thing, although it did have its moments. In its most rudimentary form, this marriage was created out of a bit of bad luck. The first time my father and mother slept together she got knocked up. Due to the barbaric society of the time, wedding bells of course began to ring. My mother says, "When I first found out I was pregnant, I seriously considered jumping off a building. But then I thought that with my luck I would be pregnant with two broken legs. And few things could possibly be worse than being pregnant, crippled, and living with your grandfather." So much for the "Gidget Gets Married" scenario.

In spite of this, my mother and father did not marry at an exceptionally young age. She was seventeen and he was nineteen. That is still about the average where I am from. There is an old saying that goes something like, "A bride is not a bride without a little bulge." I could mention that my wife was bulging a little, too, but that would be jumping ahead in the story and might make you overly anxious.

My father is generally a very self-contained man with a great sense of propriety. My mother used to say, "your father is the most civilized man I know." To her, "civilized" was an epithet. I must agree that he is civilized sometimes, but his exterior can fool you. When my mother divorced him, he drove his truck into the community center through the front door, executed a right-hand turn that people say must have been almost impossible, and then drove out through the side door. Now I think that we were all fortunate that he did this at ten at night when there was no one in the center. All he had to do was pay for new doors for the center and get his truck repainted. He was a very passionate man, but he did not know how to express it properly. My father was (and still partially is) crippled; he does not really know how to express love. This was the reason that I hated him for many, many years; this and the fact that after her divorce, my mother's bitterness toward him grew exponentially for years until she had no concept of him as a person. Instead, he became for her a stereotype of cold brutality. One of the verbal clubs she used to beat me with was, "You're just like your father." I heard this constantly for five years. This was a club that I was finally to take away from her; no one can beat you with a club that you do not provide yourself. I wish I had known that earlier.

My father is a prejudiced man. He is prejudiced in an old-time southern way. He is also a counterexample to the idea that prejudiced people are not intelligent. My father's family has always had an axe to grind against Indians. It is little wonder, then, that all of his Indian ancestors over the years suffered a profound racial and historical transformation, until finally I was no longer even permitted to ask about the dark-skinned people in our family pictures.

When I was a child, my mother worked in a sewing factory. At the time, I had a variety of baby-sitters, all of whom I didn't like. However, fate finally threw me a bone, as it is wont to do, and I finally did get one that I liked. Her name was Levina, but I called her Mama Harjo. She was a Creek woman who lived in a small company house that had three rooms. It was an old house, as there had been no companies located in Wetumka to build houses in over forty years. And it was a house that I loved almost as much as I loved Mama Harjo. Mama Harjo and I had a wonderful life together in her house. She kept other children, but I was her favorite. She said so. She even began to teach me Creek. I remember that I loved the way the words tasted and would walk around saying them constantly. This was my undoing.

My speaking Creek brought about the end of my being kept by Mama Harjo, because one day, my father said to my mother, "You get someone else. She's turning him into a little Indian." So that was the end of Mama Harjo. But I have heard it said that if the Catholic Church has you 'til you're five, you're theirs for life. I think that the same thing must be true of being Creek. And if my father could keep me away from Mama Harjo, he could not keep me away from my family, half of which was Indian, and he could not dictate the people I associated with in school, most of whom turned out to be Indian.

He also could not change where I lived. Oklahoma is an Indian state, the state of Sequoyah, both rabidly multicultural and zealously monocultural. Oklahoma recently celebrated the year of the Indian, in 1992, and in 1989, it observed the one hundredth anniversary of the "land run." To celebrate, Indian children were asked to dress as pioneers and reenact the taking of their ancestral land. Paradoxically, white children in Oklahoma now wish to dress in

Indian regalia and dance in Indian ceremonies, some of which celebrate Indian victories over white people. In scholarly terms, we are caught in what's called a narrative conflict. We move in the silent interstitial spaces left for a people displaced and finding a home in their displacement.

This is where my family and I are from, and as the Creek author Linda Hogan has said, we are in a process of "always coming home." It is probably appropriate to think of my story as a travel narrative—one of those strange little stories that explorers used to tell about exotic people and strange locations and how they survived only through wits and cunning. It is impossible for me to separate my own adventures from those of my family. We are all tightly connected, and what might be considered distant anecdotes by others are actual parts of me. When I talk about my family, I am always talking about myself as well.

As a very young girl, my grandmother was taken to Catholic schools and given to the nuns. Her family was too poor to support her. They could not buy her food and shoes. The Catholics took her, even though she was not Catholic, because at that time they were still in the business of converting Indians "by any means necessary." When my grandmother would not kneel to pray, the nuns locked her in a broom closet. Aside from the fright of leaving home and being locked in a closet, my grandmother—like many Indians—was prone to serious ear infections and developed one in the days she spent in the broom closet. Her infection became so serious, and the pressure so intense, that her eardrums exploded and ran blood. When the nuns finally came to let her out of the closet, it was only to force her to clean the blood out of her own ears. The nuns did not help. No one has ever said if grandma knelt to pray after that. She will not talk about it. Knowing her, I assume she didn't. This is where formal Western-style education begins in my family. Where it stands now is with myself, a graduate of Dartmouth College and one dissertation away from a Ph.D. from Stanford University. I have spent most of my education like my grandmother, refusing to kneel. Kneeling in Ivy League institutions is a different matter than kneeling was for my grandmother. So that is what this history of personal education is going to be about: it is going to be about how not to kneel. It is also about the price you pay when you refuse. My grandmother paid with her ears; I paid with something quite different.

My grandfather had an experience different from either my own or my grandmother's. He went to the country school near town and was judged gifted (though that wasn't the term they used back then). He was treated well throughout school, and by the time he graduated, he had a love of words, a love of language. New ideas were rare fruit to him. He lived for his ideas and not from them. He was a strong man and worked construction. He ran a bulldozer and a motor grader, and to take the sting out of the work, at night he would travel the world in his mind. When I was a child, he had a paper globe with the oceans in deep black and continents and states in color. He would have me spin the globe and place my finger on a country. I never hit on a country that he did not know something about. There were times when I would picture myself small enough to slip inside the globe. Sitting in the center, I would look out through all of the countries of the world. I would imagine the sun shining through the translucent pastel countries and playing across me until my skin was a map of the world. This was the sort of education I had from my grandfather; landscapes and languages were his domain. He spoke Muscogee, English, and Spanish, and he taught me about the country around Wetumka. My grandfather taught me geology and archaeology by showing me places to find fossilized tree roots and ocean shells. He took me out to the old cemetery outside of town and showed me where my relatives lived. He taught me about soil by taking me to dig potatoes with him. He also gifted me with a love of words, beginning, as he had done with my mother and aunt, with the word "metempsychosis."

Now literally, metempsychosis has to do with the transmigration of souls, but for me it had to do with something quite different. It was a ticket that my grandfather granted me into the world of language and its power. It all has to do with his reasoning. Papa Lloyd taught me to understand metempsychosis as a way to protect me from schooling. He said, "Your teachers don't know this word. Now you know something that your teachers don't. You know a lot of things that your teachers don't. They aren't any smarter'n you. Don't ever believe that your teachers are any smarter'n you are. They're older so they know some things that you don't, but you know some things that they don't." I suppose any long and obscure word would have done, but metempsychosis is the word that I remember starting me on my collection of words.

I came to love words the way my grandfather did. I loved the

way they tasted, the way they felt. I learned to read at about age four and read insatiably. I was starved to read. I recall stealing books from the classroom in first grade and taking them home because
you could not check books out of the school library in the first grade. I would put them under my coat and smuggle them out. I remember vividly the lump I would get in my throat, because I was raised in a family where stealing was not tolerated, but I also remember just having to have those books. In the second half of first grade, they granted me library privileges after I proved that I could read the books, and a library card brought an end to my criminal career.

It was only in the second grade that I learned that Indians don't read. The person who taught me this was Zelda Morris. Even with my vast storehouse of words, I can think of no words sufficiently venomous to describe her. Let it suffice to say that she was cold and brutal enough to beat a second grader for reading "too fast."

The rest of my grade-school career was hit or miss. Some teachers I bonded with immediately, some I did not. Mrs. Osborn was a teacher whom I loved as only a fourth grader can love a teacher. Mrs. Osborn was that rare Oklahoma teacher who prized and valued Indians even though she was not one herself. Her music class was the only place that Creek culture was allowed to intrude into our school. She and Mrs. Yahola taught the music class to sing Creek hymns, and they took us out to the Indian churches to sing them. I recall getting ready to get on the bus to go out to Thlopthlocco, edging up to Mrs. Osborn in a shy fourth-grade way, and giving her a necklace that my mother had beaded. She kissed me on the cheek in front of the whole class, a major embarrassment for a nine-year-old, but a memory I hold very dear.

As a small child, both in and out of school, mostly I tried to be unobtrusive and collect information. I would always listen, believing somehow that if I had enough information, I would be safe. I would listen around the corners of doors or sit quietly until the adults became too drunk to notice and would absorb everything and store it away. I don't know why I came to associate knowledge with safety. I only know this fused into and pervaded my education. Abetting this was a drive to understand the way things work and to collect knowledge. I have always loved things that were curious and new and beautiful.

This is how my grade-school education proceeded. It was good and bad, but by high school, it had become simply bad. I honestly don't know when my adolescence began. I understand that some people can provide you with the exact hour and day. I am not one of them. My life runs along a continuum. I hope it is one of constant development; at least I like to think it is. Not a smooth continuum, but more punctuated equilibrium. I basically went along steadily on one tangent until a crisis or event caused me to change course. I don't know of a pivotal event that signaled adolescence. I can only paint you a picture of how I remember it.

Sitting in your room alone, you have covered the windows with aluminum foil in order to block out all of the light. You do not like light in your bedroom, because it creates a web of shadows in the middle of the night. You have already figured out that it was not the dark you were afraid of in your childhood; it was the shadows in the woods outside your bedroom window. You have carried this fear into your adolescence. Only total darkness can alleviate it, so that is what you have created. You are waiting for sleep to come and it does not. It often does not. You usually sleep during the day or afternoon. You feel exhausted all of the time but not in early night. Instead your thoughts race, but not in the usual way. They are in a slow race. They are weighted and plod through your mind unstoppable, unwilling to give you peace, yet uselessly slow. Spiraling and painful, they continue on.

To escape the isolation, your ears seek out noise. They hear fighting in the kitchen. Your father is pounding on the kitchen counter, slurring his words already. Your stepmother's voice is rising, until you finally hear her yell that you are not hers. Your pain peaks although you know that this is merely drunk-speak. You sneak into the hallway and turn on the air conditioner. Its hum almost drowns out the sound. Back in bed, you put the pillow over your head. You squeeze it tighter and tighter until you are unable to breathe. Only after you have no more breath to give up do you lay the pillow aside and hope that the screaming has stopped.

Now you have the tone for my adolescence. I don't feel that I need to go into it any further. My adolescence was pain. My escape from this was reading. I read everything that I could get my hands on, and in every spare moment. I would read during lunchtime instead of eating. In every school, I searched until I found a hiding place where I could read undisturbed. This was not always easy, because after my parents' divorce, my mother got an itchy foot; I moved and changed schools six times between sixth grade and high school graduation. My life was in constant flux, and this was not a simple thing to deal with. As I changed schools, I began to attend less and less. I would cut school and go to the library or go to the movies.

My mother saw no value in attending school more than the minimum time necessary to make good grades. She said that grades were like money: they bought you things. Based on this philosophy, we struck a deal. I was required to attend school for no longer than it would take me to make A's. It was my mother's contention that all other time invested was wasted. I discovered that I could make A's by attending school two to three days per week. The remainder of my time I spent researching or watching television. On the research end of things, I would pick a topic and go to the library. I picked topics like cryogenics, black holes, the Cree Indians, riboflavin, and Australia, just things that caught my interest. I would then set about learning everything available on the subject. I had a craving for knowledge that was not being met in schools. My schools were more war zones than educational institutions. Like my grandmother in Catholic school, I would not kneel, and so I was left to fight.

My fights at school were very physical. It seemed as though I had to fight all the time. The other Indian kids were the only kids that I never fought with at school. They were my friends. I spent a lot of my time fighting with the whites; the black kids I only fought with once—then we established a mutual respect. The white kids I fought with perpetually, year after year. Strangely, I didn't notice that they were all white until later; I just noticed that they were brutal. I always won, but that is not surprising. That is what I was raised to do.

I also believe that I have a fighting nature because I am a mixed blood. I have read various authors who say that it is in the dynamic. Now being a mixed blood is not an unusual condition in Oklahoma, nor is it particularly interesting. It is only when you have it slapped into you that the peculiar nature of the arrangement comes to the forefront. For me, this came in class one afternoon in the fall of my junior year of high school.

I was sitting at my desk staring out the window as many of us often did (school being the challenging thing that it is in rural Oklahoma), when I began to pick up on a conversation between two of my friends. They were bitching about the benefits that Indians received. Their complaints ranged from "free health care" to the pencils and notebooks that were delivered to the Indian kids by the government. I had just received mine two weeks before. Finally, they centered their complaints on Indian houses. They complained endlessly about the fact that Indians got their houses free and about the fact that it was their tax money that paid for the houses. I found this interesting, since I knew that neither of them had ever paid a tax in his life; you generally don't as a junior in high school.

After listening to their tirade for a while, I felt compelled to barge in. After all, I come from a long line of "fools who rush in." I reminded them that I was Indian and that my family lived in one of those houses. I had also intended to tell them that the houses were paid for out of tribal money and that nobody's taxes had anything to do with it, but I didn't get the chance. Instead I was told, "We weren't talking about you. After all, you have some human blood, too."

These were casual friends, and it was readily apparent in the way that they phrased their response that they were actually trying to show solidarity with me. Lift me up a bit as it were. My reaction was to give them what my brother terms my "go to hell look" and turn around in my desk. Their conversation drifted on to who they wanted to take out and who they thought would win the upcoming football game—leaving me to my own partially human thoughts.

The one place I did enjoy spending time when attending school was the library. The librarian and I became good friends. When walking past the library one day, I was asked if I was going to take the PSAT, a test for high school juniors to gauge their chances for getting into college. I told her probably not, because I didn't have the two dollars. She told me she would give me the two dollars if I would take the test. I agreed because I liked taking tests. They were games to me and I loved games. It is still amazing to me that two dollars properly spent can change the entire course of your life. I did very well on the test and started receiving information and scholarship offers from universities across the country. This was something that was outside of my experience. I come from a world that is very small and very old. To me, New York and Mars were approximately the same. They were places that you see on TV and places where no real people live—infinitely expansive but with no more depth and reality than the TV screen itself.

I always tell people that my admission to college was happenstance: I just happened to be in school the day they were administering the PSATs; a librarian just happened to remind me and loan me the money to take the test; I just happened to do well, which made me a National Merit Scholar, which brought me letters from expensive colleges. I then tossed my letters in the air and the one from Dartmouth just happened to come out on top. This is how I picked my college. I only applied to one. I had never heard of it. I was sure, though, that being a small college in the backwoods, it would be desperate for students, so I did not apply anywhere else. I only realized after I got to Dartmouth that other people had worked and planned for years to go there. Some had hired coaches for the standardized admissions tests and had had their parents fly them in to look at the place. Others had applied to seven or eight different places. I recall thinking what a pain that would be and wondering why they had bothered. Many of these questions were answered upon my arrival.

My first impression of Dartmouth was that it was beautiful and cold. I was picked up at the airport by a junior who was Ojibway. He was friendly and I was freezing. Coming from Oklahoma in September, I didn't expect the chill and had packed my coat in my suitcase. My suitcases were lost at the airport in St. Louis, leaving me in a new place, a thousand miles from home, with only the shirt on my back. After walking around some and getting to know the place, I went to my room. I remember lying on a military-style bed with no sheets in a freezing room wondering just what I was doing there.

That was my first impression of Dartmouth and I guess that is what Dartmouth is to me: a random assortment of impressions with no specific chronological order. In a sense it is personal event and spectacle. I suppose this is true for everyone. Pervasive among my impressions is a strong sense of alienation from Dartmouth. This began the day after I arrived, when I received a notice from the Deans' office that I was to meet with a dean at 12:00 the next day. I could not believe how rude that was; back home, you never simply told somebody to show up one day in advance, and seldom was a week enough warning. We just didn't do things that way. I felt my sense of correctness assaulted, as a city person might feel if all stoplights were to start changing colors at random. It was one of those things that was so unconscious that I could not have told you why it struck me as rude if asked; it's one of those subtle cultural/regional "differences" that are so deeply ingrained that you have to trip over them to bring them to light. This happened to me quite often at Dartmouth. On a regular basis, I felt as if I and the other students, as well as the professors, were existing on very different planes of reality.

I should say before I go on that writing about my time at Dartmouth is difficult for several reasons. The primary one is that after my graduation, I made a decision to remodel Dartmouth in my house of memory. It seems that many of us did that; when I meet with other Indian alumni, we remember the place fondly. Much like all alums, we have sealed up certain rooms, shifted a few doorways, and recast our experiences in a more pleasant hue. We remember our friends, and even our memories of our competitors grow fonder. Contradictions that once loomed enormous may not have been resolved, but they have been lived through. I think that Indians have a gift for this. There is so much pain in our histories that even the worst a small college has to inflict pales in comparison.

The "Indian symbol" provides a good example of this process of not forgetting specific events, but rather refocusing attention only on certain aspects of them. I think of it little these days, but at one time it commanded much of my attention and energy. The Indian symbol—a degrading, stupid-looking caricature of an Indian that was usually found drunk near a rum barrel—was the unofficial college mascot for many years, looked upon with pride by many old alumni. When I looked at it, though, I saw too much of home to find anything funny or heroic about it. Let me give you an example of what it feels like, since so much of its effect is in what some elders call the unseen world.

Imagine your grandfather. He has raised you with love and respect and given a great part of himself to you. He stands very straight, and the dignity of his presence is almost palpable. Grandfather once lived very vitally, and it still shows in his humor and stories. He has a gentle wit and cares about his family and the world. His spiritual strength brings forth light. This is grandfather.

Now people have come to visit grandfather. He invites them in and offers them food. They do not accept, but instead, begin to jeer. They say taunting things that are aimed to hurt and destroy. But this is not enough; they grab grandfather and shave his head.

They paint his face with stripes and draw a scowl from the corners of his mouth. Still not enough, they take him and push him into the mud outside. You look at grandfather and realize that they have not diminished him. They did not have the power, but the world itself is now a smaller, darker place. This is how the Indian symbol made some of us feel.

Now I realize that the symbol was not and is not the most pressing issue facing Indian society, but seeing it is like walking past a stinging nettle; you chop it out of your path only to have it return from the roots. Its persistence only serves to underscore a contradiction that every Indian who has ever attended Dartmouth has felt to some degree. Dartmouth College, since its founding, has alternately used, courted, tossed aside, enticed, mocked, ignored, and, occasionally, educated Native Americans. In some ways, it is almost a mini-America.

The Indian symbol was a general challenge to the Native American community at Dartmouth, but there were many personal challenges as well. I recall being out dancing one night with a friend of mine, a beautiful Indian woman from Denver. My roommate (a student from New Jersey whose informal motto was "Yeah, I'm an asshole. So what?") was at the party as well. After a few minutes of dancing near my roommate, my friend Jo asked if we could move away from him. I asked her why. She said that he was pinching her and feeling her up. Well, where I'm from, you don't do things like that. But as a freshman, I didn't know clearly what to do. I thought about it a while and then looked him up and down and told him he should apologize to her. He said he didn't have to and that it was none of my business, so I hit him a couple of times to emphasize the point. Then I was really confused, because at Dartmouth, you just don't hit people. Mental cruelty of all kinds is protected and tolerated by established rules of conduct, but physical violence, no matter to what end, is deplored. At home, the reverse is true; decent treatment of people is encouraged and, if the situation requires, justifiably demanded through physical coercion. Unsure, I called home and spoke to my grandfather. He said that I had done "just right and if they were decent people they'd understand." How could I tell my grandfather that I was in a place where by many of the values I was raised with, people were not only not decent, but not even sane? Fortunately, it never came up.

But I also took to parts of Dartmouth like a duck to water. It was all about learning and things that were new and beautiful. The first class that I took was "Folklore," an anthropology course. Anthropologists delight in the unique, and the professor who taught this course was really the first non-Indian I had ever met who valued Indian culture. At that time I hadn't spent much time thinking about culture. It was just a given. I recall, though, being very excited at the age of eighteen to meet someone who was Jewish. I had seen some Jewish people on TV and was certain that there couldn't be very many of them, since I had never met one. At that time, for me, all the world was Indian; it was only later that I was to realize the rare and beautiful wealth that we hold onto.

One of my friends described Dartmouth as a fantasy land. In my freshman year, this was how it seemed to me. The work was stimulating but not especially burdensome. I have always loved the stars, and in my first term, I found a perfect combination of courses: "Folklore" and "Stars." But it should be clear by now that what I loved was not the physics and astronomy, but the poetry of the stars. Black holes are places where time itself stops and things become infinitely smaller and no older, an eventual horizon past which there is no force in the universe that could allow one to escape. The romance of these astrological concepts was incredible and fit in so wonderfully with the folk stories of the people who came out of the earth and the ancient spiders hanging fire in the sky. But as far as the math went, I was in way over my head. My math education had stopped after Algebra I in the tenth grade. Sadly, they expected more at Dartmouth. Upon making a D on my first exam, I was determined to leave the college. Fortunately, the Native American Program director took me in hand and reassured me that "Stars" was neither the last nor the most important course I would take in college. I got an A in "Folklore" and a C in "Stars"; not terribly unique.

What was unique about my freshman year in college was Val. Years later, I find it hard to write about her, but Val was an important part of the lives of many of us who attended Dartmouth at that time and her story is very much a part of my own. When I first saw Val on my second day at the college, she was so beautiful she literally stole my breath away. She was wearing a green army surplus coat that she had decorated herself with streaks of spray paint and red handprints. When she asked me if I was going to the NAD House for a picnic to welcome new students, I, of course, said yes.

Val was Yup'ik from Alaska. When she entered Dartmouth, she
was a poet, a singer, and a person with the most boundless raw energy I have ever known. By the time she left the college, a couple of years later, she was addicted to alcohol and cocaine and physically and emotionally battered. By the age of twenty-seven, she was dead from drinking antifreeze. Much is said about walking in two worlds, about being "bicultural." These discussions are little more than mouthings of academic platitudes. Val, like myself, thought about the world in a way that I can only superficially describe. I was not raised with talk of career paths and planning ahead. When I thought of the future, it was only a matter of days or weeks. I did not plan to finish college or go to graduate school or get married or have a son. I was raised thinking that things happen, and people adapt if they can. No one exercises much control over the world, and it is only those who are gullible who delude themselves into thinking that they do. My main concern was and is what happens to my family and community. My education, more than anything else, helped me to redefine and expand whom I include in my circle of concern.

All in all, my education has been a rather selfish thing. It took me away from my family and tribe and I did it just to satisfy my curiosity. I was a poet inseparable from momentary tribal dreams when I left, and I am a better poet now. Being away led me to understand the incredible wealth I was raised with. I recently went to the wedding ceremony of a Native friend of mine from Dartmouth. He began the ceremony by saying, "My family and I would like to welcome you. We've lived in this neighborhood for about thirty-five thousand years." That statement alone causes you to think in ways that are difficult to reconcile with Western education. This, I think, is the paradox that killed Val because she could not reconcile it. I try with greater or lesser success.

I would like you to understand that my experience at the college was not universally bad. On the contrary, Dartmouth provided me with gifts too numerous to count. The foremost among these are my ex-wife and my son. My ex-wife is mixed blood like myself. She is Slovakian, Irish, English, Italian, and some nameless Massachusetts Indian tribe. What all these things add up to is a strikingly beautiful woman. She has flowing brown hair with red highlights, eyes the color of polished amber, and a body that won't quit. In addition to all of the aforementioned things, she speaks four languages, graduated at the top of her class, was a state champion athlete, and upon giving birth, immediately got up and walked back to her hospital room.

Diane and I might have been considered star-crossed lovers. It was almost a storybook formulation. She was a near-white girl from a wealthy family who had all the money in the world to give her, but very little love; they insisted on the best from her and usually got it, one way or another. They had great plans for her: to follow in the finest tradition and become a powerful, self-concerned doctor whose only loves were money and control. And her family must always take a distant second place, so as not to interfere with her work. I was a poor Indian from Oklahoma whose family seldom had enough money, but always had enough love. My family aspired that I stay out of prison, but beyond that I was free to make my own way. Now as it happened, I loved Diane the near-white girl and she loved me and that was how things stood until one night I loved her too much and she became pregnant. When she told me this, it did not surprise me in the least, because that is how things work in the real world. Since her pregnancy was a fact, Diane had some decisions to make. I say "Diane" and not "we" because I believe that while a baby is inside a woman's body, all choices should be hers. I did tell her though, that if she wanted to have the baby, then I would have a say; the baby would not go up for adoption. If she wanted no part of it, I would take it back to Oklahoma and raise it myself with the help of my family. I had the benefit of knowing that my family loves children and that a new baby would be greeted with joy. This gave me a security that many white people, including Diane, unfortunately lack. Well, to make a long story short, Diane decided to have the baby. I was happy and hesitant and unsure and proud and a million other things all stirred together in one big pot. I think Diane was the same way. I was also feeling very good in a way that only living up to a difficult conviction can make you feel. The upshot of it all was that we went ahead with our plans for her to have the baby. We also decided to get married. Our fraternity provided the scene.

Diane and I belonged to the same co-ed fraternity, and our wedding was the event of the season. Our nuptials were paid for out of the social budget, and it seemed like half of the campus turned up. It was a mighty fine time. Diane was beautiful in green velvet, and I have to say that I made quite a striking figure in my mismatched jacket and beaded bolo tie. My brother the preacher came all the way from Oklahoma to New Hampshire to perform the ceremony, and all of Diane's family showed up. We had decided to let her parents attend on the condition that my brother and I could cripple them if they acted ugly (they didn't). It was a grand affair and seven months later, my son Scot was born. He is the finest thing Diane and I have ever done together, and between us and my family he is one loved chebonni. Since then, Diane and I have divorced, but that seems like a happy place to stop.

A Kiowa elder once told me that the victories to be won today are educational. Most of the time now, we fight with words. Dartmouth College taught me to use words as arrows, a skill which led me to Stanford. But I was not comfortable or happy in this academic environment, and it took me a while to figure out why.

For myself as an Indian academic, the problem of locating "home" within the academic structure was serious. More than any people in North America, Indians can point to a piece of the world where home lies, and they can often even trace it back to specific rocks, trees, and bodies of water. The university is not where we point. We cannot adopt academia in the way Euro-Americans can. Having no concept of links that cannot be broken, Euro-Americans can pull themselves up by the bootstraps and plant themselves firmly in the academic community, a community historically conceived to take care of them. Aside from a few minor scrapes and disharmonies, they fit academia like a hand sliding into a glove. What, however, can an Indian do? What can Indians do when the glove is tailored to the white hand, and the white hand is already happily inside it?

One of the things that an Indian can do is leave, and we do so in droves. Indians have the highest university dropout rate of any group in the United States, on the undergraduate, graduate, and faculty levels. This is not surprising to either the academic world or the Indian world. I'll attempt to explain why this is so.

As a constant and enthusiastic user of computers, I have occasionally come across programs that have serious bugs. These are programs in which you attempt to do something that the program is purportedly capable of doing, yet actually is not. The commands are there, and the computer should be able to perform the task. In fact, the computer will insist that it is able. On the Macintosh, this results in a system error. The system error is the bane of the Mac user's existence, because it offers only one solution: turn off your computer, lose everything you have recently put into it, and start again from the beginning.

This is the situation of the Indian who stays within academia: the academic structure insists that it can accommodate you, and even gives explicit instructions on how this can be accomplished. You enter the system, begin to give input, and then out of the blue, you get a system error, incapable of correcting itself. As the user, you learn merely to avoid using that particular function. Unfortunately, the only way to discover a system error is to stumble across it and be sent back to the beginning.

Indians come from a place where the primary program is different and has been running for an incredibly long time. Most of the bugs are worked out. Indians enter academia expecting a fundamentally functional program. They press keys labeled "voice," "expression," "meaning," "creativity," and "use," and expect to find that something extraordinary happens. Instead, the machine stops. So Indians go home, a place that Euro-American academics have often forgotten exists, or they stay in a world they never made and don't fully understand.

After leaving Stanford partway through my Ph.D. program in education, I was hired as executive director of The Native American Preparatory School (NAPS). I took the job in order to protect our children from the type of Western education my family and I have endured. I refuse to believe that education must be painful and cruel.

The Native American Prep School took me many places, and my "education" continued. I flew across the country from New York to L.A., had meetings at private clubs and on yachts where no one looked like me, and asked people to donate money to Indian education, because Indians are the people of the future. And then I would go home and cleanse myself and vomit, because that is what you do if you are Creek and believe in our traditional ways and find yourself living in a world that is increasingly strange. Then I would return to work and laugh myself through another day, clinging to thirty-five thousand years of dances and stories and philosophy and thought and the comfort, joy, pain, and work that its survival implies.

The chairman of the NAPS board, like many wealthy older people in Santa Fe, lives in a security-controlled condo. As executive director of the school, I often went to visit him. In the beginning, I was consistently stopped at the gate by a series of white men, and each time I told them my business. When I told them that their tenant and I worked together, they would ask exactly what I did. They would ask where I lived. They would ask how long I expected to be there. I told the same people the same things for two months. I got to know them well by sight, and I would have thought that as I came and went twice a day, they would have gotten to know me, but such was not the case. Each time, they said, "We'll have to call and get confirmation."

One day, about two months into this process, I arrived late for my appointment, and as is so often the case, desperation became the mother of invention. I was stopped and they asked who I was. Out of irritation, I sarcastically responded, "I'm the gardener. Who do you think?" This changed our relationship in a way that I could not have anticipated. The guard at the gate thrust a pass at me. "Here," he said, "remember to bring this with you." He stepped back into the guardhouse before I could explain that I had been joking. But I now had a pass that would allow me to go anywhere in the complex. Sometimes, with all the education and degrees in the world, you're still just the gardener. A gardener is a respectable thing to be. My grandfather was a gardener. He raised potatoes, and I raise money. So maybe the guards had me pegged after all.

I once read a story in which one of the characters refused to let reality take shape. Through the sheer power of his denial, things would begin to realign themselves and reality would reshuffle itself. He was not an Indian, but he might have been. I should not be here. We should not be here. I read that we were all supposed to be gone by 1910 or 1940 or 1970. It seems that for people who have outlived the end of several worlds, it is only denial and laughter that keeps us going.

I have been told that there are ceremonies going on in Native America to call people home. There is an in-gathering and those who walked, crawled, or were carried away will be brought back. I had to go away to know that my education was my grandfather and grandmother and aunts and uncles and cousins, and that the land and the turtles who live on it were my education, too. I was schooled in the cold mountains of New Hampshire, and in California, but I was educated in a warm green forest in the rolling hills of Oklahoma. Simply put, I am a rare bird trying to combine a traditional Muscogee life with an Ivy League education. When I go to work, whether it is as a teacher, grant writer, beadworker, or poet, I go to war. I seek to protect people and cultures that are beautiful and unique and timeless. But mostly, I seek to protect children who should not have to kneel; children who might be my grandmother, my son, my friend Val—or me.

According to legend, there is a little yellow deer who lives in the forest. If you are very still and very fortunate, he will come and whisper secrets in your ear. This is my son's name, Eco Lvne-ce— Little Yellow Deer. Scot often whispers secrets to me, and in exchange I have taught him to say "metempsychosis." If I do my job well, my son need never leave the forest.

Bill Bray's given name is Fus Hutke Chupco, which translates to "Great White Bird," referring to the crane which originated the Stompdance. Creek and Choctaw, he is also an adopted member of Arbeka Talledega, one of the four mother towns of the Mvskoke Confederacy.

Bill is a published poet and 1989 graduate of Dartmouth College, where he double-majored in English and anthropology modified with minority studies in education. He also earned a certificate in Native American studies. He has a master's degree in education from Oklahoma City University and has completed his doctoral coursework at Stanford University. In addition, he holds a Ph.D. in Cultural Resource Management.

Bill was the founding director of a school for gifted Native American students in Santa Fe, New Mexico, and he is currently the CEO of Este Mvskokvlke Momen Hopoetvke, a tribal corporation that assists traditional communities in achieving cultural and economic sovereignty. He is often to be found on his porch in Okemah, Oklahoma, reading a good book, beading, or watching his son, Eco Lvnv-ce, who is a delight to his eyes.

▼▼▼▼▼▼▼▼▼

DAVINA RUTH BEGAYE TWO BEARS

I Walk in Beauty

Sleet pelted down from a steel-gray sky. It was a cold Thanksgiving Day in Winslow, Arizona on November 28, 1968. Anita looked out her window from her bed at the Indian Hospital. The naked branches of the trees rattled in the wind, but Anita was happy. She thought again about the birth of her first child, and curled protectively around her newborn daughter. At the first sight of her baby in the delivery room, Anita had cried, "Oh, look at my shiny baby!"

The name "Shiny" has stuck with me, but my real name is Davina. Like my mother twenty-six years ago, I face the ultimate challenge of childbirth and parenthood. My husband and I are happily expecting our first child this year. A family of my own is something that I've always wanted—a family free of alcohol abuse, poverty, and divorce. Our baby will be born in Wisconsin, my husband's traditional native homeland. He is Wisconsin Winnebago, or Ho-Chunk. I am Navajo, or Diné. After we graduated from Dartmouth, we traveled across the country to Arizona, where we lived and worked for four years. I was able to enjoy being with my immediate family after being away from them while back east attending college. Now it is my husband's time to enjoy his family after eight years of being away from home.

While in Arizona, my husband and I had the unique and gratifying opportunity of working for the Navajo Nation Archaeology Department. The contract archaeology we were exposed to instilled in us valuable, practical knowledge concerning cultural resource management. My experience with the Navajo Nation will always be precious to me, because it gave me the opportunity to work for my people and to learn to speak more of my language, and because it introduced me to the beauty of the land that makes up the Navajo reservation.

Now we are applying our education and experience to the Ho-Chunk Nation, as they begin to develop and grow in this area. It is my husband's turn to work for his people, and to learn from them.

Our interest in cultural resource management took root while we were both students at Dartmouth. I perceive cultural resource management as a way to maintain and preserve a group's language, culture, and traditions—a challenge facing many Native American tribes today. My interest in this area was greatly encouraged at Dartmouth and through Dartmouth's Native American Program, Native American studies department, and anthropology department, where I learned more than I could imagine about Native American culture, history, and current affairs.

Whoever thought that I would attend college back east? Not me, although I am the daughter of college-educated parents. My real dad and mother met in 1966 at Northern Arizona University, where I am currently finishing up a master's degree in anthropology. My mother graduated after eleven years of hard work; my dad never finished.

As a college student and in general, my mother did not trust any man. Although she befriended many of her male suitors, she was not interested in having a "boyfriend." Then she met my dad. He was different, and intrigued her with his intelligence, sophistication, sarcasm, and in-depth knowledge of life in the Navajo world and in the white world. He was unlike any other person she had ever met.

For the first part of my life, we lived, or tried to live, as a family—a mother, father, and four daughters, of whom I am the oldest. My father was never home like a parent should be. I remember tramping through deep snow when I was three in search of dad in the seedy bars of downtown Flagstaff. It was common for him to leave us to fend for ourselves with no money for rent, food, school supplies, whatever. Who knows what he did on his excursions? My mother rarely followed him to his "drinking get-togethers." The times he did make it home, he was often drunk out of his mind. His stays with the family varied from a few days to a few months, then he'd disappear again—no note, no warning, nothing. Often he would get a job, then take the paycheck, leaving us penniless. The whole process repeated itself again and again like a broken record. But my sisters and I were always happy to see him. I loved it when we were all together as a family.

My dad had many friends who believed in his potential—professors, co-workers, etc. Time after time they tried to support him with job opportunities, academic extensions, and numerous second chances, because they saw him as an inquisitive and intelligent person. But he would always let them down by quitting and then drinking.

I ask my mom questions about him often, because my dad is no longer living. He passed away in a drinking and driving accident in 1985. He was never happy on this earth. The predicament of Native Americans—primarily their loss of land, language, culture, and traditions—plagued him, driving him to liquor, despair, and finally to his untimely death. To my mother, he often patiently remarked, "You are so innocent. You just don't understand." She, faced with the reality of raising four girls and the trials and tribulations of his alcoholism, found his remarks infuriating and of no practical use or help. Neither my mother nor her four daughters could rescue or change him.

However, I learned from my dad in many ways. First, he influenced me not to be what he was—an alcoholic. I'm sure that I'm not the only Indian person who experienced this life while growing up. Many children go through the same, or worse. Native Americans have the highest rate of alcoholism of any ethnic group in this country. My father's life showed me that alcohol means you can never live happily or accomplish your goals. He could not hold a job, finish school, support his family's basic needs, or even try to live life in a good way. He tried, but was not successful. Second, and more positively, my dad instilled in me a love for books and reading. My mother tells me that he began reading to my sisters and me when we were very young. I remember him reading books like *The Secret Garden* and *The Wizard of Oz* for our bedtime stories. Despite my dad's faults, I cannot stop loving him, and he will always be my dad. But, unlike my dad, I will not let myself get swallowed into a black hole of depression and drink myself to death.

My mother's example of perseverance was our saving grace and my standard to follow. Instead of giving up on her education, she went from class to class, semester to semester, and year to year. It was to our advantage that she stayed at NAU; otherwise we would have had no place to live. She worked odd jobs and kept us clothed, well-fed, well-mannered, loved and happy. What more could a child ask for? We didn't care that our clothes were all secondhand or from the church donation box, because deep down we knew that our mom would always be there for us. Children need love, care, and support from their parents. My mom was all of that to us. She was the person who came to all of our school functions; she made sweets for our bake sales; she helped us with our homework or found someone to help us; she cooked dinner every night and made sure we went to school every day. My dad's drinking was always a problem, but she did not let it get her down, just as she doesn't let any bad news or crisis get the best of her even today. In my eyes, my mother always comes out on top with her kindness, generosity, and grace intact. She is the backbone of who I am today; if it weren't for her, how could I have survived? I remember one time, however, that my mother did briefly let go.

My teeth were chattering, I was so cold—but I kept watch and tried to look calm. Cars were easily seen from the huge sledding hill that we six girls were huddled on. Sledding was fun for the first hour; my two cousins and three sisters screamed and laughed at the top of our lungs as we raced down the hill dipping crazily and sometimes crashing into snow. Our "sleds" were plastic garbage bags, but we didn't care, we were going down that hill fast. But that was an hour or so ago, when our jeans were still dry and we were warmed by the activity. Now we were pressed close together for warmth under our plastic bags against a tall ponderosa pine tree. All of us were soaking wet. Our socks for mittens weren't working anymore. We were freezing. I felt embarrassed as warmly dressed white people passed us in their stylish snow suits, boots, mittens, hats, and scarves, asking if we were okay, or where our parents were. If they had really wanted to help, they could have taken off their snow suits and given them to us.

One by one the cars went by, none of them my mother's blue Dodge Colt. As I listened to the girls whimper and cry, I thought of my mom's behavior over the past couple of weeks. Every now and then I uttered a comforting phrase, "She'll be here soon, don't worry. The laundry should be done soon," but even I began to wonder if she had left us for good. I would never have thought this before, but it was as if she was changing into a different person. At night, I crouched next to the heater, which was connected to the living room, and listened to my aunt and mother as they partied with men I did not know. I had never been so mad or scared in my life. I hated what my mom was doing. She began smoking and drinking and, worst of all, she was doing it in our own living room! Yeah, dad drinks, but not mom, too! It was a nightmare coming to life. It felt like the world was being turned upside down and inside out. I felt myself begin to panic, because I realized my mom was giving up, just like my dad. Her eyes were different, she seemed like she was in a daze. My mind raced as I thought about my sisters and me. Who is going to take care of us now if both mom and dad drink? How are we going to live? Are we going to wander from family to family looking for care? How could my mother do this? Why do people have to drink? Finally, I saw the Dodge, and I watched it as it inched its way up the hill, making sure it was really my mom. Yes, it was her. I yelled, "Mom's coming!" We all ran toward the entrance of the park, and straight for the car. I looked in the back and saw the laundry was neatly folded in plastic bags. I felt so relieved that she had done what she had said she was going to do, and that she had come back for us. We were all smiling

I Walk
in Beauty
▼

again, and crying tears of joy, as we surrounded her. "Mom, Mom, it was so cold!" "We were freezing!" "I'm tired!" "I'm hungry!" She began to cry, too, and hugged and kissed us all.

She told me later that that day brought her back to reality. We shocked her out of her depression when she saw us there frozen and looking like a bunch of drowned rats. At that point she realized that her purpose in life was her children, and that she could not give in to despair just because she felt like it. We were depending on her, and she couldn't let us down. And she didn't. After that day, she stopped acting "weird" and became "normal" again. At least that is how I thought of her, and I knew that it was a miracle. I think to myself, would I be where I am, or who I am, if she had failed to change that day? Or would I, too, be a drunk, giving up on life, because of the example set by both of my parents? I know that all of my strength is a result of my mother's love, care, respect, and encouragement. I am who I am because she chose not to give up. Many parents do.

Unfortunately, my mom and dad divorced in 1978. It was for a simple reason—my mother did not want us girls to grow up hating and disrespecting my dad. She thought that while we were still very young, we should still love, care for, and have some respect for him, and she did not want us to lose that. Otherwise, she said, she could have gone on living the way we had. It was this same year that she also met my stepdad, a nuclear scientist, who lived in my home community on the Navajo reservation. He had befriended a very powerful Navajo medicine man, and was living out this dying man's last request. The medicine man wanted the Navajo children of my home community to stay at home. He was tired of seeing young Navajo children bused out to boarding schools, where they would forget their Navajo teachings and be away from their loved ones. It was his dream to build a school in our home community that would not only teach the regular subjects, but more important, teach the culture and language of the Navajo. He asked my future stepdad to do this, and it was being done. My mother's home community on the reservation was having a dinner in his honor, and in a shade house, among all my mother's relatives, he and my mother fell in love.

I guess I was prejudiced, because I could not believe that my mother would replace my father with a disgusting, rude white man—and that's what I thought of him. I'll be the first to admit that I could not stand anything about him. I was the oldest and therefore knew my real dad the longest, so of course I would react this way. Before I knew what was happening, my mother and step-dad were married, and we moved to my home community of Bird Springs and began attending Little Singer School—the result of the medicine man's dream. It was and is a spectacular accomplishment—a school composed of two geometric domes facing east, powered by wind generators and heated by solar panels from the sun. Everyone in the community pitched in and worked together to build this dream, and my sisters and I were lucky to be part of the first class.

It is ironic that it took a white man to bring my mom and us girls back to our "roots." We had lived on the reservation before, but that was in Tuba City, my dad's home community. Thus, it was my stepdad who was responsible for a very precious time in my life. In Bird Springs, we lived with our maternal relatives, which is a Navajo custom, for the first time. It was during this time that my sisters and I learned to read and write in Navajo, listened to Navajo being spoken all the time, and discovered more about what it is to be Navajo. Although my real dad was fluent in Navajo and knew the culture, he did not pass that knowledge on to us. My mother did the best that she could, but she is not fluent in Navajo, although she understands it. She knows the values Navajo women hold, and that is what she passed on to my sisters and me. We were so happy during this time. I thought of my dad often, but we never saw him. He knew where we were, and we got mail from him once in a while, but he never came to visit.

Life with my stepdad, although difficult at times, was a learning experience in and of itself. He accumulated hundreds of books for our growing library, and my sisters and I always had plenty to read. My mother encouraged us as well by making sure that we visited the library in Winslow, Arizona. My stepdad was also into every electronic gadget imaginable, and worked to acquire the latest innovations in computer software and hardware. He was self-sufficient and pursued several business ventures during this time. Good came out of each one, even though they failed financially. We were always with my mom and stepdad on their business trips, and traveled to places we never thought we'd ever get to on our own. I'll admit that life with my stepdad was always interesting and a constant wonder. Although I found him extremely annoying most of the time, what he gave to my mom, my sisters, and me can never be measured or appreciated enough.

Thus, I learned from and was influenced by all three of my parents—my dad, mom, and stepdad. However, at a very young age, I knew that I wanted to excel academically. Why do poorly in school, when you can just as easily do well? Why not try your best and challenge yourself to do better each time in everything, mental and physical? If you fail in one area, you may succeed gloriously in others. As I reached junior high and high school, I was further motivated to do well academically because of the negative stereotypes that I encountered. Many people believe that all Indians do is live off the government in a drunken stupor. This mentality was unfortunately passed on to their children—my classmates. I always wanted to be a good student and to challenge myself; I was always trying new and different things. I do not like to sit back and let opportunities pass me by. I may be scared to death, intimidated, and embarrassed, but I know that I can do it, and that it will be good for me. "It" can be anything. I may not win or succeed all the time, but at least I've challenged myself to do something different and new, and I've learned and matured because of the experience. Of course, to do this, or even to think this way, you need a solid foundation and someone who believes in you. For me, it was and is my mother and family, and now my husband.

I was always a good student, and by junior high knew that I wanted to graduate in the top ten percent of my high school class. As a high school student, I purposely took the hardest courses offered, because I knew that it would be good for me in the long run. By my senior year I was ready to go to college at any one of the three big universities in Arizona, where I had been accepted and offered scholarships. One day, however, my high school counselor called me out of class to meet Colleen Larimore, then the Dartmouth Native American admissions recruiter. I was one of two students who my counselor thought should meet Colleen, and I remember sitting in a deserted classroom watching a video on Dartmouth. I had heard of Dartmouth before in passing, and I knew that some Navajo guy was rumored to have gone back east for his college education. I thought it was interesting that a Native woman was all the way out in Winslow recruiting Native American students for a college in New Hampshire, and that is the reason I followed through with the somewhat intimidating application process. I toiled over the essay, rewriting it several times. I chose to write about the phrase "no pain, no gain" as my personal quote. At the Flagstaff mall, my mom and stepdad ate lunch with me as I sealed the envelope to my application. We made a special trip from the reservation that day to mail my Dartmouth application by the deadline. A couple of months later, Colleen called me at home and asked me if I would like to visit the college for free. I couldn't believe it! Of course I said yes—this was a big deal for me and my family. My first airplane trip ever was my visit to Dartmouth.

Leaving Flagstaff was scary, and I cried a little when I saw my family waving at me through the airport window. The little plane I was in bounced amid the fluffy white clouds; the turbulence was bad. "Are we going to crash?" I thought to myself. It reminded me of driving on the dirt roads on the reservation, with all the bumps and dips making my stomach tickle. I smiled in delight and uneasiness.

My trip to Hanover began with paranoia. I was convinced that I would get mugged and lose my ticket. So I patted it every so often in my purse to reassure myself that it was still there, safe and sound. But once in Boston, I relaxed. The people talked funny, and the air smelled like fish, but I was feeling great. I made a friend, a Mohawk student who was also participating in the admissions office fly-in program. Talking with him made the four-hour layover in Boston go quickly. While I wasn't looking, he swiped my ticket, and I never knew it until he asked me where it was. In a panic, I searched my purse frantically, and then saw him staring at me, clearly amused. "You took it! Give it back!" I shouted in relief. I felt like an imbecile, that it took no more than a friendly conversation with a guy to put me off my guard.

At last we took off for Hanover. We landed in a small airport, similar in size to Flagstaff's. Right away I spotted two Indian students there to meet us. One guy was light-skinned and tall, with wavy hair and a pointy nose. The other student looked Navajo. They were laughing and snickering at something funny, and welcomed us coolly. They continued to entertain themselves with inside jokes and humor, ignoring me, as we loaded our luggage into their car and sped into the pitch-black night.

Navajo was being spoken to me out of that blackness, and it shocked me so that I didn't hear what was said at first. I blurted out, "I don't speak Navajo." I thought to myself, of all places, why the hell does this have to happen to me here in New Hampshire, 2,000 miles away from home? It is highly embarrassing for me to admit that I can't understand Navajo to another Navajo who speaks it. But the two students carried on with their jokes and snickering, oblivious to my embarrassment. "This is going well," I thought to myself, "what a great first impression I must be making—a Native student who can't even speak her own language. They probably think that I prefer not to speak my own language, or that I prefer not to be recognized as a Native woman." I agonized about what they were thinking about me as we drove on and then dropped off my friend.

Suddenly, the Navajo guy asked if I wanted to stop off at the Native American House, because he needed to find out where my host lived. I acquiesced. Instantly, visions of Indian students madly studying, crouched over their books and calculators, frowning in deep thought danced through my head. I imagined them in well-lit rooms, where bookshelves lined every wall. At the Native American House we descended a rickety staircase into the basement, and my vision shattered. No books? No studying? Several students lounged around a glowing TV, each casually gripping a bottle of beer. Cigarette smoke filled the air. I tried to compose myself, as I was offered a smoke and a beer. It was like a cold bucket of water had been thrown on me, and, in shock, I managed to decline their offers.

For someone who attended study hall in the BIA (Bureau of Indian Affairs) dormitory every night, and never "partied," it is not surprising that my first encounter with college life shocked me. I thought that every person would be studying their brains out, especially since this was an Ivy League school and a weeknight. Was I actually that naive? Some students do, and others don't. My first "reality check" of many during my stay at Dartmouth occurred that night at the Native American House.

My host during my stay at Dartmouth was a Navajo woman from Shiprock, New Mexico. It surprised me that other Navajos were actually this far away from home and succeeding. She and her friends and roommate took me around campus and entertained me during my trip. I visited a Native American studies class with her. Only four students were present, and they were engaged in a class discussion of the film "Broken Rainbow," which documents relocation on the Navajo and Hopi reservations and the strip-mining for coal. Never in all of my high school education had we talked of similar subjects or current Native American issues. I was impressed and dumbstruck with this spectacular experience and discovery.

Most of the NADs (Native Americans at Dartmouth) were happy to meet me, and their enthusiasm to show me a good time was contagious. To me, the Native American students were the most sophisticated, intelligent, and outgoing Indian people I had ever met. The whole of Dartmouth radiated a seductive power. I could sense the seriousness, tradition, and prominence of this institution, as well as the pride the students held in it. I experienced a kind of intellectual ecstasy—I could feel that the whole campus was there to educate and that the students were there to learn. I knew by the end of my trip that I belonged at Dartmouth, among students who were like me. I felt motivated to learn, face new experiences and challenges, and meet new people, in order to broaden my horizons and open my mind. Back at my high school in Winslow, Arizona, I wore my newly purchased Dartmouth sweatshirt with pride. A classmate asked if I would like to be interviewed about my acceptance to Dartmouth on the local radio station. I agreed, and my parents heard me in Bird Springs. I remember wondering if anyone cared or knew where or what Dartmouth was. But it was a great feeling to know that I was on my way there. I could feel it in my bones that I was going, even before I received my acceptance letter. I think of it all as a dream come true, especially since I only applied to "see what would happen."

When I returned to campus as a first-year student, I was tested like never before. I think an omen arrived in the mail before I went to Dartmouth—it was a message printed on my achievement test scores: "Based on your performance on this exam, you will represent the bottom ten percent of the student body at the college of your choice [Dartmouth]." For someone who graduated in the top ten percent of her high school class, this was alarming news. What a way to build a student's confidence! I wonder if they actually thought they were doing me a favor with that little bit of information. To this day, I curse the standardized testing company that sent me that letter, because their message became lodged in the back of my mind—a constant reminder of just where I stood. At least that's what I thought.

During "Freshmen Week" incoming students get a head start on life at Dartmouth and take placement tests. It was during this time that our Undergraduate Advisor (UGA) group held its first meeting. I had just finished moving into Woodward, an all-female dorm. The UGA group was designed to help freshwomen/men during their first year at college. Most of the women in my dorm belonged to my group.

We decided to meet outside, and shuffled onto the front lawn, scattered with bright red and yellow leaves. As we sat in a circle, I promptly began to freeze my ass off on the damp grass. The sun was out, but it was a chilly fall day.

Our UGA, a sophomore, smiled sweetly and began to explain a name game to us. As I looked at all the unfamiliar faces, I felt afraid, intimidated, alone, and different. I was, of course, the only Navajo or Native American person in our group. A pang of homesickness stole into my heart. Our UGA finished her instructions and we began.

The rules were to put an adjective in front of our name that described us and began with the first letter of our name. The object of the game was to introduce ourselves in a way that would help us to remember everyone's name. "Musical Melody" said a proud African American woman. A friendly voice chirped, "Amiable Amy," and everyone smiled in agreement. I couldn't think of an adjective to describe me that began with D. I racked my brain for an adjective, anything! But it was useless. "Oh, why do I have to be here? I don't belong here with all these confident women. Why can't I do this simple thing?" I remember thinking. My palms were sweating, my nose was running, and my teeth began to chatter. I looked at all their faces, so fresh, so clean and confident. It was finally my turn. I still couldn't think of an adjective. In agony, I uttered "Dumb Davina." "Nooo!" they all protested. Amiable Amy interjected, "Why not *Divine* Davina?" I shot her a smile of gratitude, but I was horrified and embarrassed. How could I have said that and been serious? Talk about low self-esteem.

My first term at Dartmouth went well academically. I received an A, a B, and a C. But I was lonely, even though I was friends with several women in my UGA group. It was hard for me to relate to them, because I felt they did not know who I was as a Native American, and where I was coming from. They also didn't understand my insecurities. How could they, when they believed so strongly in themselves?

I look back at my first year at Dartmouth, and realize that I made it hard on myself. I took it all too seriously, but how could I have known then what I know now? It took me years to be able to think of myself in a positive light. My mother always told me, "You are no better than anybody else. Nobody is better than you." Unfortunately, at Dartmouth her gentle words were lost in my self-pity.

Going home for Christmas almost convinced me to stay home. I was so happy with my family, but I didn't want to think of myself as a quitter, nor did I want anyone else to think of me that way. I came back to an even more depressing winter term. My chemistry course overwhelmed me and I flunked it.

Chemistry was torture, and I could not keep up no matter how hard I tried. A subject that I aced in high school and actually liked did me in that term, and made me feel like a loser. What went wrong? It was just too much information too fast. I was depressed, and my heart was not really in the subject. Finally, I accepted my predicament. I'm not science material, and that's that.

Why did I do so horribly? My notetaking skills were my downfall. They were poor at best. The crux of my problem was trying to distinguish the important facts that I needed to write down from the useless verbiage quickly. By the time I got to writing things down, I'd already have forgotten what the professor had just said. In this way, valuable information slipped through my fingers. Not only were my notetaking skills poor, but so was my ability to participate in class discussion. At Dartmouth, one was expected to follow everything that was being said, think fast, take notes, ask questions, and finally deliver eloquent opinions, answers, and arguments. It was beyond my limited experience and self-confidence to do so. "*Say something!*" I screamed mentally, but it was useless. Fear paralyzed me in class. Outside of class I'd talk, but not in class amid the stares of my peers. My freshman English professor and I would have conversations in her office lasting two or three hours, but in her class, when faced with all my peers, I became mute. Once Michael Dorris, my Native American studies professor, asked me outside of class why I did not speak up in his freshman seminar on American Indian policy. I was tongue-tied. Incredibly, I felt that if I spoke up in class, I would be perceived as stupid. It did not help matters that the discussions there utterly lost me most of the time during my first couple of years at Dartmouth.

On one occasion I did speak up—in an education course, "Educational Issues in Contemporary Society." It was a tough course with tons of reading. Participating in the weekly seminar was a significant part of the grade. I never talked to anyone in the class. But the professor was always nice to me, saying "Hi" whenever we ran into each other. That day was just like all the other days of the past few weeks. Seated around the oblong table were about fifteen students, the professor and a teaching assistant. The professor did not lead the discussions; he was there as a participant just like us students, and we determined the content of the seminar. I came in, sat down, and my classmates began to express themselves, taking turns at center stage. I looked from one student to another and wondered how they made it look so easy, wishing that I could, too.

On this day I sat next to my professor, and as usual was lost. The words, ideas, arguments, and opinions whirled around me like a tornado in which I was mercilessly tossed. Too many unfamiliar words, analogies, and thoughts were being expressed for my brain to comprehend, edit, sort, pile, delete, save, etc. But this was nothing new—all of my classes at Dartmouth were confusing to me and extremely difficult.

Out of the blue, as I sat there lost in thought, my professor turned his kind face toward me and asked "Davina, why don't you ever say anything?" His question was totally unexpected, but not malicious. Rather, it was asked in a respectful tone that invited an answer. Everyone stared me down; they wanted to know, too. I was caught off guard, but thought to myself: this is my chance to explain why I am the way I am. I began hesitantly, frightened out of my wits, but determined to let these people know who I was and where I was coming from.

"Well, I have a hard time here at Dartmouth. I went to school in Arizona. That's where I am from. I went to school in Tuba City, Flagstaff, Bird Springs, and Winslow, Arizona. So I've gone to school both on and off the Navajo reservation. The schools on the reservation aren't that good. But in Flagstaff, I used to be a good student. Bird Springs, which is my home community, is where I learned about Navajo culture in sixth and seventh grade. I got behind though, because the school didn't have up-to-date books. I mean we were using books from the 1950s. I really liked it though, because I learned how to sing and dance in Navajo and they taught us how to read and write the Navajo language. I learned the correct way to introduce myself in Navajo, so even though I got behind and had to catch up in the eighth grade, it was the best time of my life, and I learned a lot about my language and traditions. Then when I went to eighth grade and high school in Winslow, I had to stay in the BIA dorm away from my family, because the bus didn't come out that far. So the dorm was for all the Navajo and Hopi students who lived too far away on the reservation. Winslow was a good school, but I don't think I was prepared for an Ivy League school like Dartmouth. I mean it's so hard being here so far away from home. I used to be in the top ten percent of my class—now I'm at the bottom of the barrel! Do you know how that makes me feel?"

I couldn't help myself and I began to sob. My words were rushing out like they had been bottled up inside for too long.

"It's awful. I feel like I can't do anything here and that the students are so much smarter than me. It seems like everyone knows so much more than me. All of you, it's so easy for you to sit there and talk. It's hard for me to do that. I envy you. I feel like I'm always lost. I hardly ever understand what you guys are talking about. It's that bad. My notetaking skills aren't that good either and it causes me a lot of problems in class, makes me get behind. I mean we never had to take notes like this at Winslow. And it's hard for me to participate in class discussion. I mean at Winslow we had to, but not like this. My teacher would put a check by our name after we asked one question. We didn't sit around a table and talk like we do in here. We didn't have to really get into a subject. We didn't even have to write essays. I only wrote one term paper in my junior and senior year. My English teacher would always tell us how much writing we'd have to do in college, but he never made us write! I'm barely hanging on, but here I sit and that's why I don't participate in class discussion."

I finished my tirade. It was quiet. Nobody said a word. Then my professor leaned over and jokingly admitted, "Don't feel too bad, Davina, I don't understand what they're talking about half the time either." We all smiled, and it was as if a great weight had been lifted off my shoulders. I'm so glad he prompted me to speak that day, and his comment helped me to put it all in perspective. Not everything a Dartmouth student says is profound. It was in this class that I received a citation, which distinguishes a student's work. My professor wrote, "Courage is a sadly lacking quality in the educational world we've created. Davina dared to take steps on behalf of her own growth (and ultimately for her fellows) in an area where she could reasonably expect to be tripped by an insensitive and dominating culture. It was a privilege to accompany her." For Education 20, I received a grade of D with an academic citation, simultaneously one of the worst and best grade reports a student can receive. "Only I would receive such an absurd grade," I said to myself in exasperation, but I was proud despite the D. After that day in class, my self-confidence went up a notch. In my junior and senior years at Dartmouth I began to participate in class little by little. By the time I hit graduate school, you couldn't shut me up.

During my first year at Dartmouth, I did not find much comfort with fellow Native American students. Why was I so lonely? Isn't that what the purpose of the Native American Program was—to make students like me feel at home? Wasn't I having fun attending NAD functions and parties? To be honest, I participated, yet I did not feel accepted or comfortable among the other NAD students. It was partly due to my lack of self-confidence. Besides, it was apparent that they already had established friends and, except for a few of them, did not seem too concerned about the welfare of new students. I was an outsider, not yet a team player. Although I often talked to Bruce Duthu, the director of the Native American Program, I still felt at a loss around the students.

Finally spring term arrived after a long, dark, cold winter, and I made a new friend. This time it was different, because with Cheryl I felt at ease. She was a fellow Indian woman. We could relate to one another, and she at least had some idea of where I was coming from. However, it was the Dartmouth Pow Wow that really began my initiation into becoming a full-fledged NAD.

The night before the Pow Wow was a balmy one. As Cheryl and I sat on the marble steps of Dartmouth Hall, we alternately criticized and laughed about Dartmouth life. She lit up a cigarette with a practiced hand and offered me one. I accepted and tried to be cool like her but my lungs refused to cooperate, and I coughed out the smoke. She chuckled at my pitiful attempts, but I didn't mind. I was smoking with a friend and was finally happy. At length, we got up and headed toward the Native American House, or "The House," as it's fondly called. We entered the front door. The House was quiet and peaceful as I stepped into the study room. On my left, grocery bags full of food lay haphazardly abandoned and ignored. Where was everybody? We were supposed to be dicing up tomatoes, onions, and cheese, shredding lettuce, and most important, making fry bread dough. I knew that it would take a lot of work to do this for our Indian taco booth at the Pow Wow, so I rolled up my sleeves and began on the tomatoes. At length, a few more NADs trickled in. "Look at Davina, she's so motivated. Oh, I better get up and help, you're making me feel guilty," Bill teased. After everything was chopped, diced, and shredded, we called it quits. But early the next morning, I went straight back to the House, worrying about the fry bread dough. We needed to make enough to feed several hundred people, and that would take time. I began to mix the appropriate amounts of flour, baking powder, salt and warm water, kneading the dough to the right consistency. Cheryl came down from her room upstairs at the house and joined me. After we'd been there awhile, Richard, a Navajo guy, came to help. I was secretly happy that I'd beaten him to the job. Navajos are supposed to rise early and he was late. Did I catch a look of embarrassment on his face? He lined a trash can with a garbage bag and we poured in our dough, Cheryl's Winnebago dough mixed with my Navajo dough.

After the dough was made, we rushed to the Pow Wow grounds at Storr's Pond—a grassy camping area about a mile from campus. Already a line had formed and customers were waiting patiently for their authentic Indian food. We lit our butane stove, put on the cast iron frying pans and loaded them with chunks of white lard. The day steamed, and so did we, all day long. I didn't get to see much of the Pow Wow, as the line to our popular Indian taco stand was neverending. I slaved away, and in the process, relaxed in the familiarity of making fry bread. A fellow NAD would pass me a nice, cold Coke every so often to quench my thirst. We flapped dough with our hands, joked, laughed, and sweated as each golden round of fry bread was snatched from us for the next hungry customer. By the end of the day, I was covered from head to toe in flour, my back and shoulders were tight, and my feet hurt, but

I was at peace and happy. I sensed a feeling of camaraderie with the NADs for the first time. The day was ending; I got a backrub from a NAD medical student, and it was time for the '49.

The "host drum" group and their family brought cases of beer and began to sing Kiowa '49 songs of romance and pretty Indian girls. We gathered in the picnic area and built a huge bonfire. I drank a beer, my first since coming to Dartmouth, then bravely tried a wine cooler. I visited with the family of the host drum, and we laughed loudly together under the twinkling stars. Soon the singing coaxed us into a round dance. The wine coolers took my shyness away, and my feet stepped in time to the rhythm of the drumbeat and the words of the song.

After a couple of hours my eyes and body drooped with fatigue from all the hard work, the drinks, and now the dancing. I wanted to take a hot shower, wash off the smell of grease and smoke, and sleep. A NAD asked if I'd like a ride back to my dorm, and as I was leaving, several people thanked me for my hard work. After eight months at Dartmouth, I finally felt like I belonged and was a part of the Dartmouth Native American family. Never underestimate the power of fry bread.

It's amazing how much my life changed after that day at the Pow Wow. Now I couldn't wait to attend all the NAD functions, visit with other NADs, and enjoy my time at Dartmouth. I wondered if everyone had to prove themselves to the NADs like I did. Did I prove myself? Or did I just become relaxed enough to finally have a good time? Maybe it was both.

Friction did exist in NAD, as people always complained about NAD being too much of a clique, shunning those who were not "full bloods" (full blooded Indians). I know who I am, a Diné, even though some idiot will always say, "You don't look like an Indian." Well, excuse me for not wearing war paint, buckskin, and feathers. How someone can be ignorant and arrogant enough to know what an Indian "looks like" is beyond me. I've suffered through too damn much not to be an Indian. But I also know and understand the beauty of being Navajo—the strong matrilineal and clan ties; the lessons in my grandmother's strict admonitions; the taste of broiled mutton freshly slaughtered; the feel of dirt in my hair; and the love and wisdom of my mother. How I've lived is Navajo, even if I don't speak and understand my own language fully. How can anyone quantify what part is Navajo and what part is not? I just am. I think some people question what part of them is Indian and what part is not, and that's not healthy.

My sole problem at Dartmouth was that I did not possess self-confidence. I often looked down on myself, thinking that I wasn't good enough, smart enough, sophisticated or rich enough—whatever—to be a part of the Dartmouth family, my UGA group, or a part of NAD. That was always my problem. It took time for me to rise above my self-defeating attitude.

My sophomore year was so totally unlike my freshman year that it's comic. We had a huge and awesome class of incoming Native American freshmen and freshwomen, or '91s, as they're referred to (by the numerals of their year of graduation). All of a sudden, enthusiastic young NADs were popping up everywhere, thirsting for friendships and a good time. I promptly began befriending them and having the time of my life. Aside from the friends I had made in my UGA group, the NADs were about the only people I hung out with. Why try to make friends with people who don't seem to be interested in you? Why make that effort? I'm not sure why it works out that way, but it did in my case. I can honestly say I never really got close to a white person, other than my roommate. Why is there such a boundary between groups? Was it just me, or was it everybody? I remember getting drunk a couple of times at frat parties, and having long conversations with white people, but then I would never talk to them again, and they weren't my friends.

In the fall of my junior year, I changed my major from visual studies to anthropology. Professor Deborah Nichols became my mentor. I enjoyed her courses on the prehistory of North America. Ever since I can remember, I wanted to go back in time to see what life was like before Columbus. Also, I loved learning about other Indian tribes. Before I came to Dartmouth, I thought that all the Indians east of the Mississippi were extinct—killed off or removed by the United States government. My eyes were opened at Dartmouth. Dartmouth gave me a strong and true sense of Indian pride. Where else could I have taken classes specifically focusing on Indian life, history, literature, and culture; met and listened to Indian tribal chairpersons, scholars, performers, and artists, as well as traditional elders? The principal chief of the Cherokee Nation, Wilma Mankiller, Dartmouth's own Michael Dorris and Louise Erdrich '76, the Lakota educator Albert Whitehat, and members of the American Indian Dance Theater, were just a few of the people who spoke and/or performed at Dartmouth through the Native American Program, Native American Studies Department, and NAD. Dartmouth's commitment to Native people inspired me to finish my education and to develop and nurture my own growing desire to work for my people or people of other tribes.

Professor Nichols encouraged me to look into the field of archaeology. But after a summer at a field school at Wupatki National Monument in Arizona, I decided that I was uncomfortable excavating the places where Indians once lived and had died—anyway, it goes against Navajo religion and teachings. As Professor Nichols did not want to lose my interest, she presented other options in the field of anthropology. She pointed out that I could help Indians get the remains of their deceased ancestors back, as well as their sacred and ceremonial objects, which were being held in museums all over the country, or I could work on repatriation and reburial issues. Through research for a term paper, I learned more about these issues, and was instantly converted. Anthropology need not be the field most Indians love to hate. Instead of being an anthropologist who takes away from Indian people, I will be an anthropologist who gives back—through work with repatriation and reburial, or in other ways.

My interest prompted me to apply for the senior internship at Dartmouth's Hood Museum of Art. It was an intimidating prospect, but I decided to go for it anyway. I was accepted as one of only two senior interns. It was a glorious experience. I was able to handle the Hood's collections of Native American material objects as I helped transfer them from Webster Hall to a new storage annex at the Hood. I had the privilege of co-curating a major exhibit on Native North American basketry, which entailed conducting research on each and every basket in the collection.

The Native American Program was the reason I chose Dartmouth, and it was the reason I stayed. When I speak of the Native American Program, I am also including the Native Americans at Dartmouth student organization and the Native American studies department. NAP was the basis upon which I received my education. NAP ensures that Native youth who were raised in remote areas on Indian reservations, often living in poverty, and not able to receive the best education that money can buy, are given a chance to excel at an institution such as Dartmouth. Many Native students attend Dartmouth because they know that with such an education they will be better equipped to serve their home communities or other Native communities. I am such a person.

NAP ensures that Native students are taken care of. They are not forgotten or ignored. It is hard enough getting through college, but it is even harder when you are 2,000-plus miles away from home and you hardly have contact with any other Native people, aside from students. Although I may have felt ignored by other Native students at first, that was partly my fault, as I did not reach out.

Although Dartmouth strives to keep all of its students, some do not make it. My inner strength is my family, as I mentioned, and my beliefs. I believe that we should leave the past behind us—grow from it, learn from it—but go on with your life and do the best that you can. Why not try to make life better for yourself and others? Why waste our time hurting ourselves or others? Just live your life in a good way, the way you want to live it, and be happy. Enjoy it while it lasts.

I've always felt that way. I guess that's why I try to do well in everything I do. I'm not saying that I am better than anyone else. I'm just saying, do what you want to do in beauty. My people have a saying that we use in prayer, "Walk in beauty." I just realized that's what I always try to do: live in a beautiful way.

Davina Ruth Begaye Two Bears grew up in beautiful northern Arizona, a proud member of the Diné Nation. She graduated from Dartmouth in 1990 with a major in anthropology, and the following year, she was chosen as a teaching intern at the Northfield Mount Hermon School in Massachusetts, where she was a teacher, student advisor, and coach.

Upon returning to Arizona, she began working with her tribe as an archaeologist, and in subsequent years served as a student supervisor for the Navajo Nation Archaeology Department. At that time, she began taking courses toward a master's degree in anthropology at Northern Arizona University. In the future, Davina plans to continue her work in anthropology and pursue her Ph.D. in the field.

Davina married Brady Two Bears, a member of Dartmouth's class of 1991, and together they moved to Wisconsin, where they reside with their daughter, Brenna. They are currently expecting their second child.

▼ ▼ ▼ ▼ ▼ ▼ ▼ ▼ ▼

RICARDO WORL

A Tlingit Brother of Alpha Chi

When I think about my childhood and the place
I grew up, I marvel at how I ended up at a liberal arts college in
the northeast. When I was small, I thought that everybody lived
like Tlingit Indians. Juneau, my hometown, is a small town built
on the site of a Tlingit Indian village. Tall mountains, blanketed
by a lush rain forest, drop steeply to the green-tinged saltwater
channel. Houses and buildings are nestled close together on the
slopes. I remember being accustomed to gray and rainy days. My
neighborhood was near the waterfront. In fact, we could see the
short bridge that crosses the channel to Douglas Island from our
front window. The neighborhood was fun because there were many

other kids like me—Indians, Filipinos, and a mix of both. Our parents usually knew each other. The streets were fun because there were always lots of deep mud puddles and plenty of rocks to throw. Not too many cars came through that way, so we felt pretty safe. A trailer park was located down the block. I recall being amazed at the number of people who could live in one of those trailers. Some houses were new and well kept. Most were older, rundown and filled with lots of stuff in the yard.

My family was always happy and laughing. I grew up around all of my aunts, uncles, grandparents, and cousins. Family gatherings were as common as the rains in Southeast Alaska. Grandpa and Uncle Sam were always cooking and making us eat. My addiction to fried rice must have started with them. In good Tlingit tradition, Uncle Marcelo would take my brother and me out fishing every summer. Salmon was abundant in the Juneau area when I was growing up. Uncle George taught us boys how to be tough and the importance of hard work. When he wasn't at work, he would wrestle with us or pick us up with one arm. One time he impressed us immensely when he lifted one side of a Volkswagen bug completely off the ground with me and several of my cousins inside. Uncle Frank always had pretty girls with him so I didn't mind tagging along to play the part of the cute little nephew. Uncle Joey would take the time to play with my brother and me, which was amazing, because he was a teenager, and the teenagers usually didn't hang out with younger kids because it wasn't cool. My aunts made certain that we stayed out of trouble by keeping us busy with outdoor activities. Auntie Carmen took us up to the glacier or to the beach whenever it was sunny. Auntie Nancy brought us berry picking and clam digging. She taught us about plants, birds and animals. My sister was the oldest in our family, so she got stuck baby-sitting my brother and me when we weren't with one of our aunts or uncles.

Mom made certain that we were exposed to as many experiences as possible. When I was only in the second or third grade, my brother, sister, and I were enrolled in art classes and tap dance lessons. I never knew until recently that my mother had to scrounge up the money to pay for them. She was determined to give us as many social and cultural experiences as we could afford. My brother and I were always getting teased about being in dance lessons because we were the only boys in a class of what seemed like hundreds of teenage girls. None of the other kids in the neighborhood had to go through such humiliation.

My perception of the universe was based on my experiences growing up in Juneau with my family. My father was in the Coast Guard and worked as a bartender evenings and weekends. We never felt like we were poor. We always had food, a clean home, school clothes, and a car. I didn't realize that many kids were poor. Now I realize that most of them were Indian. My understanding of wealth had a meager beginning by Dartmouth standards. What we lacked in material wealth was made up for in happiness and strong family ties and values. We were taught to be respectful of others. We could never get away with speaking to or treating anybody harshly. We learned early that our entire family was responsible and accountable for the actions of each of its members. We had to be especially nice to non-family members, because there was a good chance that they were members of the opposite clan, the Ravens. Tlingits are divided into two main groups—the Eagles and the Ravens.

The Tlingit clan system is extremely complex. There are many rules, customs and protocols regulating clans and their members. The first, and most important, rule is that every member of your clan is your relative, like your brother or sister. Therefore, you may not marry someone of the same clan, even though they may not be biologically related to you. An Eagle must marry a Raven, not another Eagle. We grew up knowing that someday my brother, sister, and I would have to marry someone from the opposite clan, so we never took the chance of offending someone who could turn out to be a future in-law. In fact, Mom would always remind me that I was arranged to marry a Raven girl named LuLu. I still blush at the thought.

Sharing was ingrained into our thinking and behavior. We learned at an early age that when you share, it always comes back to you in a good way. Sharing what you have is also a way to increase your status and gain the greatest respect. In Tlingit tradition, wealth and status are based on the premise of sharing. When a Tlingit clan hosts a potlatch, they spend months saving money and preparing gifts, traditional foods, and art objects. During the potlatch, the clan's wealth is given away, or redistributed, to members of the opposite clan. The greater the amount given away, the greater the status of that clan and its members. This type of sharing ensured the welfare of the community and created unity between families. My aunts and uncles still tell stories about how hard they had to work all summer to harvest and prepare traditional foods that my grandmother would then give away to other families. Even though years have passed, many of the elders remember and acknowledge the generosity of our family.

When we were guests at someone's home, we were expected to behave in a manner that was appropriate and reflective of our family's status. If we were in the presence of elders or if we were attending a Tlingit ceremony, nothing less than perfect manners were acceptable. Acceptable behavior meant being respectful, dignified, and attentive. I don't recall that anyone ever said anything directly to us about how we were supposed to behave. We just knew by the way our parents looked at us, by the mood of the people in the room, or by the way other kids were acting. If we were behaving inappropriately, we could sense it. Perhaps the best way I can describe it is to liken it to telepathic punishment emanating from the adults in the room.

The best times we had were when we went camping, fishing, or down to the beach at low tide to gather food. Tlingits do not view fishing, hunting, berry picking, or clam digging as sport or recreational activity. It's more of an opportunity to learn important lessons about life or to reinforce values. Harvesting traditional foods is usually a family or communal activity. It is a time when uncles give advice, nephews ask questions, and elders share stories. We learned a lot from the stories and legends that were told to us over and over until we knew them by heart. I remember hearing the stories about Raven, the trickster who brought us water, the sun, the moon, and the stars. Other stories taught us the Tlingit belief that humans and animals alike have spirits, and only our outer appearances separate us.

Our sense of spirituality and our connection to the land were things we learned and experienced each time we were out on the water, in the woods, or on the beach. Spirituality wasn't anything that we talked about or were taught directly—we learned it over time. My reverence for the land and its people is the strongest value I possess and I cherish it.

Prior to junior high school, things were a little less clear when it came to interacting with non-Indian folks. I assumed that the awkward feelings I'd get in school, restaurants, grocery stores, art classes, or other places with mostly white people were caused by the place, and not the people. The body language and mood of people in these places were difficult to read, making it a real trick to know how to act or what to say.

The romantic notion that everybody was brought up like Indians faded when we moved out of Juneau and I quickly learned that non-Indian people think differently. My family relocated to Anchorage in 1970 so Mom could complete her undergraduate degree. Anchorage was the first city I had seen, so I was awed by the lights and the tall buildings. About three years later, Mom received a fellowship to attend Harvard. We moved to Cambridge, where we lived for three years while she worked on her graduate degree in anthropology. Throughout our stay in Cambridge, we would frequently visit with Indians from other states. I learned how to get around on the subway and how to mingle with the eccentric 1970s-type intellectuals at the many receptions we attended with Mom.

Just when I thought my exposure to diverse cultural experiences had reached a climax, Mom asked us what we thought of moving to Barrow, Alaska, so that she could study Eskimo whaling. The next thing I knew, we were hundreds of miles above the Arctic Circle, living in a one-room shack with no running water, television, or flush toilets. For the next three years we lived in this community of less than one thousand primarily Inupiaq Eskimo inhabitants. By this time, my sister was off to college in Washington state. My brother and I had to learn to stick up for ourselves, as she had always been our bodyguard.

Living in Barrow was one of the most exciting experiences of my life. The Inupiaq way of life was hunting, fishing, and whaling. However, the community was on the verge of serious transition. Barrow and several other villages in the region had just formed the world's largest municipal government, which included in its tax base the world-class oil fields of Prudhoe Bay, the starting point for the Trans-Alaska pipeline. We were there to study the "socio-economic impact of oil development on Eskimo whaling" for Mom's dissertation. By the time we left Barrow and moved back to Anchorage, my brother and I had had our fill of "cultural enrichment" and were looking forward to a lifestyle that was a little more mainstream. My brother took off for college while I completed high school in Anchorage.

During the summer, my brother, sister, and I always went home to Juneau, where we would fish and spend time with our relatives. We were also members of a Tlingit dance group that performed for the tourists on the many large cruise ships that frequented Juneau. We'd spend our days outdoors or hanging out with family.

Whether or not to go to college was something I never had to contemplate. The fact that we would attend college must have been drilled into our heads at birth. My brother had started college a few years earlier, my sister was in college, and Mom had finished graduate school and was working on her dissertation. I was fortunate to have so many role models and people with high expectations around me.

I was certain college was going to be a continuation of the mental torture I had suffered during the application process: the SAT, essays, financial aid forms, alumni interviews, and all the other stuff necessary to get accepted. My brother, who was in his second year at Humboldt State in California, told me horror stories about the study habits of college students, about how he had to sleep in his car and live off peanut butter or spaghetti because money was so tight. I had little reason to believe that college would be fun.

I arrived in Hanover for the first time in the fall of 1980. My aunt, her husband, and my two younger cousins gave me a ride from Boston, where they were living at the time. It was warm, humid and overcast. The campus was still green, and turned out to be much smaller than I had envisioned from studying the map sent to me by the admissions office. I was somewhat familiar with the geography, climate, and architecture of the region from having lived in Cambridge ten years earlier.

When my aunt drove away, it struck me that this was the first time in my life that I was alone without another family member. I was in a community where I did not know a soul. It took all my willpower to overcome my nervousness. It got easier when I thought about having the opportunity to test my independence.

I recall many insecure moments in my freshman year when I didn't fit in or understand what was going on. For instance, the guys in my dorm were always talking about a singer referred to as "The Boss." I had never even heard of Bruce Springsteen or his music until I arrived at Dartmouth. The way the guys were talking about him, and the frequency with which I heard his music, made me wonder how many other things I had never heard about while growing up in Alaska.

Another instance of my Alaskan naiveté, which I seemed to demonstrate frequently, occurred after a great evening I had partying at an upscale Connecticut country club. During the day, it was one of the finest golf and tennis facilities around. By night, it was transformed into a beachfront establishment for wining and dining. In one section of the club, a string quartet performed classical music, catering to mostly older people. Another section of the club featured a hot jazz band. The younger members congregated here for dancing and socializing. This was my first introduction to this sort of social setting. I wondered why we didn't have one in Alaska. I told my friend that this place was so cool that when I got back to Alaska I was going to open up a country club. He laughed at me and explained that country clubs weren't like restaurants or franchises, but rather were owned by local governments. He still teases me about my dream of owning such a place.

On numerous occasions, my being from Alaska was a novelty to others. I remember being at a friend's dinner party in his summer home in upstate New York. One of the guests was absolutely fascinated with me because I was from Alaska. The whole table had been listening to our conversation when she looked at me with a straight face and asked, "Well, if you're from Alaska, where did you learn to speak English so well?" I looked at my friend for help because I didn't know if she was serious or if I should laugh. After a long silence, her husband elbowed her and politely changed the subject. My friend and I get a kick out of that story now, but at the time I was at a total loss for words.

Regardless of these differences and difficulties, I was able to succeed in college. I had learned to convert being eccentric into being exotic and to capitalize on my differences. Besides, there were so many fun experiences during college that I didn't have time to be consumed by the insignificant or negative events.

My dormitory, Smith Hall, was a small, all-male dorm with about fifty guys. We were adjacent to an all-female dorm, Woodward, which faced another small all-male dorm named Ripley, our rivals in any sort of dorm competition. My freshman-year room was a one-room double. There was just enough space for the bunk bed, two desks, two dressers, and a small refrigerator. My roommate, Marty, was from Boston. He had sent me a letter at the end of my senior year in high school to introduce himself so we wouldn't be total strangers when we met in college. Marty had attended prep school and was a pretty good hockey goalie. His father was a Dartmouth grad. Marty was the perfect roommate for me. He was very patient with my naive questions about East Coast culture, sports, music, books, and protocol. Marty was always on top of the important stuff like freshman meetings, academic requirements, and registration paperwork. He knew which fraternities were having parties and he was an excellent role model when it came to study habits. My Dartmouth experience would not have been the same if I had ended up with a roommate who wasn't responsible or kind enough to show me the ropes. Marty played an important role in my effort to balance the Indian world with the Dartmouth/non-Indian world. The short time we spent as roommates made a lifelong impression on me. During that time I learned to communicate and interact effectively with non-Indian people. My family and my experiences at Dartmouth taught me that social and economic contrasts between Indians and non-Indians may get in the way sometimes, but should never prevent you from learning from and enjoying life.

I would venture to say that an equal amount of my learning in college came from my social experiences outside of the classroom. The variety of individuals I became friends with provided me with knowledge and lessons more valuable than any textbook. Certainly some of the more memorable moments took place at parties and during play time. However, the more meaningful experiences occurred during uncensored dorm room discussions or during student organization meetings. I had four years of watching America's finest in action; we became masters in diplomacy, goal setting, and problem solving.

I didn't truly understand the significance of Dartmouth's being an Ivy League school until I began to understand the quality of individuals I worked with and became friends with. I was able to determine what was important to know and what wasn't. In high school I had learned to watch for cues of proper etiquette and other social nuances. I learned to differentiate between those who were sincere, and those who were not, and what was appropriate behavior and whom I could trust. However, the Dartmouth community and social sphere were far more complex than the public high school I had attended. Throughout my four years at Dartmouth, I somehow managed to become comfortable and fit in without sacrificing my Indian identity or values. I suspect that my values and childhood in Juneau, Alaska, were not typical of most other Dartmouth students. I was expected to return home and put my skills to work for the benefit of the Indian community. I remember fellow classmates asking me what I would be doing after graduation. I explained to them that I would be returning to Alaska. They couldn't understand why I wanted to return to Alaska, where there seemed to be few career opportunities and not much social life. Many of my friends had interviewed for jobs in New York City, Boston, and Chicago. They were willing to live wherever the best job offer placed them. The concept of living anywhere but Alaska had never crossed my mind.

Many Dartmouth students viewed college as a stepping stone or a prerequisite to building a successful career for themselves. For me, it was different. My mission would be accomplished by graduating. My upbringing didn't prepare me to maximize the academic and career opportunities available at this college.

I had no idea what my major would be when I arrived in Hanover. Many first-year students already knew their major, and some had even selected their courses for the next four years. My high school counselor advised me to try a wide range of classes when I got to college. He felt I should find out what I was good at and what I enjoyed the most. By the middle of my sophomore year, I discovered I didn't have a strong desire to pursue any particular area of study. However, anthropology was a natural choice for me. Mom was an anthropologist. I grew up around anthropologists. I had even participated in my mother's fieldwork on Eskimo whaling. My grades were average when it came to all my other courses. I got clobbered in introductory economics, was skeptical of my religion course, and just barely reasoned my way through philosophy. Although I could manage science courses, I didn't have any real interest in them. By process of elimination, I determined that anthropology would be my major.

Dartmouth did a wonderful job of creating a sense of community. Our sense of devotion and sense of pride in the college was established during our first term on campus. Freshmen participated together in camping trips, sat together at football games, and constructed the homecoming bonfire. We felt this same unity within our dorms and with the college as a whole. Students had plenty of opportunity and choices for joining clubs and participating in campus activities. We had expectations and stereotypes for individuals depending on which dining hall you chose to eat at, which part of the library you studied in, which sport you participated in, which dorm you lived in, which fraternity or sorority you were a member of, and which major you chose.

My transition from Alaska to college would not have been as comfortable, nor as successful, without other Indians. My friends through the Native American programs became my surrogate tribal members. Without connection to other Indians, my self-confidence and identity would have been severely challenged. Some members were uncertain about my participation with the Native American group because of stereotypes associated with my fraternity. Since graduation I've learned that this type of skepticism is not exclusive to Dartmouth, nor is it uncommon among Native American tribes.

I was fortunate and thankful to have had Indian mentors like Arvo Mikkanen, Steve Healey, Professor Michael Dorris, Grace Newell, director of the Native American Program, and my classmate Mark Chavree. My four years at Dartmouth were the only time in my life I was not around other Indians on an everyday basis. There were so many instances where I would be at a social function, restaurant, convention, or meeting where I was the only Indian, and sometimes the only minority, attending. For nine months at a time, I would live, eat, study, and party with guys whose values and priorities contrasted with my own. Being with Indian friends helped me keep my values, my humor, and my life complete.

I made my life more complicated when I joined a fraternity that had earned the reputation of being "pro-Indian symbol." Dartmouth's unofficial mascot at one time was the Indian. The administration had officially discouraged use of the Indian symbol. However, Dartmouth has a history and a taste for "old traditions." Students who wore Indian-symbol hats, jackets or T-shirts, and who used the "wah-hoo-wah" and "scalp-'em" cheers at football games were perceived to be rebels defying "the administration" and trying to keep a Dartmouth tradition alive, regardless of the fact that the symbol and cheers were offensive to Native Americans. It was an example of institutional racism at its worst. Pro-Indian symbol students believed themselves to be somehow detached from their irresponsibility and insensitivity because it was a college tradition. Alumni seemed to encourage its use, and "everyone else" seemed to be wearing Indian jackets.

I spent hours, usually on a one-on-one basis, with my fraternity brothers trying to understand them and then trying to explain to them why using the Indian as a mascot was wrong. I know that my efforts and the words that came from my heart made an impact. I let my friends and classmates know I objected to the use of the Indian symbol. But I refused to let the issue consume all of my time and energy because Dartmouth and Alpha Chi Alpha had so much more to offer.

I joined Alpha Chi because of its many positive attributes and because of its members. Alpha Chi had an extensive membership of campus leaders, scholars, and athletes, as well as a history of community service. My best friends today were my brothers in Alpha Chi. Some of the best experiences in my life were with them, and some of my most meaningful lessons came from them. A good portion of my time outside of studies was spent at the fraternity or in fraternity-related activities. Vacations, ski trips, football games, dorm parties, movies, meals, workouts, and campus functions or ceremonies were usually done in the company of one or more of my fraternity brothers.

My senior year, I lived in the fraternity house with twenty other guys in my class. Unlike in dormitories, where the college took care of everything, we were responsible for everything—cleaning, maintenance, financial management, fire inspections, college standards, and security were all in the charge of residents of the house. Our parties were always fun, but we had to deal with the mess and the exotic smells the next morning. We knew how to have fun and we would play hard, but we also knew when it was time to work and study hard. The discipline and intensity my fraternity brothers had when it came to studies was a positive influence on my own work habits. Their attitudes toward work helped me establish a high standard, which carries over into my career today.

Graduation was a mental and emotional blur for me. Commencement was loaded with pomp, ceremony, tradition, and personal reflection. After four years of fun, independence and personal growth, I found it difficult to accept that I was about to give up the security and comforts of Dartmouth and my friends. I was too busy thinking about all the good things I would be leaving in Hanover to really think about the significance of my accomplishments, the details of the graduation ceremony, or my immediate future. I was envious of my classmates and fraternity brothers who had landed jobs in Boston or New York City, where a substantial number of Dartmouth alumni worked and lived. They would be able to room together, get together after work, and attend Dartmouth football games in the fall.

When I moved back to Anchorage, I was no longer surrounded by twenty of my best friends. I no longer had the daily exposure to intellectually stimulating experiences. I was no longer part of a community whose members had similar interests or were socially compatible with me. I remember feeling lonesome for the longest time. I had made my choice. I wanted to come back to Alaska, which my friends could not understand. They questioned the availability of any meaningful work experiences. I could have looked for work in one of the cities, but my commitment and desire to serve Alaska Native people was stronger than my desire to live in a city, away from home, where my work would only benefit me and not others in my community.

I was passing up the opportunity to live in a big city with a competitive, fast-paced, cosmopolitan lifestyle. Instead, I would be living in Alaska, where access to the great outdoors, the long, dark winters, and seasonal industries influenced the pace of work and life. I have no regrets about my decision. In the ten years since graduation, I have kept in touch with my fraternity brothers. Although at times I am envious of their professional success and personal growth, they tell me that they are envious of me—that they wish they could live in a place as peaceful, safe, clean, and breathtaking as Juneau. A close friend who has been very successful with an investment bank confided that he wished he could have a job where he could see how his work directly impacts or benefits a community. He marvels at the thought of being able to go boating or hiking after work, which I can do because the Alaskan sun doesn't set until 10:00 P.M. during the summer.

My career objectives have been like a continuation of my role at Alpha Chi. To this day, I take every opportunity possible to help non-Indian people understand and accept as much as they can about Indians, our culture, our values and our situation in the modern world. At the same time, I try to make Indians (including myself) understand the same sorts of things about white people. I could write a book on how many ways our country and environment could benefit from adopting some basic Indian values and beliefs. I could also carve many totems that would tell the stories of how Indian people might benefit from adopting certain parts of mainstream society to fit our needs. So many of our conflicts are the result of misunderstanding or misinformation.

My first job out of college was as the marketing director of a statewide monthly magazine. *Alaska Native Magazine* had been founded two years earlier by my sister and family. My mother was the publisher/editor, and my brother the general manager. Our only paid staff members were the art director and administrative assistant. The company was in serious need of a marketing director, advertising salesman, circulation manager, photographer, and reporter. I was expected to fill all these positions, since I was one of the owners and the only one without a job. Dartmouth's social and academic training gave me an advantage in meeting this enormous challenge. Although I had no formal training in marketing, sales, journalism, or publishing, Dartmouth had taught me the basics of problem solving. I was able to figure out what needed to be done and I devised a plan of action with specific objectives. I had to count on my social skills, self-confidence and intuition to do my work because I lacked the technical skills and experience. Performance and work standards were exceptional at Dartmouth. High student expectations were not limited to academics. We were conditioned to give our best effort to every aspect of our lives. I applied these principles and more to my work.

Alaska Native Magazine (*ANM*) was the only publication of its kind. It focused on the social, political, and economic issues involving Alaska Natives, rural Alaska, and Native corporations created under the Alaska Native Claims Settlement Act (ANCSA). Although we targeted our articles to the Native readership, *ANM* appealed to non-Natives as well because of its coverage of ANCSA corporations and Native culture.

ANM was not a moneymaker. The venture was a labor of love for my family and me. Our revenues just barely covered our operating costs. I remember the stress of having to hold off creditors while waiting for our next check to come in the mail. We had used all the money my parents set aside to pay for my college expenses to start up the magazine, so we had to sell off pieces of our Alaska Native art collection to make certain we could pay our two loyal staff members.

After five years of struggling month to month, we decided to shut *ANM* down. The company was a trade-off. We had sacrificed our time and money in return for the best career experience any job could offer. After shutting down *ANM*, we each moved on to our own separate careers. Mom got a job as special assistant to the governor, my brother landed a management position with Alaska's fifth-largest company, my sister started her own marketing consulting business, and I went to work as the assistant director of corporate communications for Alaska's most successful ANCSA corporation. The magazine gave each of us the experience and confidence we needed to excel in our current positions.

My entire career has been devoted to serving Alaska Native people. As early as grade school, I volunteered my time to education programs that promoted Native culture and positive Indian self-identity. In high school I served on a number of community advisory committees and worked as a counselor at a summer camp for Native kids. After college, I worked for a Native magazine, a Native corporation, a Native member of the Alaska legislature, and a tribal organization.

I had this romantic notion that after I finished school, some of our Native leaders whom I had looked up to during my childhood would take me under their wings and show me the ropes. I quickly learned that this would not be the case. In many instances, I experienced resistance instead of acceptance. Since learning this lesson, I have made every effort to be a positive role model for younger Alaska Natives. I have volunteered a substantial amount of my time organizing or participating in Native youth activities. The time spent with Native youth, like the time spent with the land, is one of my greatest sources of energy. I have asked my closest friends, who are also Native professionals, to make themselves available to Native children as well.

My experience at Dartmouth provided me with the social and problem-solving skills necessary to succeed. My family and clan members provided me with traditional values and a positive Indian identity, a task not easily accomplished given the many social ills afflicting Native Americans and Alaska Natives. When I read through these pages of my autobiography, I fear that others might interpret what I have written as simplistic or naive. Being confident with your Indian identity while surrounded by individuals and institutions who maintain values and laws that contradict your own is not simple. Utilizing elements of Western society to cultivate and protect Native American culture is not naive. In fact, Tlingits, like

other Native American tribes, have a history of cultural adaptation.

During the first part of the 1900s, Tlingits went through a period when their goal was to assimilate to Western culture as much as possible. They were willingly educated at Western institutions, and learned Western law and governmental processes. Their goal was to become U.S. citizens. While outwardly it appeared that Tlingits were rejecting their heritage, the tribal leaders knew that with citizenship came the right to vote. This was a wise decision, since the Tlingits were able to use the U.S. government system and laws to protect and gain title to ancestral lands. Today, Tlingits and other Native American tribes continue to adopt elements of Western society to ensure cultural survival. Corporations and other financial entities have become powerful tools for tribes in their quest for survival. I still believe there is merit in the thesis that economic assimilation can occur without jeopardizing traditional values or ancestral lands. Only recently have I learned that balancing my Indian world and Indian values with the non-Indian world is a complex task, particularly since both realms are constantly evolving and changing.

I wish there were an easy formula I could share with young Native Americans to help them learn how to balance the Indian world with the Western world. Our ancestors spent a thousand years structuring the tribe to ensure our survival. Our tribes are still here, with traditional values intact, after years of challenges from the Western world. We seem to be facing a period in our history where the tribes must figure out what we want to do with the strengths we have been given.

I have some of my own ideas about what we should do as a tribe. I know there are other Indians out there with their own visions of the future for their tribes. If you want to share ideas, I hope you will call me one day. I'm easy to find, since I'll be in Juneau for the rest of my life. And if, in the future, I'm not around, you can always talk to my grandkids.

Ricardo is a Tlingit Indian from Juneau, Alaska. His real name is Guchxweina. He is a member of the Thunderbird, or Shungookeidee, Clan who originate from the village of Klukwan. His ancestors come from the House that was lowered from the sun.

He is also known as Ricardo Worl. He graduated from Dartmouth College in 1984 with a degree in anthropology. Upon graduation, he went to work for his family company, Alaska Native Magazine, *as marketing director and editor. He is currently a loan officer and corporate relations officer for the National Bank of Alaska in Juneau. Ricardo is president of the Alaska Native Brotherhood Camp #70. He coaches Native Youth Olympics, which are traditional Native games. He is married to Lisa Worl, also a Tlingit from Juneau and a graduate of the University of Oregon.*

▼ ▼ ▼ ▼ ▼ ▼ ▼ ▼ ▼ ▼

◦ GEMMA LOCKHART

First Morning Light

   The White Mountains around Dartmouth College
opened doors to me because of the Black Hills around Rapid Creek.
South Dakota is my home; I was born of and from Dakota Land.
Dartmouth College became part of my story strangely and seren-
dipitously.

  From the center of the Black Hills, clean waters spread sparkling
lights through our lands. Melting Dakota winters give way to high
country mosses seeping moisture with a pulse. Drops turn to trick-
les, then to brooks, finally becoming trout streams running cold
and deep and fast.

  Rapid Creek is the greatest of these streams, meandering east from the Black Hills, into the Cheyenne River. Soon the Cheyenne's shallow pathway meets the Missouri River where water moves colder, deeper, faster.

The Missouri winds its way to the Mississippi, where currents from our lands swirl out to waters 'round the globe. I tell you these things so that you might understand where I come from, and my perspective in relationship to the woods of New Hampshire and Dartmouth College.

In South Dakota, the point of contact—the date when cultures met for the first time—is not so long ago. Major markers in history are as close as a story from grandma or an evening with grandpa. The telling can come in a song.

Sure as there can be conflict and war when cultures meet, there can also be love. My brothers and sisters and I came to be born in the Black Hills through strength of love binding our Irish father and Czech and Sicangu Lakota mother.

"To be Lakota," Grandmother told me once, "means to have a Lakota heart." I have always known who I am, and the alliances of my heart.

A little more than one hundred years ago, our homeland was not yet a state. The Black Hills and surrounding waters are part of what was known briefly in history as Dakota Territory. These lands hold the character and heritage of both American Indians and non-Natives. The victory of the Sioux and Northern Cheyenne against General George Armstrong Custer and the U.S. Cavalry at the Battle of the Little Big Horn happened just west of here. The massacre of Chief Big Foot and his band of people at Wounded Knee took place just south and east of here.

In Dakota Territory, one of the first medical doctors to arrive from the East was Daniel Geib. About Daniel Geib I know only that he had a grandson who was also educated in the east. This young man became a brain surgeon and eventually returned to serve the community closest to my home in the Black Hills—Rapid City, South Dakota.

Thirty years or so ago, his grandson, Dr. Wayne Geib, arrived in Rapid City and came to live along rapid waters two miles and more downstream from my family's log home in the canyon of Rapid Creek. Wayne Geib was a Dartmouth man. He loved and believed in the college on the hill above the Connecticut River. It was the best, he said, a place like no other for the opportunity it provided to expand the mind. Excellence of education is what he had in mind.

The people of this land who knew and worked with Wayne Geib say he was the best: a person like no other, with extraordinary clarity and brilliance of mind. They say this land has not seen a surgeon the likes of Wayne Geib before or since his presence here. I hardly knew him, though he was the kind of fellow one cannot forget—stern and serious in my memory. What I remember more is my mother's great friendship with his wife, Skip Geib.

The two of them shared a joy that emanated in dancing eyes and the warmth of women's laughter. Sometimes they moved as a pair, attending country school meetings to work for change and bring quality local education.

Through this friendship, my family came to know of and consider Dartmouth College. I was not recruited. No one came looking for me. It was happenstance related to friendship and place that brought to me an awareness of Dartmouth College. When it was time to apply to college, there was only one place I wanted to go: the University of South Dakota. A young man whose gentle songs caught my heart was enrolled there. No question. I intended to follow him to Vermillion, South Dakota, along the edge of the Missouri River.

But the voice of my mother was powerful to me. She encouraged a letter to inquire about admission to Wayne Geib's alma mater and the place of his heart, Dartmouth College. I agreed to look into it but secretly knew where my path would lead. Just for the fun of it, I wrote to Harvard, too. When all was said and done, I applied for admission to only three schools; all three accepted me.

What happened next was pivotal to my life path. An invitation and a plane ticket arrived from the Native American Program at Dartmouth College offering me a visit to Hanover, New Hampshire. This invitation—as with all invitations that open the way for individuals who would not otherwise have opportunity to leave their homelands and be part of the larger world—are seeds that sow meaningful change in society. So it was for me with this invitation from the Native American Program at Dartmouth College.

The journey away from the Black Hills to our nation's eastern seaboard, then north to New Hampshire's Connecticut River Valley, changed me. On this journey, I heard a call. The call came from the woods of New Hampshire. The woods whispered to me as I walked on paths circling Hanover, around Occum Pond, along tangled banks of the Connecticut River. The forest was alive with some spirit familiar to me. Though words fail here, I became aware the woods of New Hampshire wanted me there.

I did not expect this. Nor did I expect to see the likes of Deborah Prairie Chief on that initial visit to the college. Deborah was a forerunner to me—a Cheyenne woman finishing up her freshman year. To see Deborah Prairie Chief was to see likeness and feel the warmth of Lakota people from home. She had black hair tumbling past her waist. Her stance was Western, respectful. She met the world with gentle laughter, and filled me with laughter, too. Her presence served as a sign; it was a powerful way to realize Dartmouth College could be a place for me. That's how I came to the White Mountains and Dartmouth College.

There is a certain false phenomenon in Indian country called "Indian time." Indian time means natural time; it means one comes and goes as one pleases, without regard for discipline connected to a clock. Tick tock. It can be an excuse to be less than professional, some would say passive-aggressive. Indian time mainly has come to mean "late." Yet, if you listen to the oldest stories and values among Lakota people, you know that if something matters, an individual makes sure to be on time. If something is very important, then one shows up early.

I arrived at Dartmouth College early, eager to partake in the tradition of my future college. I came for a walk in the woods, better known in Hanover as a "freshman trip." For those unaware of the famed freshman trip at Dartmouth College, it is an extended hike through the wilds of the White Mountains. The freshman journey—and preparation for the journey—is an important experience in beginning life at Dartmouth. First, one must define oneself. In terms of hiking and camping experience, the student must say if she is 1) a beginner, 2) an advanced beginner, 3) intermediate, 4) advanced intermediate, 5) experienced, or 6) advanced experienced.

No doubt about it, I was advanced experienced, especially compared to the east, where people were pansies and did not understand the wild, rugged, and free life of South Dakota. But just to be safe, and especially to be humble, I claimed that I was only "experienced" in mountain climbing.

The next thing I knew, I was hiking up the base of Mount

Lafayette, a 5,000-plus-foot-high shrine in the White Mountains. There were six others on the trip, and we were all adorned with forty-pound packs on our backs.

Packs on our backs! I had never carried a pack on my back in my entire life! When we hike in South Dakota, we hike freely. We hike far and fast, but we do not carry forty-pound packs. The heels of my hiking companions disappeared into the woods as I fell very far behind the others. I was in over my head; my legs hurt, and my back throbbed in pain. My pride was gashed. I was not pre-pared for this—a tragedy in the New Hampshire woods! A great, granite rock held me as I cried, out of my league by my own doing.

One of my hiking associates came running back through the woods.

"What's wrong?" he inquired.

"I can't make it. I've never carried a big pack like this before. I'll go back to the road and catch a ride."

"No! Let me see," he said as he looked over the harness and heavy load.

"You don't have the waist strap buckled!" he declared in dis-belief.

"What?" I asked. He shook his head, grabbed the strap and rigged my pack tightly around my lower waist, distributing the awkward weight comfortably and evenly. With a yank, he pulled it tight and buckled the strap.

His help changed everything. We climbed on together, and somewhere near jetting granite and sky, we joined up with the others.

Ours was an eagle's view. Humbled to be present at such a height, I was again aware of something powerful and strange on the land. Clouds took away valleys, the mountain landscape, and all else we could see. We walked on, heading downward against free vapors, wind, and cool air.

The hiking trip was a foretelling of sorts. Though I had fallen far behind in my first steps of Dartmouth life, my will to endure miles, mountains, and the days that followed was unmatched by any other heart in our party.

I must note here that the young man who came running back through the woods when I could not continue did not complete his education at Dartmouth College. He left before the completion of our freshman year, feeling there was another place better suited for him. Yet Dartmouth might not have been a place for me, had it not been for his help. Falling on the trail can be a perilous moment. To that man and all men and women willing to fall back on their journeys to lend a hand, I salute you; you are warriors and the finest of friends.

On the first official evening of my Dartmouth career, I went to Webster Hall—a great auditorium on the northeast corner of the campus green—feeling somewhat small in comparison with the others. They were different from me; they dressed differently, spoke differently, and looked different—all fancy and happy and bright. I admired my classmates—without knowing them, I admired them. They were at once excited and in command. This was their night.

A striking fellow walked onto the stage and up to the speaker's podium. He was John G. Kemeny, the president of Dartmouth College. This was a man who deserved attention, a student of one of the great masters. His association with Albert Einstein made me especially attentive to thoughts of the universe spoken through him on this first Dartmouth evening. Kemeny spoke as if the world were a delicate place. He tried to tell us something that perhaps we could not hear.

"Tomorrow, you will begin wasting the most valuable opportunity and time of your life."

How could he say that? He did not know me.

I walked away from Webster Hall into the night shaking my head. I did not agree. But John G. Kemeny was something to hear and see. Spirited intelligence gleamed from the strange man who flashed light and challenged thought with his way and words. Light years in front of me, John G. Kemeny. He disturbed me. He stirred life in me as I walked toward my dormitory room. I walked toward Occum Pond, safe. It seemed I had come a long way.

Long before I knew about a place on the planet called Dartmouth College, there was a confusing "something" which had come to be connected with attending this formerly all-male school in the New Hampshire woods. That "something" was the Indian symbol and its companion "wah-hoo-wah" war cry chanted at football, hockey, and basketball games.

It was difficult to know what to say about the Indian symbol. How can you talk about a feeling that resembles a foot in the center of your stomach, a punch to your middle that makes it hard to breathe? You feel it, but you don't know what to do because you didn't do anything to deserve it.

I stayed quiet about the Indian symbol for the longest time. The Native American students who had more seniority and experience stepped up to voice the feelings of us all. By "us all," I mean the Native American students who chose to be part of the family known as NAD—Native Americans at Dartmouth. Then one day an English professor pulled me aside.

"Gemma, I'm having lunch on Wednesday with Mr. Calvin Trillin, who writes for the *New Yorker*. He's coming to Hanover to listen to different sides of the issue of the Indian symbol," he said. I did not look at him. "I wonder if you would join us."

"I need to think about it," I whispered.

"By all means, take your time, call me anytime Monday or Tuesday." He smiled and left.

Wednesday brought a feeling that resembled an edge. I agreed to go to lunch. Before long, Calvin Trillin, my professor, and I were sitting in a quiet Vermont inn across the Connecticut River from Hanover. The center of my being conveys significance or importance through an inner feeling when the well-being of all the people is at hand. This particular day, I felt the meeting was important.

During lunch, I heard a little sound.

Creak.

Creak. It happened again. They kept talking.

Creak. They paused. They heard it too.

Creak.

Suddenly, Calvin Trillin disappeared. My professor jumped as if someone had poked him. Staring at the floor on the other side of the table, he exclaimed, "Good God, man, are you all right?"

Calvin Trillin was lying on the floor in the center of many sticks! His chair had disintegrated beneath him. He was all right, though slightly stunned. The abruptness of it all was funny, and I responded with laughter. The waitress brought the writer a new chair and we casually continued with the lunch.

"I've been here for two days," Mr. Trillin addressed me, "and I do not understand what the big problem is with Dartmouth's Indian symbol. I see and hear that there are two sides to a little disagreement, but I do not understand why some people feel there is a big problem. Could you help me?"

He looked directly at me.

I would speak directly to the man who fell with his chair, for my mother had taught me that in the world of business, one must look another straight in the eye.

"It's a big problem, Mr. Trillin," I replied, "because there are American Indian nations throughout the United States. These nations have urgent issues facing their families: education, health, housing, food, and water supplies. Many of our people are poor in a material sense. Our American Indian tribes must come to Washington to directly face the government of the United States. At the same time, many of the leaders of the United States—the Representatives and Senators and their associates—come, and will continue to come, from Dartmouth College. Sometime, one of them will be sitting behind the table at a Congressional hearing when an American Indian comes forward to speak on behalf of the humble people he represents making a request for honest human needs. If, at this time, all the Dartmouth-educated person can think is, 'Wahhoo-wah,' then my friend, the Indian symbol at Dartmouth is a big problem."

"I see," he answered.

I reached for a glass of water. I did not say more. I felt related to water, little and weak.

Dartmouth College was a place of paths. Each individual chooses the path to take, the door to enter, or the one to pass by. The college on the hill in New Hampshire lent me two strengths. The first was my Dartmouth family, the inner circles of Native Americans at Dartmouth.

They came equally from the west and east. The Penobscot woman, the Cherokee man, the Cheyenne woman, the Navajo man. Their laughter and stories touched New England. Card games, ball games, and lawn games kept the joys of home in us. We knew why we had come to Dartmouth College: we came to help our families and the communities we loved. And in doing so, we learned truths of our collective tribal past.

Michael Dorris, a Modoc and a professor of anthropology, lit the academic way, providing aspects of the second strength. What we learned in Native American studies we had not known before: the Jesuit journals of the frontier West; the smallpox-infested blankets placed in the hands of innocent bands of Native peoples; the forced sterilization of our women; the dark and official hand of this nation upon Native people.

At Dartmouth, we cried, and we learned to be stronger than strong. We wanted to go home, but we had each other and in this circle of strength we found a way to stay.

Two other people on the faculty of Dartmouth College revealed themselves to be outstanding teachers and friends. Noel Perrin, professor of English, was my greatest teacher of writing. He found a way to convey what it is that brings writing to life—how attention to the smallest detail makes good writing great.

This man meant much to me, not only for his literary skills, but because he loved the land, and he walked his talk. A teacher of environmental journalism, he sugared his own maple trees, drove a solar-powered car, and built and maintained a stone fence through the woods near his Vermont home. "Good fences make good neighbors," said the poet Robert Frost. I have not found another teacher the likes of Noel Perrin on this journey of life.

John Hay, professor of environmental studies, stood out as a man who understood what was really important—the birds, trees, waters, fish, and animals of the natural world. He reminded me of some medicine men from home. Walking with John Hay was like walking with a person who knows how to listen to the world. "Where else should we go for our directions?" he asked. "Hasn't the earth been calling us for a million years?"

Since I graduated from Dartmouth College, the New Hampshire woods have called me to return. I have come back to Hanover for different occasions, but mainly to serve on the college's Alumni Council. This experience has reminded me of many things, but in particular, it has given me the opportunity to see Dartmouth "grown up," and the men and women of Dartmouth as mature adults.

In each and every one of them, I detect a lingering love of a place that has in one way or another left an indelible mark on them—one that they feel but cannot understand. It shows up in rocking chairs on the porch of the Hanover Inn, in a gaze toward the library's tower and clock, in a twinkle in the eye. They think it is Dartmouth that has touched them so, but I think it is more; it is the sum total of the spirit of that place high in the New Hampshire woods, along rapture of the Connecticut River.

Many doors open to me and to American Indian people because of Dartmouth College. Doors of academic knowledge, doors of connection to companies and corporations, doors of tribal relationships. But no door is so valuable as the one that opens the way to friends and companionship of thought: good ideas expressed freely in foundations of friendship. Not friends who are shallow and trying to hustle something, but friends who meet fellow friends side by side, heart to heart, mind to mind.

I like to think of those New Hampshire woods, the White Mountains, and the Black Hills. I like to remember that I moved East listening to voices from the land. I like to make my way now knowing that sometimes there is no way to understand reasons why our paths unfold the way they do.

And finally, as I think of the doors Dartmouth has opened and the tears and laughter which accompanied us as we crossed the thresholds, I like to remember that Ojibway saying, "Sometimes I go about pitying myself while all the while a great wind is bearing me across the sky."

To make one's way in the world means to struggle. Dartmouth does not change this. But she does have a way of lending her sons and daughters the power of a belief in education as the first morning light.

Gemma Lockhart, an Irish and Sicangu Lakota native of South Dakota, graduated with a major in English and Creative Writing from Dartmouth College in 1979. Ten years after Gemma's footsteps left the New Hampshire woods, her sister Tauna Lockhart followed. Since leaving Dartmouth, Gemma has been a television news reporter, producer of television documentaries, and newspaper columnist for USA Today and papers across the Northern Plains. She is most interested in what she does not know and feels the most important part of any communication or language is listening.

Gemma is currently president and CEO of Anpao Studios, a company that produces independent documentaries, community and curriculum creations, commercials, and mini-series for television. She makes her home with her son in the Black Hills of South Dakota.

Planted in the Ground

▼ ▼ ▼ ▼ ▼ ▼ ▼ ▼ ▼

NICOLE ADAMS

My Grandmother and the Snake

When I was four years old, my grandmother brought me out to a shed in her backyard to help with the task of cleaning that year's harvest of huckleberries. After rinsing them, my grandmother and I would pick out the stems and leaves to prepare the berries for canning.

On this particular August day, the heat of the afternoon sun forced a large snake to seek refuge in the cool shed. As it slithered through a crack in the door, I turned to my grandmother. When she remained calm and watched it slide across the floor, I followed her lead. I did not become excited, nor did I run screaming out of the shed; instead I sat by my grandma's side and watched her reactions. When I saw she did not fear the snake, I knew I need not either.

But after a minute or so of watching the snake, my chubby four-year-old legs began to swing in impatience, and I asked my grandmother if I could poke the snake to make it go outside. My sixty-year-old grandma shook her head, got up and shooed it outside, and we resumed our task. Later, my grandma would tell my mother how surprised she was that I was not afraid at all.

From my childhood I can recall instances such as this, where I learned much from my grandmother. I grew up surrounded by the strength of all the women in my family, and from their example I learned. I learned how to hold myself with dignity, and never to be ashamed of my heritage. I learned to be strong-willed and independent. And I learned how to overcome my fear. Whether it was an encounter with a snake when I was four, or facing my fear of failure at Dartmouth College as a young woman, I looked to the women in my life to guide me through difficult times.

Although I am still grappling with what it means to me to be an Indian woman, especially in an environment such as this college, I find myself constantly drawing upon the tremendous strength I have seen demonstrated by all of the women in my family. The precedent set by my mother, sister, grandmother, and aunts is not one of weakness, shame, or dependence. Rather, it has given me much inspiration to succeed, and to endure trying experiences. During my time in college, I have looked to my memories and knowledge of them to guide me through the trauma of facing difficulty and rejection in the educational system for the first time in my life.

Although I moved away from Seattle when I was twelve years old, I still consider it my hometown. Because I was born and raised there, I have come to associate it with the time of my life that was still innocent. I look back fondly at my early childhood memories of growing up there and the times spent with my parents and my older sister as a family.

When I was a child my mother always took my education very seriously. From before I can remember, she made a conscious effort to seek out the schools and programs she felt would provide me with the best possible education. When I was three, my mother learned of a new Indian preschool being developed at the Daybreak

Star Indian Center in Seattle. She enrolled me immediately, and I became part of the first preschool class. I remember hearing Indian legends being told during story time, seeing the long braids of the boys in our class, and having guest dancers visit. Because most of my classmates were Native I can't recall a single time when I felt different or isolated from them. Unfortunately, Daybreak Star was only a one-year program at the time. Soon, my mother enrolled me at St. Alphonsus, the local parochial school, where I was also happy, but this time alongside a sea of white schoolchildren.

While attending St. Alphonsus was of great benefit to my sister and me educationally, it was also a financial strain on my parents. I realize now that my parents must have sacrificed a great deal to put my sister and me into a school well beyond their financial means. I doubt that it was ever easy for my parents, but I thrived academically from their sacrifice, finishing at the top of my class.

However, the economic status of my family prevented my sister and me from completely integrating with the students we called our peers. I felt, as do all children of that age, that being different was unquestionably negative, and that conformity was the means by which I could be acceptable to them. But money, or my family's lack of it, prevented me from ever achieving this goal.

Ironically, the St. Alphonsus school uniform, intended to transform all students into identical and equal individuals, was the first and most obvious source of my financial inequality with my classmates. Although we were given the address of an expensive uniform store in Seattle, my mother stopped shopping there after the first year. Being the frugal woman she was, it was only logical to purchase more affordable clothes and create a makeshift uniform. My mother, a woman who receives untold pleasures from bargain hunting, economized and was proud of it.

Little did my mother know that my makeshift uniform, though almost identical to those of my classmates, was still of lesser quality than the rest. As each school year progressed, my uniform would gradually fade from navy to cornflower blue. By the spring quarter, I stood out unquestionably.

Naturally this did not go undetected by me. I loathed standing out in any way from my peers. It seemed to me at the time that nothing marked me as poor more than my scruffy uniform; I hated how it constricted me both physically in my rough and tumble play, and mentally as a daily reminder that I was poor.

While the economic status of my family was indeed a source of insecurity for me, it was by no means the most troubling aspect of being different from my peers. Being poor was bearable. However, being Indian in that environment was more difficult, and at times very painful.

I was genuinely shocked upon entering elementary school at the complete lack of knowledge my peers had about Native American culture. Until that moment, I had gone to school with children who were mostly Indian. To be surrounded suddenly by children fascinated that a "real, live Indian" was in their midst was extremely trying for my young mind. I cannot count the number of times my peers, upon learning of my heritage, asked me to explain what it is exactly that Indians do. It was not unusual for me to hear: "Have you ever been to a reservation?" "Does everyone live in tipis?" "Do you know anyone who has scalped anyone?"

Interestingly, it was not only my childhood peers who demonstrated this ignorance, but my teachers as well, although in a much more sophisticated fashion. I had one teacher who for four years gave me traced outlines of his feet, gently requesting that I give them to my Indian grandmother so that he could have a pair of genuine Indian moccasins. Also, it was customary throughout my childhood education to be asked to provide personal input during the one day devoted to Native Americans in history class.

Yet despite the discomfort of being different from my peers, I succeeded in parochial school. I became an athlete, participating in all sports and excelling in long-distance running. I was elected to student council, and from this small pool of children, I had good friends. I was comfortable with my routine of walking to and from school every day with my big sister.

While my school was providing me with a source of confidence, my family life was at its most undisturbed state. My feelings are bittersweet when I look back at the family life of my childhood. Much has happened since those days of being innocent enough to expect that my parents would always be together and happy, of thinking that I would always be able to come home to the small, warm, brick house on 22nd Avenue. I am sincerely grateful that I carry with me the wonderful memories of my family, though things have changed drastically since that time.

Although my parents worked hard to provide us with stability and a loving home, they were not exactly overflowing with public displays of affection. Both of my parents, from what little I have gathered, had very rough childhoods, where giving and receiving affection was an uncommon act. In turn, this affected how we as a family related and communicated our feelings. While the effects of my parents' upbringings and the hardships that they endured are clear to me, the details of their youths are not. Only rarely have I been allowed a small glimpse of their lives before their marriage. From those small glimpses I have gathered just how difficult their young lives were.

My father was estranged from both his parents for most of their lives. He was raised by his grandmother, who was also the source of his amount of Indian blood. I believe that my father's rough childhood and the uncertainty of his relationship with his own parents instilled in him a deep desire to be the best father he could possibly be. While I was growing up, there was no doubt in my mind that he succeeded.

As a child, I remember adoring my father and thinking he was the greatest man to ever live. I would run to greet him on the street corner as he returned home from work every day. He was a caring and loving father, who spoiled my sister and me in just about every imaginable way. He would never make us clear our plates if we didn't want to, and I recall being spanked only once. Every morning, my sister and I would be awakened by his off-key voice singing to us as he creaked down the stairs to our room. I can still vividly remember every word of his morning tune. My father was indeed very devoted to us, and my sister and I were proud to be daddy's little girls.

However, while I developed a very strong bond to my father, it was from my mother that I developed a sense of family as I know it. My mother's family—my grandparents, my seven aunts and uncles, a multitude of cousins—and my place within that family were central to my identity as a child. Growing up in the city surrounded by mostly non-Indians was clearly difficult for me, but because the role of my Indian family was so strong I was able to avoid turning away from my culture. While I was constantly reminded of how I differed from my peers in Seattle, visits to my family on the Colville reservation gave me reassurance that I indeed had a family and a culture of which I could be proud.

Just as her home on the reservation was the physical center of our family, so was my grandmother the driving source of strength and stability for her children and grandchildren. The comfort and sense of family that the house embodied was undoubtedly created from a deliberate and lifelong effort of my grandmother's. She spent her life instilling traditional values in her children, and was a well-respected elder in her community. She supported her children and their families through economically trying times and tragedy. She created a home that was inviting and secure, and made sure that all in her family had beds to sleep in and warm meals in their stomachs. She was the foundation that held the family together through the most difficult of times, and led her family through the most joyous experiences. My family has been vital in shaping who I have become, and my grandmother provided me with my first and strongest role model.

I can honestly say that I do not have a single negative memory of my grandmother. A petite woman with long silver hair worn in a braided bun, she was always a picture of serenity. Growing up, I never witnessed her losing her temper with anyone, and my mother tells me that I will never encounter a more patient woman. I cannot recall any time in my childhood when I did not adore my grandma.

However, it wasn't until later on in my life that I learned that my grandma had lived a very challenging life herself. My mother later told me that both my grandma and grandpa had been alcoholics when my mother was growing up. This came as a great shock to me. Of course, alcoholism is devastatingly common in many reservation communities, but I could not imagine my own grandparents as alcoholics themselves.

This knowledge, however, has only made me admire my grandmother more. I never saw either my grandma or grandpa drunk when I was a child. I never saw my grandma act any way other than serene and hardworking. By the time I was born, they had recovered from their alcoholism and changed their lives completely. One day they realized they were drinking themselves into an early grave, like so many other Indians on the reservation. With many children to take care of, they knew they had to quit, and showed incredible willpower in succeeding. I drew strength from their success in my own battle with alcohol much later in my life.

My family would make the seven-hour drive from Seattle to my grandma's house several times a year, and every holiday became a reunion time. But it was during my summer vacations that I spent most of my time on the reservation. My parents would sometimes leave my sister and me in the care of our grandma for several weeks. During this time with my grandparents and my cousins, my connection to them was deeply strengthened. I believe now that the most valuable lessons I learned about myself as an Indian woman came from watching, listening to, and respecting my grandmother.

Summertime on the Colville reservation was generally a wonderful time for my sister and me. While we did have some chores to take care of, we were left for the most part to play and act as we wished. I was an absolute tomboy with an athletic streak, and the reservation offered me a vast playground where I could romp to my heart's content. My equally rambunctious cousin Jason and I would have countless hours of football, basketball, or contests to see who could run the fastest or the farthest. We would build forts and dig tunnels, and by the evening our hair would resemble birds' nests more than the braids that we had started the day wearing.

Every year the family would travel together during the summer to gather our traditional foods. One trip would be devoted to digging bitter roots, wild carrots, and a plant bulb called camas. We would drive up to the hills and spend all day with our digging sticks and gathering baskets. The other trip was a more extensive camping excursion to the mountains, where we would pick huckleberries. Every child was given a small berry basket and sent off into the woods to fill it. Of course, we always ate more than we saved and came back with half-filled baskets and purple mouths. I was amazed at how my grandma always returned with her large basket filled to the rim, with either roots or berries.

Upon returning home from both of these trips, my sister and I would spend hours sitting in my grandma's house helping her clean the berries or peel the roots. I always grew impatient and antsy after a short time, but would watch my grandmother and be ashamed that I wanted to go play while she could sit for hours doing her meticulous work. I watched her thin brown hands carefully and quickly peel each root, and would suddenly feel clumsy with my own. Watching her more closely, I would attempt to imitate her skill, although I could never match it. While I didn't know it at the time, she was aware of my impatience, and always let me go play before the job was completely finished.

This was how my grandma taught me. Although she was a woman of few words, she was able to teach me by example what was expected of me. She taught me how to work hard, be patient, and carry myself with dignity. She showed me how being responsible and generous would help me lead a rewarding life. Most significantly, she showed me the importance of family. I always felt a strong bond to her and felt proud to be her granddaughter.

The summer before my seventh-grade year, we moved from Seattle to Vancouver, Washington. Although I was upset with this decision, it was immediately apparent to me that academically I would be able to glide through the public school system much more easily than I ever had in parochial school. At the time, though, I was too caught up in my academic success and own feelings of social displacement to realize just how difficult a transition it was for my whole family.

Beginning a stressful job in a new environment must have been extremely difficult for my mother. Until that point I had had a relatively tranquil relationship with my mother, for while my mother was never the picture of delicate domesticity, she was still able to provide a sense of security for my sister Lorrie and me. She was strong and I always knew that I could depend on her to protect me. Being depended upon was a role that my mother had grown up playing. As the eldest daughter of her family, she was expected to take responsibility for her brothers and sisters. Having alcoholic parents made this an unbelievably large task. She grew up with the idea that it was necessary for her to be responsible, dependable, and always strong. As a mother, she continued in this role.

Yet soon after we moved to Vancouver, it became clear that no obligation to responsibility would be enough to keep my parents' marriage intact. The problems between my mother and father had grown worse over the years; my mother was merely the first to admit that their marriage was not going to work, and the first to attempt to regain direction in her life without my father. Today, I do not blame my mother for the breakdown of their marriage, but as a thirteen-year-old, the fury and resentment I felt toward her was unlike any other anger I had ever experienced. I blamed her for the sudden storm of instability that surrounded me.

It was extremely difficult for me to accept the fact that my parents would never be together again, but subconsciously I had always expected it. Perhaps I would have been able to accept this more quickly had it been the only source of resentment toward my mother. But it soon became clear that there was more to the separation of my parents than just getting used to not living with my father. Soon, my mother began to date an Indian man. This sealed my hostility toward my mother, and for three years I rebelled to the point where I did not speak with her. Our already limited communication broke down completely.

It was also during this time that my relationship with my sister Lorrie changed. During a conversation with one of her friends, I was casually informed, "Lorrie is having a hard time lately. She's been very worried about being pregnant. . . . You did know that she was pregnant, didn't you?"

I was shocked. Somehow I had known something was different with my sister, but I had tried to convince myself that nothing was wrong. I had thought that I could rely upon my sister to understand and help me deal with my mother. But I knew that she now had her own issues to deal with, and that because she had not been able to tell me of her pregnancy, she was dealing with them alone.

Teenage pregnancy is nothing new to my family, nor is it at all uncommon for Native Americans in general. Interestingly, most if not all of these pregnancies are carried to term; in my experience adoption and abortion are not common. Being raised in a Native American culture, I have a unique perspective on family. I have grown up knowing the importance of extended family and children, and I know how much each is valued. While it might seem illogical to dominant society for a low-income, teenage girl to keep her child, for the women in my family it is expected. Native children are cherished. With the support and involvement of an extended family, most Indian women can care for and support their children.

Despite this tradition of support, it took a while for Lorrie to tell the family, and I know she must have gone through a lot during this time. I wish now that I had been a stronger source of support for her, but despite my sisterly inadequacies, Lorrie was quite capable of dealing responsibly with her pregnancy. Until then, she had been a wild and rambunctious teenager, but with her first child on the way, this lifestyle vanished. While in the past I had often grown frustrated with my sister, I now became overwhelmingly impressed and full of pride with how, in a few short months, she turned her life completely around. She never once felt sorry for herself, or blamed anyone else. Instead, she took control of her life. Knowing that soon a child would be completely dependent upon her, she began to take steps to prepare herself for the responsibilities of motherhood. Unfortunately, to Lorrie this meant that she needed to remove herself from the wild influence of her Vancouver friends; in the fall of my sophomore year in high school, my sister moved back to Seattle to be with my father. That January my beautiful nephew, Nathan Nicolas, was born.

I admire and love my sister more than words can express, and her absence only highlighted my feelings of alienation from my mother. While growing up we had no real sibling rivalry, and as adolescents—aside from the time I annoyed her with my sarcasm and she dumped yogurt on my head—we had a very good sisterly relationship. The months following her move were extremely difficult for me. I missed her very much, and the situation with my mother had not changed. We still did not talk. I knew that she missed Lorrie just as much as I, and that it must have been very hard for her to see her daughter leave home, but because the tension in our relationship was so great, we were never able to share our feelings with one another.

I eventually began to sense that my relationship with my mother was beginning to change as well, though there was never any pivotal event that changed how we related to one another. It was very awkward at first, but I noticed the effort she extended to renew our relationship. It was of extreme importance to me, the way she would ask me about school or take me to a movie, as I knew how difficult trying to rebuild our shaky relationship must have been for her. I sensed it all, and I was quick to reciprocate.

During all the years that I had scowled at her, and stormed out of the room when she entered, there was never a moment when I did not want to reach out to her. In the back of my mind, I always hoped for the chance to soften my rough exterior and to show her my feelings. So when she began to initiate conversations, or suggest spending time together, I quickly accepted. I did not want to hold grudges, or to remain angry. I only wanted my mother back.

This is not to say that communication lines immediately opened and all was calm. But little by little, I began to communicate with my mom, and we resumed a peaceful mother-daughter relationship. By the beginning of my senior year, she had again become an important part of my life, and I began to depend upon her as a primary source of strength and guidance.

Compared to my turbulent family life, high school had been a wonderful and stable experience for me as I was actively involved in many things. While some of my high school peers were spending their senior year researching and applying to colleges, I was readying myself for the one-page application to the University of Washington. Many of my friends were planning on attending UW, and it only seemed natural that I would, too. Then one November evening, my mother came home from work and excitedly told me about a Dartmouth College informational session in Portland that evening. She had long been telling me about one of her co-worker's daughters who had just graduated from Dartmouth, and how wonderful their Native American Program had been. As I had done previously, I smiled and nodded at my mother with feigned interest. But when it came to my education, my mother was quite persistent: she bribed me with the promise of taking me out to dinner if I went along, and grudgingly I accepted.

After the slide presentation and question and answer session, I tried to hide my interest in Dartmouth, but the admissions officers had done a tremendous job impressing me. I was intrigued by the programs the school offered, and was excited by the opportunities I might have. I applied and in time learned that I had been accepted.

My decision to attend Dartmouth resulted in a number of varied responses from my family and friends. While most were surprised, they were also quite happy for me. However, it soon became clear to me that not everyone would be supportive of my attending Dartmouth College. To begin, some of my peers in high school were very quick to credit my acceptance to the fact that I am Native American, though in the four years I attended high school with those same students, no one had addressed my Indian identity outside of history class. So it was completely shocking to me to hear comments like, "Well, you were only accepted because you're an Indian."

Unfortunately, such comments were all too common, even from my friends. One of my closest friends snidely told me one day, "I just wish they had a poor white girls' scholarship program so I could get into Dartmouth, too." On graduation day, another friend of mine took the ceremony program and waved it in front of my face, apparently strengthened by the fact that I had not made honors. It was painful for me to see how my peers responded, as I wanted to share my happiness with my friends.

Although I may not have received the support I desired from

my friends, my family more than made up for it. News of my acceptance traveled quickly, and my family congratulated me. My mother, too, was quite happy for me. It was typical of her to do all sorts of things for me, to help me prepare for my trip to Dartmouth. I appreciated her efforts tremendously, as I felt like we were rebuilding a very strong bond between us. I knew that I would be able to leave home without regrets, for I knew our relationship had been renewed, and that my mother would support me even thousands of miles away.

I will never forget the day I left for college. My mother and my boyfriend, Jeff, accompanied me to the airport to say goodbye. I boarded my plane and did not look back, and we slowly took off. Later, Jeffrey told me that my mother cried silently as she watched my plane until it was a tiny speck in the sky.

Given all the buildup, my arrival at Dartmouth was less exciting than I thought it would be. Granted, I did get excited with all the Ivy League hype surrounding matriculation, and the first-year trips got me in the mood to bond. But after I settled into a daily schedule, it became very clear that there was more to Dartmouth than ivy-covered buildings and school songs.

Everyone had told me that the first year is always the most difficult for college students, yet for some reason I was arrogant enough to think that this would not apply to me. I fully expected to arrive at Dartmouth and continue with the success I had achieved in high school. Unfortunately, I did not anticipate the tremendous workload I was undertaking, and the extent to which culture shock would affect me. It was very difficult for me to adjust to the competitive, fast-paced East Coast mentality once I arrived at college. At Dartmouth, I felt as if my classmates each had their own individual agendas, and cooperation and support were not necessarily priorities.

My feelings of alienation intensified that January when I began to experience abdominal cramps. Although they were for the most part no more than a dull pain, I made an appointment at the college health clinic. During my examination, I was shocked to hear the nurse practitioner say, "There's definitely something here. My goodness, it really is big . . . obstructive, too. You're going to have to go to a doctor at the hospital and have him examine you. He'll have to treat you for this." With no further consultation and no further explanation, I was instructed to get dressed. I was given the card of a doctor at the local hospital and told to make an appointment. I left shaken and felt very ill.

The time between my first examination and my followup appointment with the doctor seemed like an eternity to me. I remember not being able to sleep at night, and being constantly worried about what was wrong with me. Although physically my pain was still faint, the mental stress I suddenly felt was overpowering.

When I eventually had my appointment with a young, male doctor, I was informed that I had an abnormal growth on my cervix. Its cause and malignancy status was not something he could determine immediately. Instead, he scheduled me for a series of appointments to conduct tests and treat me. I left the hospital having had my worst fears confirmed. And yet, I still did not know what had invaded my body and caused the growth.

The fact that my support system was at its weakest during this time only made things more difficult. My college friendships were still in their early developing stages, and I did not feel comfortable telling new acquaintances such intimate details of my life. Therefore, I again turned to my family for support. My mother, father, and sister were all very concerned about me, and called me frequently to see how I was doing. My mother was especially helpful, and seeing her concern helped me to be strong. She would remind me of all the strong women in the family, from my grandmother who was still strong despite her own health problems, to my sister who was redirecting her life to benefit her son. "These women don't let themselves become overcome by all their ills. They remain strong, and they survive without feeling sorry for themselves. You need to be strong to get through this year. You be strong, and you'll make it through."

My doctor, in contrast, was not at all helpful in explaining what was wrong with me, and in fact caused me more anxiety than I deserved. Now I realize just how little consideration the man gave to me, and I would not tolerate the same treatment today. But as a frightened college freshman who had just left home, I followed every word he said without question or doubt, and I dismissed my discomfort with his professional manner as irrelevant.

Eventually, the results of the biopsy indicated that the growth was benign, but for the next few months the stress surrounding my health problems became too much for me to handle. My insecurity over my academic ability grew every week. I was so far behind in my work that I felt completely overwhelmed with nowhere to turn. Even my family's support could do nothing for my academic problems. Soon I neglected my work altogether.

Instead, I lived for the weekends and the relief from the daily pressures of my class and work schedule. I began visiting fraternities on a regular basis and drinking excessively. I would stay out late, sometimes all night, getting drunk and acting irresponsibly. It wasn't that I particularly enjoyed the whole fraternity social scene; on the contrary, I loathed it.

It's hard for me to understand why I continued to place myself in such an atmosphere, where I was so clearly uncomfortable. There is no logical explanation. But at the time, I wasn't thinking in terms of what was logical or illogical. I knew my feelings and actions contradicted one another, but I was so desperately searching for something to ease my worries and depression that it did not matter to me. I went to ease the depression I was constantly feeling, with the hope it would make the stress disappear. Unfortunately, I only succeeded in creating another problem.

Finally, the downward spiral I felt my life following became too difficult for me to deal with alone. As I had hesitated to tell my professors any details of what was going on in my personal life, they only viewed me as an unmotivated, ill-prepared student who rarely came to class. I knew that I had to tell them at least part of what was going on, or face the possibility of failing. But by that point I did not have enough confidence in myself to confront my professors alone. I was depressed all the time, I had fallen far behind in all my classes, and I was seriously considering giving in to my feelings of ineptness and returning home for good. It was then that I turned to the Native American Program and its director, Colleen Larimore.

Although I was extremely uneasy unloading all the events of the past three months on Colleen, I immediately sensed her willingness to listen. Her attentiveness showed that she cared about what I was feeling and experiencing. It did not take much to get me talking, as I had been carrying around so much anxiety for so long that I was just waiting for the opportunity to tell someone. I told her all the details of my health problems, of my reckless drinking and the guilt I felt from it, and of my academic problems. Finally, I told her about the explosion of self-doubt that had grown since the fall, and how I was convinced that I could not succeed in the Ivy League.

"Nicole, the admissions office is very selective at Dartmouth. They would never have admitted you unless they knew you could succeed here," she told me. "You have shown that you are capable, Nicole. You can succeed." She went on to tell me how to approach my professors and offered to help me with whatever I needed.

I did manage to finish my second term without failing any classes, although I was quite disappointed with the grades I received. It was tough for me to settle for what I had earned, knowing that I was capable of doing so much better. For months I had felt my control slipping, and constantly felt that I had no firm ground to stand on. I wanted to be as strong as the women my mother had told me about, and I wanted to be as secure as Colleen, another strong Indian woman, told me I could be. But I had failed to do so, and I was so disappointed in myself that I was willing to do anything to regain that feeling of confidence and control.

That spring term my boyfriend Jeff came to visit to lend his support. The Sunday evening before he was to leave, we came back from dinner at the Hanover Inn and were relaxing when my mother called. I could tell immediately from the strained sound of my mother's voice that something had happened.

"What's wrong?" I asked.

"Nicole, grandma passed away this morning."

At that very second, my whole life changed. It was as if all the strength was drained from my body. In that one moment, a thousand different images of my grandmother came to my mind.

I saw my grandmother sitting at her cluttered card table, slowly smoking a cigarette and watching television with her grandchildren. I saw her crouched at a huckleberry bush, picking berries with ease and attentiveness as she watched Lorrie and me playing in the woods. I saw her combing my cousin Jason's long hair into braids, her fast hands twisting the hair quickly. I saw her at the head of our Thanksgiving dinner table with my grandpa, speaking loudly to him, relaying the conversations of the meal to his deaf ears. I saw her bundled up in her cardigan, bandanna, and woolen blanket, watching me graduate from high school. I remembered all of these images in that one moment, and my sadness overwhelmed me.

"Now, Nicole, be strong. Remember what your grandma taught you. You have to be strong for her now," my mother said, her own voice trembling. "Her body just gave out. She wasn't in pain. She was just tired, Nicole. And she was ready to go." My grandmother's kidneys had failed, perhaps due in some part to the effect that alcohol had had upon them decades earlier.

I told my mother that I would fly home the next morning, and that I would see her soon. Then we hung up, and I felt deadened inside.

Throughout my childhood, my family had experienced a great deal of tragedy. I had experienced the loss of many members of my family, and knew what was expected of me during our time of mourning. I had been taught by my mother and grandmother alike to follow our traditional customs: I could not allow myself to cry until my grandmother's body had been placed into the ground. I had been taught that to cry would not only be a sign of disrespect for my grandmother, but it would also impair her journey into the spirit world. I knew I could not do that.

Immediately, I flew home to help my mother and sister prepare for my grandmother's funeral and longhouse services. I had difficulty staying awake during the final night of praying, drumming, and singing before my grandmother was to be buried. The drumming lasted throughout the night. At first light, we brought my grandmother from the longhouse to the cemetery, and the moment she was placed in the ground I saw tears fall from the eyes of my cousins, aunts, and uncles who were standing at the graveside. After more songs were sung, and more prayers offered, we journeyed back to the longhouse to complete the ceremony. It was then, leaning on Jeff's shoulder in the back seat of the car, that I finally began to cry.

By the end of the entire ceremony, I was exhausted and saddened. Being with my entire family again gave me strength to get through that difficult time, but it also made me dread returning to Dartmouth to finish my freshman year. I had no desire to return to school, and I was so deeply affected by my grandmother's death that I did not want to leave my family. But I felt that I had no choice, and so I returned alone to Dartmouth.

After returning, I visited each of my professors to explain the situation. While two of my professors were very understanding, my freshman seminar professor, a high-ranking administrator, was not. She had difficulty comprehending why it had taken me a week to travel home and take part in my grandmother's funeral. Because of her own cultural bias, she could not understand why I had not simply flown home, attended a service, then flown back to school. Taking an entire week was unnecessary and unheard of to her.

Needless to say, my attitude did not improve for the remainder of my first year. While I had begun the spring with a genuine desire to turn the tide of my dismal winter term, the death of my grandmother was the final straw for me. I gave up. I resigned myself to simply finishing the school year and returning home as soon as possible. Once I returned home, I hoped to forget about my freshman year and all the pain and disappointments surrounding it. I felt pressured and suffocated by my own stress, and I felt confined and judged with very few sources of support. For six months I had had professors—people who not only commanded authority over me but whom I also was supposed to somehow respect—repeatedly whittle away any self-confidence I might have maintained during my academic difficulties. In my mind, getting away from Hanover, New Hampshire, was the only thing I wanted to do.

I returned home in June, and soon left for Seattle to live with my father. I was still reeling with disappointment and frustration with myself, but I hoped that by finding some type of job working with the Indian community of Seattle, I would be able to regain my motivation for college and a career. Yet when I approached some area organizations looking for work, I was turned away, sometimes with hostility.

I remember one afternoon I went to one particular organization to discuss some volunteer work with the director. At first he was somewhat friendly, but within minutes his questions turned into a lecture.

"You think that going to some fancy Ivy League college is going to teach you anything about being Indian? None of that matters. Don't think you're getting any special knowledge because you're not. Just because you go to some fancy college doesn't mean you can just walk in here and expect us to take you."

It's hard for me to relate how devastating it was for me to take that kind of rejection from Indian people in my home community. Since I was young I had known that I wanted ultimately to find a career that would let me contribute to the Indian community. Now, in addition to wanting so desperately to work for these organizations, I also needed them to help me regain my direction and enthusiasm for returning to college. When I felt the sting of hostility, I was completely at a loss. I felt accused of selling out my heritage and culture in exchange for an Ivy League degree. It was a pain that I will not soon forget.

I did not succeed in finding a job that summer, and simply added that disappointment to what I believed would be a long, growing list of them. But whereas at Dartmouth I was able to drink away my worries in the company of dozens of Dartmouth alcoholics, I now was forced to realize just how out of control I had become. It was only after I removed myself from the binge drinking lifestyle of the Dartmouth fraternity system that I was able to see where my behavior was headed; I realized that alcohol had become too much of an accepted fact of my life. I also realized that my three months away from Dartmouth were an opportunity to change my habits.

Indeed, being home again and close to my family *did* serve as a means of recuperating and regaining my strength, mentally and physically. Counting down the final days of my vacation was not at all easy, yet having the support of my family helped me to decide that I would indeed return. So, filled with both apprehension and tempered hope, I returned to school in September.

Fortunately for me, the smothering heaviness in the air that I had felt during my freshman year had subsided. Academically, I again tried my "clean slate" mentality, this time with more success. Physically, the abnormal growth in my abdomen had been completely removed by treatment, and I was feeling much less of the physical strain of the stress and alcohol of my freshman year. Spiritually, I found myself thinking more and more of my mother and grandmother, and drawing strength from my memories of them. My mother's support and the memories of my grandmother again taught me how to be strong and disregard my self-conscious fears. I had decided that I would try to learn from my painful experiences and again try to succeed. If I still encountered the same difficulties and the same insensitive and degrading treatment from members of the Dartmouth community, then I would accept that Dartmouth was not the college for me.

The effect that this new attitude had upon me was profound. I found myself more able to contribute to the Native community here, and immediately felt the rewards of this new sense of community in the student group, Native Americans at Dartmouth.

While I had spent my first year immersed in my problems, I now had time to become active in the organization beyond merely attending weekly meetings. The support I have received from members of the Native community here has since become a major source of strength for me.

Little by little, I began to regain confidence in myself. The heavy weight of inadequacy that had persisted throughout my first year gradually subsided as I began to reassert myself in different ways. Although the steps I took to rebuild my self-esteem were slow and small, I nonetheless felt myself becoming gradually free of the burden of self-doubt that had plagued me for so long.

It was during this time that I had a conversation with Michael Dorris, who was spending the term with his wife, Louise Erdrich, as a Montgomery Fellow at Dartmouth. During our conversation, he gave me valuable advice that I have taken very closely to heart. I explained the difficulty with which I had experienced the rejection and hostility of that previous summer, and the doubt I had begun to feel about my ability to pursue a career in the Native community.

"You've encountered early a problem that you're undoubtedly going to face many times in your life," Michael told me. "But you have to always keep in mind that it will happen to you regardless of who you are or what you've accomplished. If they didn't criticize you for going to an Ivy League college, then they'd criticize you for only going to a state school. If it wasn't that you never lived on a reservation, it'd be that you *only* lived on a reservation. Bearing that in mind, you have to make the decision of whether or not you want to work with Indians. But I'll tell you now, the only way to deal with that is to be strong and to prove yourself to that community. Like I said, you'll undoubtedly endure some criticism. The only way to prove those people wrong is to show your determination and prove to them that you are serious in your commitment. Only then will you gain their respect."

It amazes me how single events can have such a remarkable impact upon my life. In retrospect, I see the remarkable impact of that small bit of advice Michael gave me; it provided me with the final mental boost that brought me from the wavering self-doubt of my first year to a new level of problem resolution and self-definition. I have heeded that advice many times since then, not simply when determining my future career, but in all aspects of my life.

Since that time, much has happened to me at college. My second year was filled with almost as much success and positive experience as my first year had been with failure. I have become an active and vocal member of the community, and a leader in NAD as well. Above all else, I have gained a tremendous amount of confidence in myself for having endured that first difficult year at Dartmouth. Having been through so much, I now know that I have the ability to succeed during the most difficult times. While it may be difficult, especially in a sometimes hostile environment such as Dartmouth, I have begun to drawn upon an inner strength that has its roots in the teachings of my mother, my grandmother, and the other women in my life.

At college, I have been able to use this strength as a driving force. Additionally, NAD has given me a strong sense of community from which I have gained valuable experience dealing with difficult and controversial issues with the mainstream society. Recently, we were successful in our Columbus Day quincentenary commemoration, and in our persuasion of the college to divest financial holdings in a hydroelectric project that threatened Native tribes living in Quebec. I was also elected president of NAD for three terms, during which time I had to address the recurring issues of the Indian symbol on campus, and the Class Day Clay Pipe tradition. Although it was often difficult for me to retain my patience during these dealings, I nonetheless gained both valuable experience asserting myself publicly and confidence in the influence of NAD's voice on campus.

However, serving as president of NAD provided me with much more than that. It again tested my ability to stand strong in my convictions despite the criticism of other Native students. To many students, an Indian woman who is active and outspoken is "nontraditional" and "power hungry." For being outspoken as a Native woman, then, I was labeled a "white feminist wannabe." But for me, I only know the teachings of my grandmother and mother—teachings that instilled in me a strength and an unwillingness to have other people's opinions undermine my own convictions.

With these teachings in mind, I have actually begun to enjoy my college experience. I am now able to recognize the many opportunities that are available to me as a Dartmouth student. I am currently preparing for a foreign study program in Kenya, to be followed by two exciting internships. I have strong friendships both inside and outside of NAD.

There is no doubt that my first year at college was difficult, but I did ultimately succeed. And it is an exciting time in my life right now. I am at a point where I am still forming my ideologies, and determining my future career goals. In doing so, I am incorporating the values and lessons I learned from my family, with the new knowledge my education has provided. I hope that, when all is said and done and my Dartmouth years are over, I will find that I have combined the two aspects of my life successfully. Then, I hope to use this knowledge to return to the Native community, and contribute what I can as a strong Indian woman.

I think often about the women in my life and what I have learned from them. In most ways, my own difficulties pale in comparison to what they have endured. My strong-willed sister, who has taken responsibility for her three children (my three bouncy nephews, Nathan, Michael, and Joseph) without ever falling victim to self-pity; my grandmother, who was strong enough to recover from the problems of alcoholism and hold her family together; my own mother, who has struggled to find her own independence from the rigid expectations of her youth—each has given me much pride in my identity as a Native woman.

Through them, I have gained a permanent inspiration to succeed despite the obstacles I may encounter. Native culture is to this day filled with countless examples of women who have survived poverty like I have never known, and tragedy that I could never comprehend. Yet like the women of my family, they succeed. I strive to be a strong Native woman, not only to honor my female ancestors but also to honor the struggles and successes of all Indian women today.

Nicole Adams is a member of the Wenatchi Band of the Confederated Tribes of the Colville Reservation. She graduated from Dartmouth College in 1995; while at Dartmouth, she majored in government and minored in Native American studies, in addition to being active in the Native Americans at Dartmouth and the Women's Resource Center.

She enjoys spending time with her family, traveling throughout the country, and learning life lessons from her mother. After completing a master of education degree at Harvard University, Nicole hopes to pursue a career in Indian educational policy. She anticipates that this work will take her back to her native Pacific Northwest. This essay was written in her junior year of college.

▼ ▼ ▼ ▼ ▼ ▼ ▼ ▼ ▼ ▼ ▼ ▼

ELIZABETH CAREY

I Dance for Me

I have been dancing hula for as long as I can remember. I went with Mom to her evening hula classes, held in an elementary school cafeteria. The room was large, with lots of louver-type windows and swinging cafeteria doors. We danced with all those windows and doors open, so it didn't even feel like we were inside. Nature came in to us—or was it that we went outside into nature? The light evening breeze felt nice on our hair-matted necks dripping with sweat. The sunset twilight would fade and the evening darkness would slowly blanket everything outside. A stillness would settle on the class. My mother's chanting echoed through the room and escaped through the open doors to join with the night.

Mom taught a class of ten to fifteen women, young and old. At first, I sat on a chair watching the class and trying to imitate my mother's rhythm by tapping the tops of my thighs with my hands. Eventually I got up and joined the class. I stood in the second row behind the more experienced dancers and tried to follow what they did. I must have been six or seven. Soon I felt very comfortable, and it was easy to tell stories with my hands and my body. During the years I trained, hula became for me a way of reading between the lines, a way of expressing more than just words. If I could somehow express the idea in all of its essence with my motions, then the chant would take shape visually, and would come alive nourished by my heart and soul.

Of course, I didn't think all that then, when I was a little girl. I just danced. It gave me pleasure beyond words to listen to the chant, to let it flow and pulse in my veins. The spirit over-whelmed me. I fear that I cannot do it justice in words. But I didn't realize what a part of my life dancing and movement were until I danced my first hula at Dartmouth. It was almost the end of my third year, when a friend asked me if I would perform for Cultural Expressions, a show in which people from different backgrounds present little bits of their cultures. It is produced every spring, mainly for minority prospective students who visit the college, to reassure them that minority students survive at Dartmouth and that the college does not let the white majority stifle their cultures.

Having just returned from a few months at home, I thought this would be the perfect opportunity to share my culture. But I was really nervous. I had danced on stage before—that was not the problem. I worried about what people would think. Practicing the day before, I shook as I thought about all the people I knew and didn't know who would be watching. I was afraid to open up, but I had made the commitment, so I went through with it.

I remember the looks of wonder and confusion when people saw me in my costume before I went on. It was a simple red outfit. A sleeveless top was held around my chest by elastic and fell to right above my knees. A full skirt of the same light red material sat right on my waist and also fell to my knees. I had let my hair fall long down my back and around my head I wore a golden wreath made out of yarn, which looked like smoothed feathers. I wore the same kind of wreath around my neck, wrists, and ankles. One person approached me and said, "Where are you from?" I told him that I was from Hawaii, and his eyes lit up. "You mean you are going to be doing that 'dancing' that you do there?" As he spoke, he lifted his hands in a halfhearted gesture, his left limply across his chest and his right limply extended, with droopy elbows and wrists. Then it hit me: most people in the room had never really seen the hula, not the way I learned it, only the grass skirt thing always shown on television. What were they all expecting?

My friend read the introduction for my dance:

> Hula is an ancient form of Hawaiian expression, a communication of prayer and homage to the three central forces in life: the gods, the chiefs, and nature. Hula expresses these in a deeper and more three-dimensional way than words are able to express, because hula encompasses the five senses. Through the hand movements, the flowers, the costumes, and the chants, the hula gives us an entire picture that we can touch, smell, see, hear, and almost taste. Hula is the spirit, the spirit of the ancient ones and of those yet to come communicating, expressing themselves. It is now also Elizabeth's spirit expressing herself.

I remember thinking, "Hula is my spirit expressing myself," and I don't remember what happened after that. I was dancing in my own world; everything was coming out from inside of me and I felt a huge release. A great outburst of applause jolted me back. Mentally and spiritually drained, all I could think was that I had completely opened myself up to all those people and how scary it had been.

People were astounded. "Liz, that was so beautiful!" they said, and "Why haven't you performed before?" Why? I was afraid of people not understanding, of people mocking me; I was afraid of showing who I really am. I am still afraid. Each time I dance, I think, "How much should I really show?"

That was the first positive experience I had at Dartmouth. My first two years there had been marked by strain and unhappiness. But after dancing my hula, I felt at home and comfortable. Finally, I could focus on my spirit, not only on my intellect; I could express myself not by the system's rules, but by my own. Coming to Hanover from Hawaii had been a big shock. In leaving home, I had lost my spiritual center, and trying to find it again in a new place was not easy. Only after I took that risk was I able to feel at home in the foreign land of Hanover, New Hampshire, and in the Native American community at Dartmouth.

Dartmouth provided learning for my intellect, but not nearly enough learning for my heart. The mind needs to develop, but so do the heart and soul, and here, as at any academic institution, spiritual growth and development are stunted because the system is not supportive of any real feeling. "Get the work done" is the first rule among Dartmouth students. On the surface, campus life looks calm, but it is a cutthroat environment, and the undercurrent can pull you down in one swift motion.

In the beginning, the people seemed nice, though nosy. Circles of unfamiliar faces hovered around me with their questioning, prodding, intimidating voices, their greedy eyes looking at me as if I were some sort of unidentified species. So many times I felt like screaming, "Yes, I come from Hawaii—but I am not a new minority attraction at Dartmouth!"

People would say the stupidest things. "You folks are a part of the United States even though you are out in nowhere land in the middle of the Pacific Ocean . . . right?" or "It must be awesome to go home and go to the beach all the time. If I lived there that's all I would do!" And the clincher: "I know this might be a stupid question, but do you guys really wear those grass skirts and bikini tops?"

At first I didn't mind answering the questions, but they got repetitive, and I started to get annoyed at the constant bombardment. Yes, we are a part of the United States; no, I don't spend every waking moment on the beach; and no, we do not run around in grass skirts and bikini tops. How many times would I have to say it?

To me, Hawaii is not a luxury vacation spot. It is home. Of course, I had taken the beauty of my home for granted. I had to come 2,500 miles across the ocean and then about the same distance again across the continental United States before I realized just how beautiful Hawaii really is and how lucky I am to come from such a wonderful place. I missed the beautiful blue skies bejeweled with rainbows, the flowers in the lush green valleys, and the light breezes that carry their scent. I also missed the cultural diversity visible everywhere—Japanese, Chinese, Korean, Filipino, Samoan, Thai, Hawaiian, Portuguese, Vietnamese, Puerto Rican, Caucasian—and the smiles that people from different cultures share, although naturally problems do sometimes arise in this exciting mix of diverse peoples living together.

Like everything, Hawaii has good and bad sides. Racial tensions between the various groups and within the groups themselves are subtle and sometimes hard to see. Many Hawaiians feel some animosity toward other races, especially the whites from the mainland, who seem to be getting more and more numerous, taking away land for development and destroying nature in the process. There is also tension between the poorer groups—the Hawaiians, Samoans, and Tongans—and the richer Japanese. Money, or lack of the same, is a contentious issue.

In Hawaii, humor eases the tensions; everyone makes jokes about everyone else. It is an accepted custom, and no one gets too upset or takes it too personally because they know that they can joke about anyone, too. There are jokes about what people eat, how they dress, where they live, and what kinds of jobs they hold. Some jokes can be quite mean, but most people take them in stride and come back with another just as potent. They may not be politically correct, but they allow individuals to air the inevitable frustrations that come with living among so many different peoples. Through humor, we achieve openness, patience, and tolerance.

At home, I grew to appreciate the many different cultures of my world. I learned to give people the benefit of the doubt, to believe that there is good in everyone. I may not have grown up with material riches, but emotionally and culturally, I was raised like a queen. I was allowed to express my emotions and my culture freely.

But living in Hawaii is hard. How can you enjoy all the beauty when you have to worry about getting to work on time so you can make money to pay bills? If you look under the exotic surface layer, you will see families struggling to survive in one of the nation's most expensive places to live. Imagine large amounts of development taking place and an influx of insensitive people trying to claim Hawaii as theirs. We don't mind sharing, but sharing calls for mutual respect. Greedy, profit-motivated people don't take that into account. Such people want to exploit Hawaii's beauty, and they manipulate others and drain their power. Hawaii is being crippled beyond recognition—to the point where it cannot survive without major support from the United States and other countries. Hawaii's number one industry is tourism, and without it, our economy would fail and we would suffer enormously. Tourism is the double-edged sword we continually stab ourselves with. It brings in the money, but it also brings in the development that is destroying our culture. Hawaiians are angry, but their anger has been pushed down and not dealt with—by individuals, by corporations, by the state, and by the U.S.

These issues were never raised directly in my home. Life was already too difficult, and we figured anger was not going to pay the bills and put food on the table. I did not really start thinking about these issues until I came to Dartmouth.

I was one of the lucky ones. I had food on my table and, although I don't know how they managed in a state where the cost of living is forty percent above the national average, my parents had enough money to pay all the bills and put my two younger sisters and me through private school. My dad is an industrial real estate broker and Mom works as a part-time teacher of Hawaiian culture for the Department of Education.

They are both incredibly strong people, from two very different backgrounds. My mom is from a little town called Honaunau, part of the district of Kona, tucked away among the palm trees under the beautiful blue skies of the island of Hawaii. She moved to the island of Oahu, to our capital city, Honolulu, for schooling. She was always one to blaze new trails, and this determination led her to the University of Hawaii. She never completed her nursing degree though, because of her grandmother's illness. She went back home to care for Grand Tutu, the name I call my great-grandmother. Yet she knew that she wanted to do more with her life than pick coffee beans and work at the Kona Inn, so as soon as she could, she went back to Honolulu and started working at Sea Life Park.

When I was little, Mom told me stories about how she swam with and trained the whales, porpoises, dolphins, and penguins. She was also the lady in the canoe with the dog in the little show performed every hour for the visitors. Mom also narrated the show. How I loved my mother's park stories. In one, she had been in the midst of training a porpoise when she had to make an emergency trip back home to Kona. When she returned a week later, she learned that the porpoise had died. They had done an autopsy and found nothing wrong. But my mom knew. She told me that the porpoise had died of a broken heart. My mom could tell me that story over and over again, and every time, tears welled up in my eyes and sometimes silently trickled out.

My dad met my mother at Sea Life Park. He was working at a
sea range right down the road from the park. Dad had come over from Los Angeles a few years earlier because he couldn't stand the city any longer. His urge to surf on the beaches in Hawaii lured him to Honolulu. My father has always been independent. Both his parents died when he was young, so he and his older brother moved around a lot. Dad went to one of the universities in California. He loved skiing, riding motorcycles and dirt bikes, and surfing, and he was never at a loss for a story. I always listened to them rapt with attention.

I am the oldest of three children. Three years after I was born came Victoria, and four years after that came Catherine Anne, or Annie, as we call her. My sisters looked at me as the independent one, the one who always did well, the one who never spent much time at home.

Just this past Christmas, I was home from Dartmouth for break. Annie was feeling depressed one day and she approached me.

"Peki," she said, using the shortened version of my Hawaiian name, Elikapeka, which only my little sister is allowed to use. "Peki, I am going to miss you."

"What do you mean, you are going to miss me? I just got here." I looked at her, bewildered.

"I know," she said, "but you will leave, and when you leave I will be all alone." She gave me a tearful hug. "You are going to have to come home again, Peki. It is sad without you. You are never really home. Even Victoria thinks so."

I had never thought about how they would feel with me gone. Would things have been different if I had been less independent, had been closer to my sisters, closer to the rest of my family? They have always been my source of strength, but not in the traditional ways; I have learned much from them, but I was never one to hang around with them. I love them and would do anything for them, but I don't know if I could give up my independence for them.

In Hawaiian tradition, family and home are sacred and powerful, and the oldest child especially does everything to protect and nurture the home. But I went against all of that and left my family to pursue my academic and intellectual interests. After graduating from high school, I went to Spain for a year to live with another family. Immediately afterward, I went off to Dartmouth College, all the way on the other side of the United States. At that time, I wanted to get as far away from my family as I could. I felt I needed more—I needed to see more and to experience more. But what about my family? What have I done for them in all my travels? They are very proud of me and want to nurture my adventurous spirit, but they also want me home with them. I am always with them spiritually, but they want me there physically.

How can I be with them in Hawaii, and still quench my thirst for the unknown, for travel, and for new places? There is only one of me. The pressure is especially strong now, in my senior spring, when I must decide what I want to do, and where I want to go to do it. My relatives, friends, and immediate family are all asking if I am going to come home, and sometimes it gets to be too much. Sometimes when I talk to my family on the phone, I want to cry because Annie says, "But you have to come home, Peki, because we need you. You are never home." Other times I get frustrated because they seem to hear only what they want to hear, which may or may not be what I am trying to get across to them. I have told my parents many times on the phone that I am thinking of going back to Europe after I graduate, that I don't think I will be coming home. They continually ask, "So, are you going to be coming home?" That is the ominous question right now. I love Hawaii, but I am afraid I would get stuck there.

I had never heard of Dartmouth until my mother told me about it and said they had a special program and lots of financial aid for Native Americans. I later learned that even though Dartmouth doesn't hand out full scholarships to students just because they are Native American, they still award financial aid to anyone with demonstrated financial need. My mother was persistent and kept saying, "Apply to Dartmouth! It is an Ivy League school. What more could you ask for?" Mom's eyes would sparkle each time she read that ad from the Office of Hawaiian Affairs publication: " 'Dartmouth College in Hanover, New Hampshire, accepting applications for the Class of 1992.' " She would read on, exaggerating, " 'We are encouraging all people of Native American, Alaskan, and Hawaiian descent to apply.' Go for it," she urged. "They consider Hawaiians Native Americans. You can get a great education, and you will have support from others too!"

I made the final decision to come to Dartmouth after visiting the campus in the spring of my senior year in high school. I got a call from Dartmouth: "How would you like to come up and see Dartmouth?" I was amazed. New Hampshire? I couldn't imagine what New Hampshire was like. All I knew was that it snowed and the winters were awfully cold. "Sure," I said, not knowing what to expect. But it was a free trip to a place I had never been before, so I went.

When I got there, I was introduced to more than just cold weather and the beautiful New England landscape awakening from its winter sleep. I was introduced to the famous Native American Program I had heard so much about from my mother. Everyone seemed friendly and nice. I was part of a group of ten Native students from across the United States, and one of three Hawaiians. We were paired with Native students and stayed with them in their dorm rooms. My original hostess was not able to take me in, so Geri, a Native from Arizona who was already watching one other prospective student, took me in. She showed us around campus, took us to her Spanish class, and took time off from her busy schedule to buy us Ben and Jerry's chocolate ice cream, the best I had ever tasted! She curled up with us in the comfortable chairs of her dorm lounge and explained that being a Native American at Dartmouth was not very easy. But you needed to stick it out and strive for your goals—without forgetting where you came from.

During that trip, Dartmouth was wonderful—a new place full of exciting opportunities. New England was different from Hawaii, and I liked it. No palm trees or ocean breezes, but rather forests of conifers and hardwoods running along the Connecticut River and up the hillsides. I was hopeful; Dartmouth did have all of those opportunities Mom kept talking about, and the Native American Program was there to help with the feelings of being overwhelmed. Its purpose was to act as a support group by creating a home-away-from-home atmosphere for the Native minority, while reminding them of and helping them with all of the opportunities that surrounded them at Dartmouth. That was what I saw in my short stay.

But I couldn't see everything in three days. When I returned to Dartmouth as a first-year student, I saw deeper into the school's dynamics.

While I had expected racism and other controversies in the gen-

eral campus population and from alumni, I was surprised by the
racism and animosity I experienced from fellow Natives. When I
searched for the support that had seemed to abound in the Native
student community, I couldn't find it. I felt that the students had
lied to me in order to sell Dartmouth. It took me about a term to
see the big rifts in the Native community. I saw how cliques of
people were exclusive and mean and talked about others behind
their backs. This was my first experience with people who appeared
to be my friends but who said evil things about me behind my
back.

Through the very intricate grapevine, I found out that I was
being called a "slut." At first, I didn't understand. Then slowly I
became more aware; I was a friendly person and openly hugged
people, put my arms around their shoulders, patted them on the
back, stood close to them while speaking. I also told a lot of jokes
that poked fun at ethnic groups—no harm intended—just like we
did at home. But soon I understood that this was not the proper
way of behaving at Dartmouth. Intellectually, I understood that
this wasn't home. Here people had a problem with my standing or
sitting too close, and my jokes were sharper than people were used
to. But my heart couldn't fathom the problem. Where I was raised,
touching was okay, not forbidden. I tried to let people know this,
but the rumors persisted and became harsher.

Then someone I considered a close friend stopped me and asked,
"Did you really sleep with ————? That's what everyone is saying.
That's what ———— told me." I couldn't believe my ears. Then I
started hearing from others that I was a "good lay." I was crushed.
No one wanted to know who I really was. They were too busy
spreading rumors. "Why are these people hurting me?" I asked
myself over and over. They didn't even know me.

The rumors had been started by a core group of four or five
juniors and seniors in NAD, the student group Native Americans
at Dartmouth. The other members of NAD could be really nice,
asking how my classes were going and saying that if I needed any
help I should come to them. But they were spineless because they
copied the core group when its members were around, and
wouldn't even talk to me. The core people would leave, and again
the others would approach me and ask for some help on their
Spanish homework or something. I was disgusted. If people didn't

like me, I wished they would be open about it and not hide behind sickly sweet smiles and superficial concern.

One day late in my first term, I went to the Native American House to pick up a book I had left there. I had been struggling alone with the hypocrisy for some time and I was feeling desperate to get back home to Hawaii where I was understood and didn't have to explain myself. Some of the core NAD members were sitting around talking in the room where I had left my book. When I entered, everyone became silent. I didn't want to smile at them. I was tired of putting on an act, tired of playing their game and pretending that nothing they said or did hurt me. They had been drinking, and whatever it was, it was sitting pretty strong on their breath. I was frightened. I wanted to get my book and scram. Then one of them started to mutter and laugh.

That did it. It had been a long, tiring day of work and classes, but I looked her in the eye and said sharply, "If you have a problem with me, tell me to my face. Tell me right here, right now! I am tired of your sorry games and your hiding behind rumors. If you are as strong as you think you are, talk."

As soon as I spoke, I wished I could take back what I had said, because I knew that all the mud was going to hit the ceiling. I wanted to run out of the room, out of the house, away from Dartmouth, away from New Hampshire. I wanted to go back home. I wanted to be anywhere but in that room surrounded by those mocking faces. But I stayed glued to the spot with my eyes gleaming. It was the same feeling that had made me stick it out that far. I hadn't left when things started buckling under me, and I was determined not to fail, not to let others take away what was mine— a chance at the Ivy League.

The "leader" sat up and put her beer down. She looked at me and whispered, "You're not Native enough. You're from the city, from Honolulu! You don't know what it's like to struggle. You don't even *look* Native. So don't even try to sympathize with us real Natives. You are white!"

My mouth wanted to drop to the floor. How ignorant! I was so angry that pains shot up from my stomach through my chest. But in a steadily rising voice, charged with emotion, and very controlled, I replied, looking at each one of them. "I never said I was Native American. The college defines me that way. I am Hawaiian.

I am Polynesian. I may have other blood in me, but that makes me even richer in heritage, and if you cannot respect that, then you are just as ignorant as those who cannot appreciate your heritage!" I grabbed my book. My eyes were beginning to fill. I left the Native American House, and I didn't go back for two years.

After that incident, the rumors really flew. I started to feel alone and afraid. I didn't want anyone to think badly of me, because I have always been a good, caring person. Many nights those rumors made me cry. Angry, sad, frustrated, and confused, I didn't know how to deal with all of the feelings eating away at my insides. I folded and became very introverted. I stopped hanging around NAD. Instead, I worked at the dining hall, did my schoolwork, and spent a lot of time with my boyfriend.

Working at the dining hall, which began as a simple ten-hour-a-week job, became my life for a long time. I worked there maybe fifteen hours a week, along with taking classes. I needed the money, but it was also a place where I was accepted. It didn't matter how "Native American" I was, or where I came from. All that mattered was how hard I worked, and the people at the dining hall gave me the chance to prove I was a good worker. I found a very comfortable niche there.

All kinds of people worked there—Native Americans, African-Americans, Chinese, Jamaicans, Hispanics, Indians, and a large number of Caucasians from all sorts of cultural backgrounds—English, Irish, German, French. All these people of different races and cultures united by one goal: to earn money.

I was pulling so many hours that the full-timers began to ask, "Hey Liz, do you sleep in the basement?" The few people I hung out with outside of the dining hall said, "You head to work so early, we hardly ever see you!" At the dining hall, the more I worked, the more I was respected. I couldn't find that sense of worth anywhere else. So I worked.

The work also led me into difficult situations. During graduation week festivities one year, I was busy with fancy breakfasts, luncheons, and seated dinners for the various alumni classes that came for commencement and reunions. Things were hectic, and we student caterers were working long and hard hours to make sure that the alumni were happy. It was not easy work. The dining tables and chairs, the table cloths, silver, glasses, flowers, napkins, and creamers all had to look perfect. At the same time, the food had to be prepared, the bar set up, and the food arranged. The preparation alone took three or four hours. Serving took three hours, and cleanup another two or three. We worked at least two of these events a day for ten days straight.

We were all tired, and as I recall, that spring, the fiftieth-year reunion class was very hard to please. I was tending bar at a reception being held in the lounge of the dining hall. The crowd was milling around with martinis, vodka-and-waters, and scotches in hand, discussing the murals they had just viewed downstairs, the 1930s paintings supposedly depicting the founder of the college, Eleazer Wheelock, with the "Indians" he supposedly set out to educate. I had seen the murals earlier in the day while setting up for the reception and still could not believe my eyes. I had actually started to cry as I stood there staring at the insensitive and disgusting childlike depiction of the "dumb natives," all painted with the same Caucasian features, almost naked, holding Bibles upside down and lapping up rum at the feet of Eleazer Wheelock. Because Native Americans and others have objected to them, the College covers the controversial murals with panels during most of the year, but for commencement and reunions, the panels are removed for the viewing pleasure of the alumni.

I had calmed myself by thinking, "Okay, you are working. This is a simple four-hour deal. You are getting paid, and you are working for Dining Services, so don't instigate any debate with the alums about how offensive the murals are. You have better things to do with your energy. Serve them their drinks. Stay strong."

Along with the murmurs about the "beauty of the murals," I heard many alumni say they were upset because the senior class executive committee had decided not to have the traditional "clay pipe ceremony" at the Class Day exercises. Native Americans had struggled to abolish that Dartmouth tradition, in which the seniors all gathered to "smoke" the clay pipes the college gave them and then walked past the stump of "the old pine," smashing the pipes on the stump. Because the pipe is a sacred symbol in many Native religions, many members of NAD objected to this practice. The pipe is like a sacred altar that can be used to pray to the Creator anywhere and at any time. Breaking the pipe to us is like smashing a cross to a Christian. According to College lore, the tradition was supposedly started by three Native American students who were graduating together in 1850. It is said that they danced a war dance, smoked a pipe, and then broke it on the stump of the old pine. But that cannot be true, for no three Natives graduated together from Dartmouth until 1970, and, more important, no Native American would break a sacred pipe.

I stood behind the bar, smiling and making drinks, hoping no one would ask me to discuss the clay pipe ceremony or the murals. I overheard an older woman in a small group snap, "I just don't understand those Indians. Why are they so offended at everything? If I was an Indian, I would be honored to have those murals downstairs, and I would want them uncovered for all to see all year round." I gritted my teeth in a superficial smile as she looked my way and moved toward me.

This was my test. I smiled again. I looked straight at her without really seeing her. I grabbed a glass, ready to pour her a refill. But she didn't ask for a drink. First, she hit me with the question.

"You are a student here," she said. "Now, why is it that the Indians here are so offended by everything? My husband said there was an Indian in his class who was proud of the murals. Why do you think the Indians are offended today?"

She didn't really want me to answer that question. I poured her the vodka and water she asked for, still silent, still seething. "If this woman continues to ask me what I think," I thought, "I think I am going to choke her!"

Even if I wanted to, I wouldn't have known where to start to educate her on the Native American struggle. She exuded arrogance. Everything was simple in her mind. Everything was done her way, or something was wrong. Black or white.

"Well," she said, sarcastically, "don't you have anything to say?" Haughtily, she picked up her drink and held it out at eye level, examining it carefully. She took a sip, and our eyes met. She muttered, "You don't happen to be Indian, do you?"

It was the last straw. "I do have something to say." The words came out distinct and controlled. "The college considers me a Native American. I am Hawaiian, from Honolulu. I am proud of my heritage, yet I am unhappy, as are my Native brothers and sisters— because people like you do not take our struggle seriously. And you think anyone could answer for us, taking as truth whatever is said that fits your way of thinking." I was very calm. I looked her straight in the eye. "I feel sorry for you," I said, and there was real sympathy in my voice. "It must be hard to be so ignorant."

The woman gasped, made a sharp about-face, and walked back to her group. They whispered. I looked at my watch. One more hour.

For my first two years at Dartmouth I was stuck, not really enjoying myself, feeling intimidated by many Native American students. I walked around uneasy, worrying about what they were saying about me. I was getting tired of working at the dining hall, and with schoolwork on top of it. I was exhausted mentally and physically. "Liz," people told me, "you gotta learn how to relax a little." I knew they were right, that this wasn't living, but I didn't know what else to do. Then a good friend at the dining hall said to me: "This life is your life. Do what you want to do. No one else is going to take care of you for you. I may tell you that you need to sleep more or eat more or go out more—but you decide; you're the one affected by the choices you make."

Finally it clicked. People decide what they want. I wanted happiness. I wanted to wake up in the morning smiling, not dreading what the day held for me. I had become caught in the tangled web of trying to please others. But no matter what I did, not everyone was going to like me or think I was a good person. So, I decided to enjoy myself. The hard part was finding out what made me happy and finding a way to do it. It became my goal for the year and a half of school I had remaining.

The following term was an off-term for me, so I went home to Hawaii to remind myself who I am and where I come from. Home from the airport, I sat around with my family watching TV. My youngest sister, barefoot and in a pair of shorts and a tank top, was sprawled out on the floor. My father sat on the couch in shorts and a comfortable T-shirt that had been washed too many times, and my mother was at the dining room table in her sweats, barefoot, preparing for the Hawaiian culture class that she taught at a nearby elementary school. She was mumbling some things in Hawaiian about Lono, the god of the harvest. I sat on the couch. It had been snowing when I left Hanover, so I had on some black jeans, boots, and an off-white turtleneck.

I was thinking about unpacking when my sister sat up abruptly. "Change your clothes. Don't you feel funny in those mainland clothes? I mean, they're cool and everything. I like the boots—but aren't you hot?"

Caught off guard, I didn't say anything. I let my sister keep talking. "Relax. Geesh—thank goodness you're going to be home for a while, because then you can stop acting *ha'ole* [white] and be yourself again."

Was I that different? I sat there a little dazed. "What are you waiting for? Take your boots off so I can try them," insisted my sister. I could hear Mom and Dad chuckling to themselves. Was I that out of things? I guess I was. I was dying of heat, and I had a headache from the extreme weather change. I was also tired. I remember thinking, "Okay, in the next three months here I want to get my life back together again." Maybe taking off the boots and the turtleneck was a good place to start.

For the longest time the air was heavy, and I was always tired. My parents told me not to worry; the tiredness was just my body adjusting to the humidity after being in a dry climate for so long. Everyone else was so laid back, but I was used to the furious pace of academic life at college where if I wasn't going to classes and working ten or fifteen hours a week in the dining hall, I felt I wasn't doing anything. I wondered if I had made the right choice in coming home.

At that time I was going to hula classes and taking Hawaiian language in the evenings. Then I started tutoring English and Spanish at a small university near home. I was meeting new people, spending lots of time with them, and I was with my family—important things that I didn't focus on at Dartmouth. "I will have to change my way of living when I get back to school," I would think every night before I went to bed. "Remember—people and their feelings, especially my own, are very important. I am not going to fall into the trap of books and words again."

In my Hawaiian language class one evening, our teacher wrote on the board, "'A'ohe 'ike i ka halau ho'okahi." Every class she wrote a Hawaiian saying on the board and explained it to us. This evening she said, "Literally this means, 'There is not only one school of knowledge. There is not only one way to look at life.'" I thought of Dartmouth, how academically oriented and intellectual a place it is, and how one-dimensional that can be. That night in class I realized that balance and harmony require learning how to feel and express one's emotions as well as one's thoughts. It takes confidence to express yourself truly, without fear of being intimidated by others. At Dartmouth, I had been afraid of people hurting my heart. At home, my faith in myself and my heart was reaffirmed. Coming from Hawaii, I realized, I have a view that not many other people at Dartmouth have, and I should be proud and excited to share it.

Back at school, I made the difficult decision to live in the Native American House. I could be happy only if I listened to my feelings, and they told me to show these people that this Hawaiian was not afraid of them, that she could hold her ground.

The House rang with the taunts and whispers of the past. "You are not Native enough." "Who do you think you are?" I was still afraid of the cutting rumors, but most of those people who had made me so unhappy had graduated. I reminded myself of what my friend at the dining hall had said: "It is your life. Make yourself happy."

Slowly I began to express myself with NAD—very quietly at first, doing behind-the-scenes work at the annual Pow Wow. Then I decided to dance the hula for Dartmouth. Until then, I had been angry and unwilling to share my culture, and dance was my first and foremost link with it. I had felt that if people didn't respect me, they wouldn't respect my dancing. It was a harsh and rash judgment. The real reason I hadn't danced was that I was afraid of what others would say.

When I feel out of my element, performing the hula seems like selling out: the token minority providing Dartmouth with the image of diversity. Yet, in order to come back into my element, I needed to dance for other people. I can dance by myself, and I do, but hula is meant to be shared. I danced for the tourists at home, never thinking of it as exploiting my culture. It was sharing. But still, inside, I dance for me. Sharing my culture is secondary. I remind myself of this often.

Choosing the right word is too important at Dartmouth, where feelings are lost or disappear. I am always dissatisfied whenever I write something or say something, but dance and music do not focus on words for expression. "Liz, did you realize that you can tell an entire story with your hands?" someone once said to me. "They never stop moving when you talk. You are very expressive with your body. Actually, with your entire body." I was staring at her intently, and she added, "You can tell a story without even opening your mouth. Your eyes do all the talking."

Sometimes people approach me when I dance and ask, "Doesn't it bother you to be on display like that?" Yet these are the same people who ask to see me do the hula, to see me display my Hawaiianness. Being a minority student at Dartmouth is a paradox. To live, we have to assimilate and learn the dominant way of living, while also trying to preserve our traditions.

My junior year, my life at Dartmouth improved, but it wasn't an overnight process. After I became active in NAD again my junior spring, life began to look a lot more positive. Living in the NAD House made me visible to those who hung out in the Native community, and I was surrounded by the issues that plagued us: the clay pipes, Hovey's murals, the continuing battle with Dartmouth's Indian symbol. I was forced to think about them and form my own conclusions. When I danced the hula and shared my true self, I opened myself to truly experiencing all of Dartmouth: its good things—the people I have met and become close to; its frustrations—ignorant people who continue to wear the Indian symbol, knowing that it offends the same people "tradition" says it honors; its stresses—waiting until the last minute to write a final twelve-page paper on *War and Peace* and studying intensely night after night to finish up the term; the happiness—the exhilarating success of teaching hula to my dance class, having people say how much they enjoyed the class and how they would like to continue learning the hula; the sadness—the subtle racism that still exists on campus, even within the minority groups themselves, and the fact that it took me over two years to get over a racist remark. Now, when I have finally discovered Dartmouth and all those opportunities that my mother harped on when I first applied, I am going to have to leave this place. Luckily, I caught myself and took control. I made my final year at college memorable.

Why didn't I realize all this earlier? Although I am somewhat ashamed to admit it, the true reason I decided to attend Dartmouth was its name and its status. As a senior, I became deeply involved in NAD and the Native American Program, and it was the best outlet the college provided for sharing myself and my culture. I saw that many NAD students were having the same struggles with their Native identities that I had. I found others who, like me, didn't look very Native, who appeared "white" at first glance, but who knew more about their cultures than the Native-looking students. I started to hang out with these new people and found that we also shared the common bond of "lack of funds." Together, we went through the ritual each term of standing in lines—at the financial aid office, at the accounts office, then back to the financial aid office—just to beat the deadline for late registration. Whiling my mornings away complaining about bureaucracy, I made some good friends.

I wanted to make sure that the new Native students did not go through the same pain and struggle that I did, or at least not as much. As an active member of NAD, I could be there to tell them what a few true friends had told me about taking charge of my own happiness. As a senior, I became a peer advisor in the Native American Program's Full Circle program, which trains upperclass students in listening and counseling skills for crisis situations that Native freshmen might experience in this vast and foreign world called Dartmouth. By sharing my pain with others in hopes of helping them with theirs, I have been able to put my own difficult memories to rest and realize that each struggle has taught me something—mainly that I am a very strong person, capable of more than just surviving.

I have grown spiritually in this last year at college. I have found a core group of friends with whom I can be myself and talk about anything, from how my Russian classes are getting me down to the meaning of life and whether there is an afterlife or spirits watching over us. I have become very close to another Native American woman, also a senior. I met her our freshman year and respected her and looked up to her. She knew a lot about her culture and both gave and demanded respect. But we were very different from each other. It wasn't until my junior spring, when we both moved into the NAD House, that I could confide in her. I desired her friendship because she seemed to be in harmony spiritually. She wasn't stressed out over grades and competition like many other Dartmouth students. She always got her work done, but rarely would she make it the center of her life. She focused instead on people and their feelings. She was very sensitive to others, very perceptive, and intuitive to an uncanny degree. She helped me link my intellect and my spirit. On nights when I sat in front of the computer and felt threatened by a writing assignment due the next day, she would say, "Don't let the words intimidate you. Just free-write. Don't worry about it coming out perfect. It will happen. You just have to let it happen."

She taught me that it is okay not to be comfortable with words and that not everyone works in the same way. Her policy on writing is the same as her policy on life—just feel. Feel and you will live life. Even as I write now, her wise words ring in my ears. Feel and the words will come.

Dartmouth teaches your mind, but the key teacher of the spirit is not found in any academic system, but in other people. Only through others are we able to learn about ourselves. In my final term at Dartmouth, I feel some pressure to have everything pulled together, because this important era in my life is coming to an end. Maybe this way of thinking is the problem. Everything is a continuous process, a never-ending cycle, and while dividing life up into four-year intervals like college may help in some ways, it can hurt in others.

To be honest, I don't worry about finding a job. I am struggling with the bigger decision of whether or not I will go home. If I don't have anything definite planned immediately after graduation, my family will insist that I go home. But there are not as many opportunities in Hawaii as there are in the continental United States, and I could get stuck there. My adventurous spirit wants to go to places I have never seen, while a small part of me wants to go home.

The real issue I face now is, what do I really want to do? I have a general sense, but nothing is certain—life is dynamic. I will likely change my ideas. But I have one comforting thought—my spirit will remain the same. If I can identify with my spirit and balance that with my intellect, I will be okay. Until then, I will keep going; I don't know where. Twists and turns will lead me to places I have never dreamed of. Or maybe right back home again.

Elizabeth Sprague Kahalaomapuana Carey was born and raised in Honolulu, Hawaii by a loving family who instilled in her a love of adventure and acted as a strong support network throughout all of her endeavors. Liz, a Russian major, graduated from Dartmouth College in 1993, where she wrote this essay in her final year. Liz credits her experience at Dartmouth with having given her a new understanding of and respect for her home, along with a newfound curiosity about the world.

Liz currently lives in Massachusetts, where she is still sharing herself and Hawaii's

culture through the hula. In addition, she is a professional flamenco dancer. Liz believes
that life is like an ongoing dance, in which humans are dancers creating their own
choreography in search of their identities. While seeking her own identity through hula
and flamenco, Liz hopes to help others express themselves and find their souls. She
currently does this as a dancer and dance instructor, and she hopes eventually to
accomplish these goals as a dance therapist.

▼ ▼ ▼ ▼ ▼ ▼ ▼ ▼ ▼

ROBERT BENNETT

Why Didn't You Teach Me?

Success in the white world has always been easy
for me. My accomplishments never surprised me because they
were enjoyable and relatively effortless. My grandmother, however, was usually more than surprised—perhaps even astounded.
"And you're Indian!" she would often exclaim to express the
joy, happiness, and amazement she felt for me. I did well in a
white school, played varsity football, baseball, and basketball,
went out with *wasicu* (white) friends, dated *wasicu* women, attended an Ivy League school and now make a living as a professional baseball player. I was doing everything she had always
hoped I would do, but because I was an Indian, she did not ex-

pect me to have so much acceptance and success in the outside world of the *wasicu*.

I remember, when I was very young, going over to Gramma and Grandpa's house, only two blocks from our apartment in Rapid City, South Dakota, and listening to Gramma and her mother speak Lakota to each other. During my childhood years, she never taught me one word of Lakota; she always spoke English to me. All I knew was that they were talking "Indian" and I spoke only English.

When I came to Dartmouth as a young man, I realized that my life was not well balanced because I had never learned the Lakota language and culture from my grandmother. Before I came to New Hampshire, a former Boston school teacher told me that many New Englanders think that "all Indians are dead." In a frightening sense, so did I. At Dartmouth, I was shocked to realize two important truths: I am an Indian and I am indeed alive.

When I first came to New Hampshire, I was at a loss because I could not answer the questions people asked about Native American life. Hell, I could not even answer my own questions! I took a Native American studies course my sophomore year and learned more about Indians than I had in twenty years of living as one. Yet there was something ironic and troubling about the source of my newfound knowledge: I was learning about my culture and ancestors from a white professor in a white institution. That fact disturbed me and prompted me to examine why I had ended up so ignorant. That course also reminded me of a conversation I had had with my grandmother.

While at her house during Christmas break, I asked her a question that caught her off guard. "Gramma, how come you never taught my brother and me to speak Lakota?" She looked surprised and sat silent for a moment. Then, with a sad, heavy voice, she said, "Oh, I really wish I had. Mom and I always talked about teaching you grandkids. I really wanted to, but I was afraid you would get made fun of by the *wasicu*." *Wasicu* was one of the few Lakota words I understood. To me it simply meant "white people," but it can also be translated as "greedy ones who take the fat."

Her reasoning is easy to understand when you consider her childhood. My grandmother was born on April 1, 1916, in Norris, South Dakota, on the Rosebud Reservation as Clara Virginia Quick Bear, the eldest of seven children. Her blood came from the Sicangu Oyate (Burned Thigh People) band of Lakota. When she was ten years old, it was decided that she should go to school. She had learned a little English from her mother, who had gone to school for a few years, but had had no formal schooling. She had also learned the Lakota language and traditional tribal ways as well as Catholic spirituality from Old Gramma. The lessons she learned in the Catholic mission school scarred her, and eventually those she loved, forever.

Even late in her life, many of her memories of St. Francis Mission School were still vivid. She said, "It was run by all whites. They treated us very mean and I didn't like it there much. They would punish us for speaking Indian and doing Indian things. The nuns there were really mean to us and sometimes they would lock us all in one room if someone was misbehaving. There were always a few kids who were homesick and tried to run away. It would always be just a few kids but the nuns would take it out on all of us. My brother tried to run away a few times and they would always catch him and bring him back. One time they shaved all of his hair off. They did it so the rest of us wouldn't get any ideas of leaving."

I tried to ask her to tell more, but she did not want to continue. "No, they are all dead and gone and I don't want to talk about it anymore," she said. I never asked anything more about it. I was angry, but not at her. I understood that Gramma wanted us to learn the *wasicu* ways to keep us from experiencing her ordeal. I was angry that "civilization" had denied me the freedom to be what I was, a Lakota. I look in the mirror and there it is, my Indianness. Yet I did everything in such a "white" manner that my white friends and others would distinguish me as the "good Indian" and say, "You're not like them." This acceptance is exactly what my gramma wanted for me. According to her, being an Indian in a white world gets you "made fun of." And she was correct because I was already guilty of making fun of other Indians myself. I had fallen deep into *wasicu* ways.

I remember making fun of a Lakota boy for expressing his Indian identity. I was about ten years old when my brother, cousins, and I first met this boy. When I asked him for his name, he lowered his head and submissively put his hands in his pockets. Then he suddenly raised his head and proudly said, "My name is Hunkpapa." We all laughed, and I said, "What?"

"My name is Hunkpapa. It's the name of my people and my parents gave it to me so I'll never forget," he replied. At this time, I was ignorant of how many bands of Lakota there were; as far as I was concerned, we were all just Sioux. The Hunkpapa, "the Campers on the End," are a northern band of the seven bands of Teton Lakota.

"Look, guys, this kid is still trying to be Indian. Hey boy, those days are over," I said as we walked away from this proud Hunkpapa.

To all of the Hunkpapas of the world, I am sorry. My grandmother's fear became a reality long before I knew it existed. I was part of that narrow-minded and twisted attitude I have grown to despise. Now I stand as a twenty-two-year-old Lakota who is dissatisfied with that sense of white identity.

My mother is also a product of my grandmother's hurtful mission school ordeal. She is shy of her Indianness and the world's perception of it. This shyness affects her thoughts and behavior in many aspects of her life. One time last fall, we both ordered the salad bar in a Rapid City Wendy's restaurant. The restaurant provided us with plastic plates so that we could serve ourselves from the food bar. When she finished eating her first portion, she wanted to go for a return trip to the salad bar, but she was embarrassed by her messy finished plate.

"Mom, just go up and ask for another one," I said.

"Can you do that? No, I'll just wipe this one off," she said.

"What are you so worried about, Mom? Do you think that because you're Indian they won't give you one? What can they tell you other than no?" I asked sarcastically.

Her face had an apprehensive look while she pondered whether or not to get a new, clean plate. She looked around and saw another customer, who happened to be a white woman, with two plates, one messy much like hers and the other clean and full of new food. She jokingly said, "Look! She did it but she is white." She was trying to be humorous, but there was also a sense of truth in it.

"Just go up and do it, Mom. These workers are here to help you and if you want a clean plate, they will give it to you," I said in a fatherly tone. Then I snapped, "Even if you are Indian!" She gave a fearful laugh and headed towards the counter, nervously glancing back at me several times.

She looked like a shy little girl. She had a submissive pose, with her back slightly hunched and her neck leaning forward, as she handed the messy plate to the Wendy's worker. The young worker gave my mother a new plate.

"You see, Mom, that wasn't so hard," I said as she returned. "All you had to do was ask. Do you feel better now that *wasicu* gave you a clean plate?"

"Well, I didn't know what to expect. Now shut up and let me eat!" she snapped back. These types of incidents were not uncommon, and the way my mother perceived each one of them only served to perpetuate her shyness.

Despite the stultifying effects of her self-perception, my mother still has within her the strength of my grandparents. She worked hard to be a good provider and to discipline two wild young boys. My brother and I were raised, like many other Indian children, fatherless. As a single Indian woman with two children, my mother had a tough time making ends meet, but with much help from our grandparents and other relatives, she succeeded. Our struggle was not unique. Like many poor Indian people, we survived on federal money in the form of food stamps and welfare checks. Our grandparents also directed much of their limited resources to us. Gramma always kept us fed by cooking up a casserole, a pot of chili, a meatloaf, spaghetti, or soup. Gramma and Grandpa were always there for us on our birthdays and Christmas. I think every new bike I ever got came from Gramma and Grandpa. I cannot imagine how life would have been without them in our lives.

When I was young, I shared my mother's timidity. The first racial insult I can remember being directed at me happened soon after the training wheels were removed from my bike. A maintenance man, coming down the stairs of our apartment building, did not see me approaching on my bicycle. I had to swerve to avoid hitting him. I stopped to see if he was all right and to apologize, but before I could say anything he blurted out, "You fucking Indian!" That insult scared me. I must have heard many similar comments afterward, because my mother said I came to her several times and told her that I wished I were white. She would lovingly respond, "Tell them you are proud to be an Indian."

Tell them that I was proud? Proud of what? I knew nothing to be proud of, just like my mother. I was on welfare and received free lunches. I was a "savage" who killed white American settlers. I was a boogey man, a gut eater, a dog eater. I was an exile in my own land. I wasn't aware of why my *akicita* (warrior) relatives fought and died for their ways and for the land. I did not know how my people lived, and I had no pride in my Sicangu Lakota. I didn't know the power and strength of the old stories. I didn't know how the name-calling *wasicu* had stolen my homeland and killed my ancestors. Ignorance was at the root of their misdirected bigotry, as well as my own and my mother's sense of inferiority.

Thus, during my upbringing I made myself acceptable to nearly every white person by being just like them, *wasicu*. It was not an entirely deliberate effort on my part to fit in. These people were my friends and we had much in common and shared a similar sense of humor. I did what made me happy and really had no idea what my Indian identity was.

During high school, I was usually the only Indian in any group I was in: football, basketball, baseball, and all my social groups. I felt overly cautious when my white friends were "causing trouble." Because I was the only Indian, I was often singled out as the troublemaker. In sports, I had to be better than the non-Native players, and in social situations, I had to be more humble than others to avoid problems. As a result of this intentional and unintentional social pressure, I was just as timid as my mother.

Because many Indian high school students feel extremely unwelcome among non-Native students and teachers, they join together for support. I am lucky that I felt comfortable with the mainstream at Central High School, but problems came from both sides of the ever-changing racial lines.

The word "apple" is a pejorative term used to describe a Native American person who has sold out the rest of the Indians and has become "red on the outside but white on the inside." Indian students who try to do well in school are often called apples by those who think success in the white world means that you are no longer an Indian. By this definition, I fit into the apple category.

Though my behavior, social life, and school success were reason enough for other Indians to confront me, it never happened. Still, my grandmother warned me to be leery of the "bad Indians" from the reservation. "They are bad people who will stab you in the back. They are all so jealous and will try to bring you down because you are doing so good in this world," she said, very sternly. She loved Indian people, but she also remembered the teachings of the mission school.

High school never presented any major problems for me. Everything—classes, friends, teachers, sports, and dealing with other Indians—was easy. I was just like any other kid who was curious about drinking and crossing over the lines of authority. I often went to parties—Indian, non-Indian, or a mixture of both—and did my share of drinking and other stupid juvenile acts. I often drank until I got sick, but that behavior is fairly normal among high school kids. I was involved in smashing a mailbox with a baseball bat, overturning a hotel ice machine, and other small-time crimes.

All of these little juvenile acts were gradually coming to a head when my baseball coach, Dave Ploof, confronted me. "Bobby, you have a lot of things going for you. I would hate to see your friends and other associates screw it up for you." This was the best advice anyone could have given me.

I was an investment for Coach Ploof. During the next three years, I pitched on his American Legion team. I owe much of my success to him because he taught me the discipline I needed to become a mature ball player and to always play hard. He touted my baseball skills and maturity to the college baseball scouts.

I also played basketball. My senior year on the team remains one of the best times of my life. We finished with a great record and made it to the state tournament. I was the only Native American on the team and was very vocal on the court; I was perhaps our team's biggest cheerleader. But I was also friendly toward the opponents, which surprised many of them as well as the fans; I was supposed to be a mean, vicious, and dirty basketball player because of my Indian blood. People sitting in the stands gave "war whoops" and yelled insulting names at me during games, but I still played my heart out and enjoyed it.

Throughout my high school sports career, opponents gave me the war whoop when I was on the field. I was an Indian beating them at their own game, and some found that hard to accept. I think their hostility was a response to their feelings of guilt at having reaped the benefits of their ancestors' taking everything we had. Yet, their fear and hatred of Indians prevailed because they knew that Indian people would continually return to reclaim what had been taken from us. We threatened them when we became educated, voiced our opinions, lived next to them, or excelled at sports.

One event showed me the irony of my position as an Indian on the team. After a game, a white woman tapped me on the shoulder. As I turned toward her, she extended her hand and said, "I just wanted to say how enjoyable it was to watch you during the tournament. Good luck." I barely had time to thank her before she smiled and walked away. What did she mean? Could she have meant: "It was good to see an Indian play the way you did?" Or was it: "You are a symbol for other Indians to emulate?" I think she was surprised that I was even out there.

Both on and off the sports field, I was the "good Indian" to nearly everyone in my school. Being elected the Homecoming King in my senior year shows how well I fit into that image at Central High. Indians normally frightened the people of Rapid City, adults and teenagers alike. The mother of one of my better friends in junior high school, for instance, had a problem with me. Kirk's family was rich, and we liked to go to his large, immaculate house to jump on his trampoline and shoot pool. One day, as we were playing billiards, Kirk's mother asked him to go with her on an errand. She told him it would take only half an hour.

"Why don't you just wait here for me until we get back?" he suggested to me. He left the room, but quickly returned with a worried expression on his face. His mother was standing right behind him. "She doesn't want you to stay here while we're gone," he said reluctantly. I will always remember his mother standing in the doorway with an intimidating look that made me feel very unwanted. She could not wait for me to leave, so I did. That was the first time I had met her, but she only saw a strange Indian person, not her son's close friend. That memory still hurts.

I not only scared parents, but also my peers. I cannot count how many times kids moved quickly out of my way while I was walking down the halls or going through the bathrooms at school. I was an Indian and we were all supposed to be mean to the *wasicu*. When I went into stores, I always felt the eyes of the clerks upon me. I hated to go into a store unless I truly had to buy something. If I were only browsing I made a show of returning whatever product I was looking at to the shelf or rack to avoid any possible problems with the store clerks. Even now, I find myself being cautious when I go into a store back in Rapid City.

For my high school graduation, I was chosen as one of the commencement speakers by the faculty. It must have been a good speech because it made several students cry and the audience seemed to listen intently. I wondered, was their interest in my words, or were they merely surprised to see an Indian up there? Whatever their opinion was, speaking for my fellow seniors was an honor and privilege that I had earned.

The day before the graduation ceremony, another honor—a spotted eagle tail feather—was presented to me by Sidney and Shirley Keith, a traditional Lakota couple who live in Rapid City. Sidney is a Lakota spiritual leader. He and his wife performed an eagle feather ceremony for all of the Lakota high school graduates. They sang to the four directions and to the sky, the earth, and finally to us. I wish I could describe how they sang because it was so powerful. Sidney and Shirley's voices calling to the spirits through the wind was something that I had not heard in years. We all watched and listened silently.

In Sidney's aged hands were many spotted eagle tail feathers, all about a foot long with dark brown plumes that had a milky white area at the bottom near the quills. At the base of each of the quills was a leather loop attached by a twisted red porcupine quill. I knew these feathers were holy. He stopped singing for a moment and lit some sweetgrass. He "smudged" the feathers by circling them with the smoldering braid of grass in order to make them sacred and give them power before presenting them to us. He then began again with the same powerful, rhythmic singing. Though I had no idea what the words meant, I stood with my mother and listened out of deep respect. Or was it fear?

I am Lakota. Why should I have listened in fear to a Lakota eagle feather ceremony? Because I had no clue what was happening. I recognized the sweetgrass because I had seen my grandmother use it many times before when I was a boy. Seeing and smelling the burning sweetgrass in Sidney's hands brought back memories from my youth. . . .

"Why are you doing that, Gramma?" I remember asking when I saw her light a thick braid of sweetgrass during a powerful thunderstorm.

"I don't want the house to get struck by lightning. This grass will help protect the house and us," she said as she walked from room to room waving the smoking braid of sweetgrass from side to side. She would mumble a prayer in Lakota at the same time.

She often prayed in both sides of her life, the Lakota and the *wasicu* sides.

I remember, too, going to the Rosebud Reservation with my grandparents when I was a boy to see the pow wows and hear traditional Indian songs. The constant pounding of the drums and the singing filled the air and my thoughts. I watched the "real Indians" in dance attire with their big headdresses and bustles adorned with multicolored feathers, their bells rhythmically sounding with every move, their buckskin pants and shirts with colored tassels swinging, their war clubs, eagle fans, and eagle claw staffs in their hands, and their faces painted with red, black, and yellow clay to make them look terrifying. No one told me what any of it meant or how to learn to do it. When I was perhaps five years old, not knowing the meaning of a song didn't scare me, but as I aged it became a different story. At age eighteen, my own ignorance frightened me. I hate not knowing now and am still frightened.

When Sidney and Shirley's song came to an end, they turned to us and he told the story of the eagle feather.

In the old days they gave these feathers to people who did a good deed. That deed could have been anything—saving a life, doing well on the hunt, doing brave things when it came time to fight, or becoming an adult. Times have changed, but the honor in accomplishing tasks has not. You kids have done a great thing in graduating from high school and that is what this feather honors. Use it in the new world you are entering for strength and guidance.

They gave each of us a feather and shook our hands. I then had something that visibly made me more Indian than I had ever been before. The feather connected me with a part of myself that I had never known about, and I was uncomfortable with it because of my lack of understanding. That day also opened my eyes and curiosity to the spiritual world—or, in American terms, the religion— of the Lakota. Next to my Lakota blood, that feather is the most significant Indian thing I possess. It changed my perspective and attitude toward everything around me. My brother recently said to me, "When you got that feather, that's when you became an Indian. You never hung out with Indians before you got that feather." That blunt truth hit me hard. But the true significance of the feather dawned slowly on me as, indifferent to my Native American identity, I searched for my true self away from my people.

Finding friends at college was fairly easy because my ability to throw a baseball made the transition from South Dakota to Dartmouth much smoother. According to the college's baseball coach and the school paper, I was the number one baseball recruit that year. That reputation made it very easy for me to meet people. The baseball team had guys in many fraternities who knew the ins and outs of Dartmouth College. "Yeah, this guy is cool. He's a good ball player," I frequently heard. Word quickly got around among the freshmen, and I soon had friends.

Without my baseball skills, I probably would not have met the people that I did. Most of the first people I met were *wasicu*, and my identity as a Native American was never more than a passing issue to most of them. That I came from South Dakota was more of a revelation to people than my Indian heritage. Most of them had never met any Native Americans before, so they had some basic misconceptions about me. They assumed I could run silently through the forest and shoot an arrow well. They did not know enough to be intentionally racist, only ignorant.

But those harmless assumptions and jokes had another side to them that was insulting, racist, and full of stupidity. Under the shadow of such preconceptions, I have had to shed my own cultural and personal ignorance. If I had known more about my heritage and culture, then I could have defended myself better and educated those with a distorted perspective on Indians. Many conservative people at Dartmouth have felt that my presence, or any other Native American's presence on the campus, is simply a big favor they are doing us—that we do not really belong here. Instead, we should stay on our reservations, out of the way of progress and intellectual enlightenment. To many students, and to the college in general, we are only as real as the old Dartmouth Indian symbol that many people claim is a tribute to all Native Americans. People see a symbol or a costume, but often fail to see the human being under the braids, buckskin, and paint. They do not know us or how we perceive the world; people only assume that we are out of our element and need special guidance. I think no white person can ever truly understand the thoughts and feelings of a Native American; we can only ask *wasicu* to respect the Native perspective. This was evident early during my freshman fall at Dartmouth.

When Coach Walsh recruited me for baseball he had informed me of Dartmouth and its fabled beginning as an institution to educate Native Americans. When I arrived at Dartmouth, Coach Walsh and I immediately became friendly, and we often talked openly in his office. Though he listened attentively as I talked about life in South Dakota and my Lakota background, he already had some preconceptions about me and Native Americans in general. Behind my back, Coach Walsh asked one of my teammates to watch out for me. "Don't let Bennett hang out in the fraternity basements, because his people have a big problem with alcoholism. I want you to watch out for him," he said. I was very angry when my teammates revealed this conversation to me after Coach Walsh had left the college. I acknowledge the problems with alcohol that many—but not all—Indian people face, but I did not appreciate being stereotyped.

Coach Walsh's successor, Bob Whalen, also assumed that I needed help to overcome the shackles of my Indian identity. I had filed a petition to get my sophomore summer course requirements waived so I could play in the Cape Cod Baseball League. I wrote in my petition that I had always wanted to play pro baseball and that taking part in the league would improve my chances of getting drafted by a major league team. I also stated that I intended to make up the academic work the following fall. I asked Coach Whalen to write a recommendation for me.

Coach Whalen's recommendation clearly showed that he saw me as Bob, the poor, disadvantaged Indian who needed help to join mainstream American life. The first sentences of his letter read, "I am writing on behalf of Bob Bennett. Due to his poor socioeconomic background I feel it very necessary for him to forgo his summer residence requirement and play baseball." The implications of this well-meant statement infuriated me.

I was so angry that I was crying and could not articulate my thoughts when I confronted Coach Whalen in his office. I told him how his letter made me appear to the registrar and explained that I had wanted reinforcement of my own arguments, not another handout from the white man. Of course, he replied that he had meant no disrespect and that he was only trying to help. I believed his sincerity, but he is typical of many white people who do not expect a Native person to succeed on his or her own merits. I have grown tired of having to justify my presence and identity to people.

I was granted my request and, fortunately, Coach Whalen and I have grown since that incident to become friends.

Other incidents at Dartmouth forced me to confront my Indian identity. My freshman roommate was interested in my Native background because he was taking an environmental studies course in which he read the journal of Lewis and Clark. Lewis and Clark passed through the territory of my ancestors, and my roommate asked me to verify one observation in the journal.

"Hey, Bob, have you ever eaten dog?" he asked. "These guys said the Sioux fed them dog meat."

I replied confidently, "No, they didn't. I haven't eaten dog and they didn't eat it either. They were buffalo hunters, and wouldn't eat dogs. They used them to pull the travois and carry packs. They weren't food."

My roommate insisted that we did and even showed me the passage in the journal. How could I refute what was right in front of me in black and white? I was confused and also embarrassed because he now doubted my Indianness. I also doubted my own Indianness. That early lesson at Dartmouth about my own cultural ignorance pushed me to know more about my ancestors.

I met some other good friends through the Native American Program, although my initial involvement in the program and in the student group Native Americans at Dartmouth (NAD) was quite limited. NAD's activities didn't interest me a great deal. I just wanted to meet some other Native Americans in this strange place. I never thought too much about the political aspects associated with NAD because I had my own agenda. I was a baseball player, and that occupied most of my time and effort each term. Then I rushed a fraternity. The combination of the two shaped who my friends were and, despite my limited interaction with NAD, I came to know many of its members as well.

Academics took up much of my time during my first three years at Dartmouth. One class really opened up new doors for me. The class, Native American Studies 22, "The Invasion of America," made me fully aware of something that I had been lacking all of my life—a Native American perspective on my own Lakota heritage. None of my previous classes had really touched my inner self.

The teacher, Professor Colin Calloway, had studied the Abenaki in Vermont and had learned much about the Crow people and their reservation while teaching at the University of Wyoming. I listened very attentively as he spoke of his experience with the Sioux people. "I have spent a lot of time among them and can recognize the sound of their language, but by no means can I speak it," he said. "I only learned this." He said a Lakota phrase that means "bullshit" in English. I laughed aloud as he finished because I recognized one word of the phrase, *cesli*, which means "shit." My chuckle was heard by the entire class and every pair of eyes was suddenly on me. Professor Calloway said, "I see we have a Lakota in here with us. Did that sound right?" I said yes, and he continued with his material.

I had made myself the "real Indian" of the class by recognizing one word in the Lakota language. But the extent of my Indian abilities was quite limited. I became frightened of my ignorance once again. I became aware of how white I was during each of his lectures on some other tribe, and I was overwhelmed when he came to the Lakota section of the class. I did not know the Lakota were the *Titonwan*, "dwellers on the prairie," and the western people who spoke the Lakota dialect of the Siouan language. I did not know there were seven bands of Lakota or two other groups of people who were also Sioux. I did not know anything, yet Professor Calloway always looked to me for approval when he pronounced the names of one of the bands of Sioux, and I usually gave him a nod. Other people would look to me when he said something. If only they had known that I didn't know much more than they did.

In the grand scheme of Lakota knowledge, I knew nothing. After a year and a half at Dartmouth, I began to question my life as an Indian, which was really my life as a white guy who looked like an Indian. I was trying to be the person my well-meaning mother and Gramma wanted me to be: an Indian Catholic who only knew the ways of the *wasicu*.

I was searching for a personal identity before that NAS 22 class forced me to think about the path I was treading. I was trying to find my identity, but only managed to become even more lost in the blurred world of Dartmouth College. I realized how lost I was when I tried to find myself spiritually. During my first few terms at Dartmouth, my search for spirit was centered on the Campus Crusade for Christ (CCC) and the Aquinas House.

Though these groups made a great effort to treat me as a person and respected my heritage, I found it difficult to find a comfortable niche in those institutions. I can now say that my true spiritual awakening, or journey, was just beginning, and I soon abandoned white religion.

Professor Calloway's class dealt with the issue of Native religion versus Christianity. Religion was used as a tool of destruction against all tribes in the colonization of North America, and I found it difficult to accept that I was part of an institution that had destroyed so many people's cultures and lives. I did not want to be a part of that institution anymore. I wanted to learn how to be a Lakota, not a white crusader or Catholic with an entirely different culture, spirituality, language, and history.

I made the strongest attempt to regain what had been denied to me by enrolling in a Lakota language class. The professor, Elaine Jahner, had written a Lakota language book with a Lakota woman earlier in her career. She was raised in North Dakota and had a good understanding of and respect for Indian culture and thinking. She knew the sound of the language and many words and pushed us patiently.

Four students, three Sioux and one Ojibwe, met weekly with her in her office. I wanted to learn Lakota very badly because I believed the language would return some of my identity. Though I learned quite a lot, Lakota was a difficult language to pick up for a twenty-year-old whose only familiarity was with Latinate languages.

In high school, I studied Spanish, and I remember writing letters to my grandmother with little Spanish phrases and sentences in them. "Gramma, I'm writing and speaking a new language," I wrote with a great sense of accomplishment. That pride now troubles me greatly because I did not even know how to speak the language of my ancestors. I could not even say "How are you?" What in the world was I doing, telling my Lakota-speaking grandmother that I could speak Spanish well? Now I'm angry with myself for being so blind.

When I told Gramma of the Lakota class and Professor Jahner, I felt proud yet nervous. I think she may have been a bit apprehensive about my reasons for learning. "Oh, you want to be Indian so much, don't you, Bobby? But . . . ," she said. There was usually a "but" in everything she said regarding my search for identity. She did not want me to get distracted from learning the *wasicu* ways and playing their game of baseball.

Despite her warnings and hesitation, she opened up to me before I left for my junior year at Dartmouth, after doctors found that she had developed lung cancer. "Don't worry. I'm going to beat this," she told me before I returned to college. "I've been to ceremonies before and they helped me then. They'll help me now. Just go to school and don't worry about me. Just pray for me." I never knew she had gone to traditional healing ceremonies. She was even more traditional than I had thought.

I returned to school for my junior year and often thought of her. I called her to ask questions for the Lakota class, and she spoke more freely than she ever had in answering my questions despite her intermittent warnings. She started her chemotherapy treatments later that fall.

I knew the side effects of chemotherapy—weight and hair loss—so I was nervous and frightened when I came home for Christmas break to see my grandmother. However, she had changed very little. She wore a little turban and had lost weight, but her voice and eyes still had their familiar strength. We talked a lot about her childhood and how she met Grandpa. She truly opened up to me for the first time, and I think it was because she realized her time was limited. I talked to her several times about my Lakota class. She taught me how to pronounce the word "deer" in Lakota. I wish I could remember all of the Lakota conversations we had, because they were the first ever. I hated to leave her at the end of that Christmas break because I knew I would not be home until the end of the following summer. It was a long nine months without seeing her. When the time came to see her again in September, I knew the little time I had was going to pass quickly and then I would never see her again. That one week, those seven short days, we spoke of our lives together and said our final farewell.

The chemotherapy and radiation treatment had failed to destroy the tumors in her lungs. She realized her time had come, and she just wanted to go home and stop the grueling cancer treatments. During that week in September, we had several great conversations about our lives. I was always on the verge of breaking down, and every time I did she would tell me to stop. "I'm old and I'm not afraid to die. I'm just so thankful that I got to see all of you kids grow up and do so well for yourselves," she said in her strong voice as I was crying next to her.

She never wanted us to feel sorry for her. I was crying and feeling sorry for myself that night. She knew she was going on her last journey soon, and she wanted to be strong for me. One night, she made herself sit up, put her arm around me, and consoled me, the healthy grandson, with an amazing strength in her voice: "I'm not afraid; it's my time to go. Bobby, you be strong for everyone here and just use the blessings you got from God. Don't cry for me because I will be fine." She had such strength in her final months.

During one of our conversations, I asked her how the Lakotas described "life" with their words. She thought for a moment and casually said the words in Lakota. Of course, I could not understand them, so I asked her what the words meant in English. She thought for another moment and said, "I have come this far." "I have come this far" is a literal English translation of the Lakota concept of "life." The old Lakota had a very insightful perspective on the world, and those were the most profound words I had ever heard from her.

"I have come this far." That phrase hit me that night. Ironically, my Gramma spoke the words at the end of her Lakota life. When she left this existence, my life—"how far I had come"—was just beginning. I was shedding my *wasicu* version of life and beginning to understand why my forebears had preferred to die in battle to protect their ways rather than become puppets of the *wasicu* world. Now I wish my upbringing had been as Indian as possible. I grew up solely as a *wasicu*, and that angers me greatly. My "I have come this far" is far from over, and when it does end, I want to be as content and unafraid as my grandmother was. Though she suppressed much of her Indian identity to protect herself, her children, and her grandchildren during her life, she left this world content, ready, and unafraid as a Lakota. I will follow her example.

She had gone a long way in her seventy-six years and I am thankful that I had nearly twenty-two years to spend with her. At her funeral, I put a baseball next to her body, just as I had for my grandfather years before, so she could hold it for me on the other side. That way I can play for her and Grandpa and they can give me their strength. I feel her spirit every day and I have seen her in several dreams. In her life I found strength, and her death only enhances the power we find in each other. When they closed the casket and the shadow covered her face forever, I truly realized why she did not teach me. I have to teach myself and also those who do not understand.

I am angry that a place like Dartmouth was necessary for me to figure out my identity and direction in life. The college has educated me in the *wasicu* sense, which contradicts much of the Indian knowledge I have acquired recently. Dartmouth has only licensed me as an educated Indian in the world of the *wasicu*, but that learning will be valuable in helping me help other Indians and myself. I have found more of myself, more of my spirit, and in that discovery comes knowledge. Knowledge will come to me and it will be in control. I just need to keep that in mind, relax, and allow everything that eluded me as a boy to come to me as a man.

Wanbli Wanji emaciyapi na han ma wicasa Lakota yelo.
I am One Eagle and I am a Lakota man.

My journey is far from over, and one of my yet-to-be-attained dreams is to stand on a major league pitcher's mound with my hair in a braid, knowing that I have accomplished everything I ever wanted. Standing there alone, standing as *Wanbli Wanji,* will be a testimony to the struggle of Native people and the individual battle waged within all of us. Stand proud, Indian people. *Mitakuye oyasin.*

Robert (Bob) Antoine Bennett, an enrolled member of the Rosebud Sioux (Sicangu Lakota) Tribe, was born December 30, 1970, in Rapid City, South Dakota. He graduated in 1989 from Rapid City Central High School, where he participated in football and basketball. At that time, he also played baseball for the Post 22 American Legion baseball team.

He enrolled at Dartmouth College in 1990, finishing his coursework for a major in government and a minor in Native American studies in March 1994. This essay was written during his final year at Dartmouth. While in college, he played three seasons of varsity baseball, and in June 1992 Bob was drafted by the Oakland Athletics as a right-handed pitcher.

As of the 1996 season, he was a member of the Class "AA" affiliate of the Oakland Athletics, the Huntsville Stars, located in Huntsville, Alabama. Bob is also a Grass Dancer, and he plans to help Native people as a lawyer, counselor, or educator after his baseball career is over.

▼ ▼ ▼ ▼ ▼ ▼ ▼ ▼ ▼ ▼ ▼

MARIANNE CHAMBERLAIN

The Web of Life

        There is a web, intricate and beautiful, that weaves itself around everyone and through everything. It is through this web that knowledge, strength, and humility are earned. Though the lessons contained therein may seem isolated and unkind, it is through these tests that we come to realize who we are and why we are here.

As I sit here at my computer in the last week of my Dartmouth undergraduate career, I think of my mother and sister, who will ride on a train for three days from Montana to watch me graduate. What will they think of this place? Will they understand how hard it was to make it through? Will they see past all the whitewash and happy faces? Will they see the pain that I have endured and the tears that I have shed just to walk up to that podium to receive a single sheet of paper? And if they can't see it in me, will they see it in the faces of the other minority students who have cried and triumphed in their journeys?

Thinking about it, I know my mother will sit there quietly with tears in her eyes seeing through the whitewash and wealth, and I will know in that instant where the strength came from for me to get through this place. I will look around and see my friends and the women who made it possible for me to walk steadily on my own two feet. I will know where the spirituality, humility, knowledge, and courage came from. I will know what beauty is. And last but not least, I will know who I am.

Dartmouth is not an easy place if you are different. The conformity and prejudice and blind allegiance to "traditions" that persist here are enough to extinguish anyone's spirituality and confidence. In my freshman year, I was lost in this sea of conformity.

I don't believe there is anything that could have prepared me for the challenge of freshman year at this college. The loneliness of the New Hampshire hills enclosed and suffocated me. There was no place for my spirit to wander and be revitalized . . . no place for it to run free . . . to shout . . . to dance. I had grown up in Florida for the first part of my childhood, and then on my grandfather and mother's reservation in Montana. I don't remember much about Florida, but to this day I long for the rolling plains of Montana. I consider Wolf Point, Montana, on the Ft. Peck Assiniboin and Sioux Reservation, to be home. Montana is known as the "Big Sky State." This is because you can see the sky for miles—almost three-quarters of your view is sky. On the eastern side, where I live, there are no trees—only plains and badlands. The land may seem barren, but it is the same soil on which my ancestors roamed and lived lives in harmony with each other and with the earth.

At Dartmouth, there wasn't one place where I felt comfortable and at home. I felt trapped. To feel alive, my spirit must feel free. It seemed that Dartmouth handed me a key and told me to lock my spirit up. Being young and unsure of myself, I did. In high school, I had known who I was. I was conscious of my identity and understood what it was to be traditional. I always thought that if I could combine my cultural heritage with eurocentric standards of success, I could succeed. I was right; and yet I lost sight of that my freshman year when I locked my spirit and heritage away in an effort to fit in.

Looking back now at my freshman year in college, I laugh and wonder how I could have known the answers in high school, and then forgotten them when I became an "adult."

When I left Montana on the train for Dartmouth, I thought I had left my family behind. I thought that the only person I could depend on now was me. I remember thinking that I had made it this far on my own, and that I was going to take college by storm. I would make my family proud of me, and I would do it by myself. I never realized what an impact my family had on me, how much strength runs through the blood of the women in my family. When I succeeded in high school, it never dawned on me that it was their triumph as well as mine. It was not as a result of my efforts alone that I walked on that stage to receive my high school diploma. It was the constant pushing and encouragement of my mother. It was the stubbornness and strength of my grandmother. It was the belief in me of my Aunt Babe. The love and sacrifices of all three of these strong and proud women got me through high school . . . and where I am today.

We lived in the Indian housing section of Wolf Point in a house with a revolving door. It was Ohiyesa (also known as Charles Eastman, a graduate of Dartmouth) who said, "Children must early learn the beauty of generosity. They are taught to give what they prize most, that they may taste the happiness of giving." My family lives by these words. The women in my family have given and sacrificed themselves for others—friends, family, and strangers alike. My grandmother always told me that to give something away was to help someone. You didn't do it to receive something in return. To see someone happy and succeed—even if it was your enemy—was the greatest success that you could have. My mother and stepfather, Willis, have always lived by this rule.

The first thing I remember about freshman year was coming across a four-page layout in an off-campus student newspaper, *The Dartmouth Review*, on the "Indian symbol." I remember thinking to myself, "This has got to be a joke. People just aren't that ignorant." They talked about how the Indian represented "savage nobility." They thought that since Dartmouth was already famous for its drinking, why not have the Indian as its symbol? At that point, I dismissed the *Review*, and began decorating the outside of my dorm room door with pictures of Montana, my little sister, and American Indian bustle dancers. I happily left that night for the Native American House, a meeting place, dormitory, and home-away-from-home for some of Dartmouth's Native American students.

I walked into the house hoping to ask someone about the *Review*, hoping that someone would tell me that it was a joke. Instead, what I found was a bunch of Native American-looking people sitting around a drum, singing and drinking beer and hard alcohol. I remember standing there looking at them in disbelief. It is this particular image that we, as a people, have been fighting against forever, it seems, and here I was at an Ivy League college looking at this stereotype come to life. The head singer looked at me and said, "Hey, white girl, do you know what kind of song this is? You don't belong here, go back to the city."

I am the lightest-skinned person in my family: my mother had told me that most people on the street would not be able to tell that I was an American Indian and that most Indians would tease me for not looking Native. She was right, and at that moment, her voice echoed in my ears. She had told me to always stick up for what I believed in, so I did. Barely audibly, I said, "Of course I know what song you are singing. It is a slide step song. You know, back on the reservation where I am from, we are taught at an early age that you should never sing and drum while you are intoxicated. Singing is sacred." I turned to leave, starting to cry. In this one moment, I became alienated from the Native students who lived in the NAD house and were active within NAD.

During my "prospective" trip, NAD had seemed to be a strong, cohesive group on the campus. There was no mention of *The Dartmouth Review* or the hostility toward minority groups. Maybe it was my fault that I did not research Dartmouth's background carefully enough. I wanted to believe that I could fit in. Yet here I was, my freshmen year already starting off on the wrong foot with the NAD students.

Early in my freshman year, I decided to try out for the track team. In high school, I had been good at sports. I liked competition and the camaraderie of a team. If I made the team, I would have a place to take out my aggressions and let myself be free. I went to the P.E. office to get information on track and field tryouts. They told me to go and see the coach, the "legendary" Carl Wallin.

They also told me that I shouldn't be afraid, even though he looked intimidating. "Great!" I thought, "Now I get to go and talk to some mean guy." I am not confrontational by nature, but I will stick up for my beliefs and for what I want. Setting aside my fears, I went to his office to try and persuade him to let me join his team of handpicked recruits as a freshman "walk-on."

They were right—he was very intimidating. Coach Wallin is over six feet tall and around 250 pounds of pure muscle. My knees were shaking and I stumbled over my words. I asked him to let me throw for him. In high school I had thrown the shotput and discus. He pretended to test me. He said, "You're kind of short to be a thrower, aren't you?" Trying to sound impressive I said, "Yeah, but I'm quick." He asked me if I had thrown in high school and what the distances were. After I had told him, he decided to let me throw for the team and we set up a practice schedule. I remember leaving his office with my head held high and a beaming smile on my face. This was my first major victory at Dartmouth. I had something to turn to, and a chance to make friends.

I returned home to my dorm that evening with renewed enthusiasm. School was going well, but I didn't have much of a social life. I was still trying to get to know people. I didn't drink and did not feel like compromising my ideals to be like everyone else. Having lived on a reservation where alcoholism runs rampant, I have seen the destruction that the abuse of alcohol can cause up close and because of that I don't consider going out and getting "wasted" a good time. Most of the people I knew went to fraternity parties to have fun. If you had connections, there was a party every night. Between school and training for track, there wasn't enough time for me to go out anyway. Besides, I had work-study.

My work-study job was at the Dining Hall. The first month and a half of work went smoothly. Then one day the student supervisor on duty approached me and asked if the rumor he had heard about me was true. "They say that you are an Indian." I answered him honestly and told him, "Yes, I am an American Indian." "Well, then, I better go and hide all the liquor. We don't want it to disappear or find you drinking on the job." I couldn't believe what I was hearing. But then he continued, "The only reason that you got into Dartmouth is because you are Native American. We all know that you are not smart enough to get in. They lower the standards for you people!" You people? All Native

Americans are stupid and alcoholics? When was this going to end? I wanted to call my mother that night to tell her about all the things that went on at Dartmouth. I wanted to tell her about the night that I came back to my room and found "Indian Bitch" written across my door in red paint. I wanted to tell her how hard it was and how many times I had wanted to come home. But I couldn't. We don't have a phone in my house. We do not live in a tipi; we just can't afford a telephone. I guess it was a good thing that we didn't have a phone, or I might have left Dartmouth that night.

All in all, I truly believe that I could have made it through my freshman year had it not been for the end of that first term. I had found an outlet for my aggression in track and the beginning of an outlet for my spirit in the Dartmouth College Gospel Choir. Then, two days before my fall term finals, I was sexually attacked in my room by a man who claimed to know everything about me. I went to both the Hanover Police and to the college police. I spent forever at the Hanover police station looking through books with student pictures when I should have been studying. It turned out that he wasn't a student. The only one who could comfort me was the sexual assault counselor at the college. She was very kind and kept asserting that it wasn't my fault. But I already felt ashamed. Afraid to leave my room, I decided to take an incomplete in my courses. I wanted to recuperate at home and come back in the right frame of mind to take those exams.

At home, I received a letter from the man who had attacked me, once again stressing that he knew everything about me. He said that I could never hide from him—he would always find me. Being stubborn, I headed back to Dartmouth on the train. I had three days to sit and think about what I was going to do and how I was going to do it. No one was going to stop me from getting what I wanted. I had my mind made up, and I was determined.

Winter term did not go as smoothly as I had hoped. The man who had attacked me began stalking me, reminding me that there was nowhere I could hide. The college police did all they could. They came whenever I called them and checked up on me at night. However, I had no roommate, which made me feel uncomfortable and frightened. More important, I was angry because I had lost my independence. I began to stay at the NAD House. I figured it was the lesser of two evils. There was nowhere else I could go.

That term I did average academically. However, I was able to channel all the added stress in my life into athletics; I excelled at track, and was invited to travel with the varsity team down to Arizona State University to train during spring break for the outdoor season. This time away from Dartmouth allowed me to rest and rethink my goals. But my success had made others jealous. I was told by a fellow athlete that I did not matter to the team because I was just a walk-on, not a recruited athlete. At first what she said hurt me, but eventually I became angry. The fire she started in me allowed me to place that spring at the Outdoor Ivy Heptagonal Championships in the shotput, the event my detractor had been recruited for. Because of my performance over the winter and spring, I was given the "Outstanding Freshman" award for the women's track and field team.

Just when I thought that everything was going well for me, the man who had attacked me found his way back into my life. He began calling me—reminding me that I was a nobody, and that he would make sure that I knew it. I was terrified to go anywhere by myself. I locked myself in my room, hoping that he would leave me alone. The only time I remember coming out in those last few weeks of classes was to go to NAD's annual Pow Wow. My friends had to coax me to go. They promised me that they would never leave me alone, and would walk me back and forth to my room to make sure I was safe. The Pow Wow that year was an important event for me. A friend had asked me to dance the women's fancy shawl dance. I decided that I would. It would bring me back in touch with my culture and allow my spirit to be free.

I think it surprised the people in NAD that I knew how to dance. I have been dancing ever since I can remember. It is an integral part of my life. At home I traveled across the country, going from pow wow to pow wow, dancing competitively in the summer pow wow circuit. Dancing is a way of life in my family. It allows the spirit exercise and happiness. When I danced at the Pow Wow my freshman year, I was spiritually happy for the first time at Dartmouth. I felt like I embodied the dance of the fancy shawl. (The fancy shawl dance personifies the butterfly as she floats over the rocks and flowers looking for her lost lover.) I felt like I was floating, and at the same time, regaining bits and pieces of the self that I had lost.

In the middle of the dance, my choker slipped from around my neck and fell to the ground. When the song was finished, I picked it up and walked off the competition floor. According to tradition, when a piece of your regalia drops to the ground during a dance, you should disqualify yourself. I was taught the old way, so I removed myself from the dance arena. I was called back out by the announcer. He explained what had happened and why I had walked off. What he said made me proud of my courage to walk off the floor and honor the traditions that my family had taught me. He spoke of how today's younger generations do not respect the old traditions, and he said that he was proud to see one young person following in the footsteps of the elders before her.

At that moment, I was so proud of what my family had taught me. What the announcer said opened other people's eyes in NAD, and suddenly, I became an accepted member. I was sad that I had had to prove myself, but I was happy that I had finally found a family. Here was a group of people who understood what I was going through. They also struggled with the extra load of intertwining their cultural heritage with "white, male academia." My new family gave me an outlet to express my heritage through conversation, dance and crafts. I was elated. I decided that now that I was a part of NAD, I would do my best to bring in others who felt that they did not belong because of their lack of cultural knowledge or lack of "skin color." This would not only strengthen NAD but would give those who were once alienated an outlet for expression—or, more important, a chance to learn from one another.

As I was walking to the NAD House from my dorm room the night after the Pow Wow, I was grabbed from behind and shoved to the ground by the same man who had attacked me before. Terrified to look up, I curled up into a fetal position. He grabbed a handful of my hair and yanked my head back. "Can't you see that I love you?" he yelled at me. He punched me in the stomach and turned and ran. I just stayed down on the ground crying for what seemed like an eternity. When I finally had the strength and courage to get up and run, I returned to my room, locked the door and hid in my closet. The fear had returned. All I could think about was this man who had stalked me. How could he say that he loved me? I didn't know what to do, so I locked myself in my room trying to hide from him. Unfortunately, I also locked myself out of my classes. I did not pass any of my classes that spring. Emotionally and physically drained, I made the long journey home.

When I finally reached home, I had a severe case of bronchial pneumonia. When it cleared up, I moved from Wolf Point to Kalispell to live with my Aunt Babe and look for a job. During my time with Aunt Babe and my cousin Gina, I began thinking a lot about my grandmother. When I was younger, my grandmother had told me stories about dancing and shared her memories of her parents and relatives. These stories, passed from generation to generation, helped to teach us our ways of being. I had heard what she was saying, but being foolish, I had not really let it sink in. Fortunately for me, I would get a second chance.

I began asking questions about my grandmother's life and my family history. My Aunt Babe and Gina began telling me what life was like with her. They pulled out old photo albums with pictures, old black-and-whites as well as color photos. Among the familiar faces were others I stared at in wonder. Who were they and what was their relationship to me and my family? I remember one picture in particular that showed a younger Grandma, before her hands were ravaged by scleroderma. Her eyes seemed so sad. She was standing beside a pickup truck parked on the hard-packed, dusty earth. I wonder what she was thinking when that picture was taken. Her shoulders were bent as if all the problems of the world were sitting right there weighing her down. They told me that that particular picture was taken after my Aunt Helen's funeral. I knew very little about Helen, only what my grandmother had told me, and that she had died at a young age. My relatives had told me that I looked like her when I was younger.

Then one day we got a call that my grandmother had just gone into cardiac arrest, and that we needed to get to Wolf Point immediately—they didn't know if she would make it through the night. That evening we packed into my cousin Gina's car and headed home. When we arrived, my grandmother was in stable condition. We said our prayers and all went up to see her, and she was surrounded by all her children and grandchildren when she woke up. I realize now that this is what gave her the strength to survive—her love for her family and our love for her. When she was well enough to travel, it was decided that she would come back to Kalispell with us and we would take care of her. I was excited—here was my second chance. I was determined that I would not only hear but would really listen to what she said. We often don't appreciate the knowledge of an elder until it is almost too late. I was so glad that I had another chance. Not long afterward, my grandmother did pass away. People came from all over for her wake. While we were passing out cigarettes and coffee (my grandmother had demanded that anybody who was going to be present at her wake be sober), some of my mother's siblings went into my grandmother's room and began looking through her things. When I walked in, I saw my grandmother standing there, clear as day. She just looked at me and shook her head. I left immediately, and the others followed me out. They told me that I had gone deathly pale and that I was trembling. They said that I had scared them. I laughed and told them that Grandma was in there watching them. They did not know what to say.

Later that night, I went into my grandmother's room with my Uncle Ben. He began straightening the room up. I was speaking to Grandma. I remember that she had once told me that when she died she wanted to be buried with the things of her daughter Helen that she had kept. I told Uncle Ben that the bag that had Helen's stuff in it would be at the bottom of a barrel that contained sheets and towels. He laughed and asked me how I knew this. I told him that Grandma had told me in a dream where she had put it, and that is where we found it. I had had dreams before that had come true, but this was the first dream that had a real impact on me. I knew that my grandmother would be with me wherever I went and would help me whenever I needed help. The strength she left us with would give us the determination that we needed to accomplish what we set out to do.

Knowing that I was not alone anymore, I felt confident in returning to Dartmouth with renewed strength and the wisdom of my relatives. I returned in the spring of my sophomore year. Things went pretty smoothly that spring. I passed my classes without any worries; more important, there were no more appearances by the man who had attacked me. I wasn't listed as a student in the campus computer, which made my address unobtainable. My phone number was unlisted.

With the approaching international "celebration" of the Quincentennial, or Columbus's so-called discovery of America, NAD began changing. We started planning activities to commemorate the Native peoples who had inhabited the "new" world before the colonizers had arrived. NAD became a group with a distinct purpose. We set aside all differences between our nations and worked together as a group.

One of NAD's greatest coups came during the spring quarter later on that year. NAD petitioned Dartmouth and its students to drop the so-called clay pipe tradition from Class Day ceremonies. In this 100-year-old tradition, all the members of the graduating class broke imitations of sacred pipes against the college's famous "lone pine tree" stump, supposedly to symbolize their "breaking" with the college and moving on to another phase of life.

Ever since its inception at the college, NAD had been petitioning the college hierarchy to eliminate this tradition from the Class Day celebration. Due to pressure from alumni and right-wing students, the College repeatedly denied these petitions. In the spring of '93, NAD held a campus-wide information and discussion session concerning the clay pipe to explain why this particular "tradition" was considered by members of certain tribes to be religiously offensive. I honestly believe that the Dartmouth community thought that we as Native people should embrace this tradition because they believed it was paying homage to us.

It was hard trying to make the mainstream community at Dartmouth understand what we were saying. Being Native Americans, we certainly understood the value of traditions and the importance others place on keeping cultural traditions alive. But this particular tradition was rooted in a myth, a story about three pipe-smashing Indian graduates of Dartmouth who apparently never existed; instead of honoring us, it mocked us. During the campus-wide discussion session, we compared the pipe to a crucifix and to a menorah. We tried to show non-Native students how the pipe fits into Native American religious life by comparing it to an item of similar significance in contemporary Christian and Jewish societies. Unfortunately, the non-Native students were not grasping this basic concept and the discussion session was in danger of disintegrating. Being a religion major with a certificate in Native American studies, I decided to stand up and try to relate the symbolism of the pipe in a different Judeo-Christian perspective that non-Native students might better understand. The gist of what I said was that in my family, we regard the pipe as a portable altar. The smoke from this type of altar serves to carry our prayers to the Creator. I am not sure if what I said made an impact or not, because I left the discussion session soon after I spoke to study for an exam I had the next morning. But we must have said something right, because the Dartmouth community shortly thereafter chose to eliminate the clay pipe tradition from Class Day exercises. Not to be outdone, however, *The Dartmouth Review* advertised and sold clay pipes to individual students who wanted to continue the tradition.

About the same time that NAD pulled together, track became much more important to me. With hard work and determination, I became the number one hammer thrower on the team and a nationally ranked thrower in the United States. I qualified for the U.S. Mobil Outdoor Track and Field Championships that year and competed successfully. The U.S. meet determines who makes the U.S.A. national team that travels to the World Championships, and ultimately who makes the Olympic team that represents the United States. It is a hard meet to qualify for, considering you are competing against the best track and field athletes in the United States—including world-class athletes like Jackie Joyner-Kersee, Gail Devers, Michael Johnson, and Carl Lewis. It was an amazing experience. I could not believe that I was competing at the same meet as my high school role models.

At the end of my senior year, I still had two more terms of academic work left to complete before I could graduate. Naturally, I decided to complete those two terms during track season so I could compete. I had an excellent start, setting the stadium record at Arizona State University for the hammer throw and simultaneously setting the school record for Dartmouth College. Owing to an injury, however, my season was cut short. After graduation, I will have the chance to compete again at the U.S. Mobil Outdoor Track and Field Championships. I plan to continue throwing after graduation, and hope to qualify for the 1996 and/or 2000 Olympic teams.

Again, I find myself sitting before the computer in the last week of my college career. In composing this narrative, I have relived some of the best and worst moments of my life and my Dartmouth career. I would be a fool to believe that I made it this far by myself. Through all my ups and downs, my family and my friends were right there, no matter what. They have enriched and enlightened my world and have made Dartmouth the beautiful place that it has become. Now, graduation is right around the corner. I have to ask myself, "What have I really learned about myself as a Native American student and as a woman? What have I taken from this web of life and what will I leave behind for it?"

I don't know if it was harder being a woman or being a person of Native descent on this campus. At the beginning of my Dartmouth career, I was very shy and quiet. I didn't speak up much. I think because I don't look like your stereotypical Native American, I experienced more abuse for being a woman then for being Native. However, as I matured and found my voice, others started to view me as a Native American woman. They saw who I was through what I believed.

I went through most of college like any other poor, young minority woman—misunderstood, angry, and eventually outspoken. Dartmouth gave me a glimpse of the real world. It is hard to be a person of color on this campus. It is also hard to be a woman on this campus. I know what it is like to be a woman of color in a place that does not really want you there if you're not willing to keep quiet and conform. Dartmouth was the last Ivy League institution to go co-ed, and that was not until 1972. There are still sentiments of bitterness from the alumni who wanted the college to stay a single-sex institution.

At times, it seems like you cannot fit in anywhere as a woman. Even within a minority group, there is prejudice against its own women. Many people say that feminism destroys the unity within the minority group. I think that there wouldn't be any unity in the minority group if there weren't equality among the sexes. It's not feminism that prohibits the group from reaching its goal. NAD as a minority group accomplished many of its original goals, such as eliminating the clay pipe ceremony, once it became a united group. Women and men worked together and shared the responsibilities. In their quest for respect, the talents and abilities of the entire group (men and women), not just half the group, were utilized and that is what made us successful.

I've had men in NAD tell me, "Woman? Make me fry bread," and "You are just a woman, you should be walking at least ten paces behind me. You do not deserve to be my equal." I laugh at that last remark. My grandmother always laughingly told me that the women walked behind the men. It's always been that way. And if they hadn't been behind the men telling them where to go, the men would still be lost today.

The discrimination doesn't stop there. As I mentioned before, sports have always been an important part of my life. Discrimination against women exists on the athletic field as well. I am not a small girl. I have been solidly built ever since I can remember. It is only natural that on the track team, I compete in the field or "strength" events. I have been lifting weights all my life in the hopes of becoming a world-class athlete. Early on in my track career at Dartmouth, I recall lifting heavy weights in the weight room that was reserved for non-varsity athletes' use. While warming up, I noticed that there was a male student lifting about the same weight that I was. However, what I didn't realize was that he was lifting his heaviest and final set. I asked him if I could work out with him. He laughed and said, "Do you realize how heavy this is? You might hurt yourself." I assured him that I had stretched out thoroughly and that I knew what I was doing. After I finished my warm-up set and was just about to add more weight, he called me a "fucking freak" and walked out. I remember feeling so badly about this incident that I started a diet that very day, only to break it later that month when a fellow female athlete reassured me that I wasn't really a freak of nature.

A couple of months later, while practicing, I was told by the men's lacrosse coach, "Get off the field, little girl, women aren't real athletes." To this day, that quote has remained embedded in my brain. Is there any middle ground for the female athlete? On one end of the spectrum, if we are too strong and threatening to men, we are "freaks," and on the other end, we don't deserve respect as real athletes because we are just "little girls."

During my years at Dartmouth, I have been fortunate to have met some very strong women from a wide variety of racial backgrounds. These women have blazed a path through this college, making it a little easier for each entering class of women to feel more comfortable to excel. They chose not to close their eyes to what was going on and to speak up for what they believed in. My success here was derived from the many other women who made it through Dartmouth before me. These women helped me realize that I have a voice, and that one voice can make a difference if it is joined with other voices.

My one voice, along with those of other Native women, makes up one strand of the web of life. Individually, these strands may not seem strong, but together, they form a web that is almost impossible to break. The strength that I draw on comes from the web not only of my ancestors, but also of the women here at Dartmouth who have gone through, and are going through, situations similar to mine. When I leave, I hope that I can leave the strength that I borrowed from the web reinforced so that others can make it through also.

When I walk up on that stage to receive my college degree, there will be minority women from all walks of life sitting in the audience and among the graduating students. There will be Native American families watching their daughters and sons receive their degrees. And among those families, I will see my mother and my little sister. I know that my grandmother and my Aunt Babe will be there in spirit, and in that instant—through the web of life—I will know what beauty is.

Born in Glasgow, Montana, Marianne Chamberlain spent her early years in southern Florida. After her parents' divorce, Marianne, her brother, and her mother returned to Montana, where her mother remarried, giving Marianne two new stepsisters, a stepbrother, and a younger sister. She graduated from Wolf Point High School in Wolf Point, Montana, in 1989. In September of the same year, she matriculated at Dartmouth College, where she was an active member of Native Americans at Dartmouth and the Dartmouth Women's varsity track and field team. Marianne graduated from Dartmouth in 1994, with a degree in comparative religion modified with Native American studies. This essay was written during her senior year at Dartmouth. She is a member of the Ft. Peck Assiniboin and Sioux tribes, and her Indian name means "Woman who walks the sacred path."

Through her involvement with Dartmouth track and field, Marianne met Kurt Cohen, the captain of the men's team. Currently, she lives in Stamford, Connecticut, with Kurt and their daughter, Alexandra. Kurt is a consultant with McKinsey and Company, and Marianne remains at home to raise Alexandra. In the near future, Marianne hopes to pursue a career in secondary education and coaching.

Coming Full Circle

▼ ▼ ▼ ▼ ▼ ▼ ▼ ▼ ▼

ARVO QUOETONE MIKKANEN

Coming Home

The clarity of the air, along with the brightness of the sky both during the day and at night, is something that makes the Wichita Mountains otherworldly to me. Rising out of the plains like great mounds of rough, rounded boulders, the Wichitas have been an important and even magical place to me since childhood. I remember my fascination as I watched a mother buffalo and her calf lumbering along, unbound by fences and corrals, and recall my amusement when I tried to sneak up on the prairie dogs in the prairie dog town before they jumped into their burrows. I remember that, sometimes, when it was very quiet, I could hear their shrill barks in the distance over the whistling wind through the knee-high grass in the fields surrounding the mountains. I always enjoyed visiting the Wichitas when I returned to Oklahoma in the summertime for visits with my family.

It is also curious that these mountains have such beauty not only in the spring when the grasses are lush and green, but also in the winter when the grasses are golden brown and dry. When driving through the refuge that surrounds these mountains, one cannot look out across the fields without imagining what they must have been like a hundred and fifty years ago when the plains were still open and there were no fences, electric wires, or roads.

These mountains have always been an important place for the Kiowas and Comanches, not only because they were primary landmarks in the last tribal reservation, but also because so many of our ancestors are buried in the mountains in unmarked graves under the heavy rocks and boulders and down in crevices—places where no one has trodden since they were placed there hundreds of years ago. I also wondered how it was that the Kiowas and Comanches lost these lands. My curiosity about this was sparked by conversations with my grandfather about the old treaties and the many laws affecting the tribes.

Today, when I return to the Wichitas, it reminds me of my childhood visits to Oklahoma and the time spent exploring the lakes, rocks, and fields of the entire area. Sometimes I also recall how it came to pass that I am now here in Oklahoma. I guess I just could not get enough of the Wichitas and the rolling plains of Oklahoma; or maybe it was an inner longing for a place where I felt that I belonged or that was meaningful or significant to me. I was a bit lost in high school and looking for a direction in my life—something that would be important for me to do—and it took some time to find that goal. Ironically, I think it was primarily an education at a small liberal arts college on the border of New Hampshire and Vermont that brought me back to Oklahoma. This is the story of that journey.

The journey began during the summer immediately before my senior year in high school, when a subtle panic began to set in. Everyone I spoke to inquired, "What are you going to do after you graduate? . . . Where are you going to college? . . . What are you going to do with your life?" I did not have a definite answer. I assume that in the back of my mind, I thought planning for my future could be put off for a while. However, the closer I got to graduation, the more I realized that the time to act was now upon me and I had some important decisions to make. During my senior year, I spent a lot of time working in my high school's closed-circuit television station. From the time I was a freshman, I had worked in the television production facility in a variety of technical positions. Falmouth High School, in Massachusetts, was built in the mid-1970s and was a modern "high-tech" school equipped with a three-channel television studio that provided programming, news shows, announcements, and special productions to the faculty and students. The station was connected to the community cable network, and its broadcasts could be seen by the public as well.

Eventually, my long hours of after-school work at the TV studio, as well as my training and interest in creating different types of TV programs, resulted in my being selected to be the general manager of the station. At that point, it seemed that television would play a big part in my future. When the time for graduation came, I really had no idea what to do for a career other than to pursue a position connected with television production.

Unfortunately, my guidance counselor did little, if any, "guiding" during our few sporadic meetings throughout my high school years. I actually felt at times that I was nothing more to him than a number on some manila file folder. I don't really blame him—I felt that he was a good person who had some interest in my future, but he didn't know me well enough to suggest what would be in my best interest from an educational and career standpoint. Needless to say, I didn't receive much direction from him.

Unlike many parents, who push and prod their children into a particular field, my mother and father were very open and supportive of my interests and life goals. The issue of what I would do after high school was, therefore, squarely "in my court." I appreciated that sense of freedom, but without a definite path set out for me, it was that much harder to make a decision about something so vague as "the future."

While I was still in high school, I had secured a part-time job working for a private television production company, relying upon my experience in video production. The company originally started in a local entrepreneur's basement with a home video recorder and a hand-held mini-camera, and quickly grew into a substantial business with a half-dozen employees. I ended up doing almost all of the camera shooting, editing, and composition of the various productions ranging from sports events to travel documentaries. This work first made me realize that not only could I have fun working in television production, but I could possibly make a living at it as well. I also preferred working in the air-conditioned videotape editing studio at fifteen dollars an hour to working for minimum wage in the hot sun at the golf driving range where I had previously been employed. As a result, most of the universities that I looked at, and considered applying to, were those that had an active program in television production.

Unlike many other students, I didn't really have a concrete plan from the beginning that I would go to college. I guess I always assumed that I would go to college, although I never made a specific decision until right before my senior year in high school. A big concern I had was where to get the money for a college education. Both of my parents worked—my dad as an electronics technician and my mom as a nurse—but we were an average middle-class family, without a trust fund or a tremendous amount of savings to pay for my education. In fact, we had only moved into our first house when I was a junior in high school. Before that, we had lived in either an apartment or a mobile home. Moving into our own house was a big step for us, primarily because it was the first time that we had a permanent place that we could call our own.

After I decided that I would go to college, I set out to try to research every scholarship, grant, and fellowship that I could find so that I could accumulate enough money to help me pay for my education. My mom and I had a Saturday morning ritual where I would go to the local public library and read for a few hours while she went grocery shopping. It was during one of these many research sessions in search of college funds that I discovered the path that led me to my college.

I sorted through tattered boxes, dog-eared books, brochures, and flyers piled in stacks describing countless scholarships and fellowships available for everyone from professional bowling league members to the descendants of Civil War veterans. I recall reading a publication dealing with scholarships available to Native Americans, and remember something catching my eye. It described a small, liberal arts, Ivy league college that was looking for Native American applicants who could "adjust to a small-town New England environment." I thought to myself, "Well, that sounds like me." I was a Kiowa/Comanche living in a small town on Cape Cod, Massa-

chusetts. I figured that I had adjusted fairly well to a New England environment, since that's where I had lived since third grade, except for the summers and holidays that I spent with my extended family
in Oklahoma. The union of my dad, of Finnish descent from Massachusetts, and my mother, a full blood Kiowa/Comanche Indian from Oklahoma, led to the unusual situation of my being a Plains Indian on Cape Cod, Massachusetts, of all places.

Although I was proud of my Finnish background and was familiar with that side of my family, it was somewhat difficult for me to forge a Native American identity since I was only immersed in Indian culture on those occasions when I returned to Oklahoma. It just so happened that we lived near a small Massachusetts community called Mashpee, home to a Wampanoag Indian community. While I had some classmates and friends who were descendants of individuals from this tribe, I really didn't feel all that close to their tribal culture, since it was so different from the Plains culture that I was familiar with. Moreover, the Wampanoags, through almost 500 years of acculturation and intermarriage, had very little left of their own traditional culture. While I did go to some pow wows and other events in Mashpee, it felt somewhat foreign to me as a Kiowa/Comanche.

I ultimately applied to several universities known for their television production programs. Almost as an afterthought, I completed my application to Dartmouth College, even though it didn't fit my "mold" of being a school with a known degree program in television production and it cost two or three times the amount of other schools I had considered. I sent off the application and really didn't know what to expect.

To my surprise, I was accepted to Dartmouth in the spring of 1979. Fortunately, my searching for funds had also paid off and I received several scholarships from private foundations, from the Kiowa Tribe, and from the federal government. Of course, I had saved some money from my old job at the golf driving range and from my video production position. My parents had also saved some money to help me, and I sold my rusted-out, 1966 4-wheel-drive truck to help pay for some of the expenses.

I traveled to Hanover, New Hampshire, on a spring day and visited the campus. Dave Bonga, a Chippewa and the outgoing director of the Native American Program, gave my mother and me the grand tour of the campus. This visit was the first time I had actually seen the Dartmouth College that was not on the glossy cover of a brochure. In actuality, it looked much like a brochure, with all of the scenic beauty, bright white buildings, and foliage. It seemed unreal and fantasy-like. I decided to accept the offer and enroll. With this step, I had made the plunge, not knowing what to expect.

Not long afterward, my mother shared with me the fact that her dream had always been for me to go to Dartmouth. I was somewhat surprised and perplexed by this, especially since she had never told me, nor had she encouraged me to apply specifically to that institution. In any event, it was clear to me, as it was to her, that this was an opportunity that I could not let pass; despite the expense, I figured that I would go and try my best.

During that initial visit, I also had arranged an informal internship with a local television station in the nearby town of White River Junction, Vermont. After my visit to this backwoods broadcasting facility located in the basement of an old motel complex, I felt I could still hold fast to my goal of going into some aspect of television production. Like the old cliché, I felt like I could have my cake and eat it too.

My first experience with college life was the freshman trip that took twenty of us on a three-day hiking excursion through the White Mountains of New Hampshire. I enjoyed this experience with the outdoors and despite my mosquito bites, calluses, and sore back, I joined in with the hundreds of other students in a rendezvous with the various other freshman trip groups at a lodge at the foot of one of the mountains.

The rendezvous at the college's mountain lodge was the culmination of our trip and the opportunity to eat our first home-cooked meal after three days of hiking and surviving on powdered soup, canned meat, and crackers. Our long-awaited meal consisted of scrambled eggs dyed green (in honor of Dr. Seuss, an alumnus of the college), green orange juice, and burned sausages. Somehow, despite the unusual color, we all appreciated having some real food. We were introduced to many of our classmates in this rather unusual fashion, and it served to draw us closer together. Afterward I felt that this was preferable to the bland introductory lecture you might expect in a traditional university orientation.

When I arrived on campus to begin classes, I was relegated to one of the groups of dormitories with an early 1960s-style cinderblock decor which was certainly at the bottom of any student's preference list. Not surprisingly, these dorms were primarily occupied by freshmen and a few unlucky sophomores. During my freshman year, I attempted to adapt to this environment with other students from various cities, regions, and states. However, by spring term, I came to the conclusion that I had little in common with these students and sought housing elsewhere.

Our dorm was a curious mix of jocks, computer whizzes, and hard-core "partiers" who could stay up half the night reveling and then pass a three-hour midterm the next day with flying colors. I had a somewhat difficult time adopting the mentality of the so-called popular people in our dorm who, perhaps because this was their first opportunity to be away from home, displayed what may politely be described as the worst aspects of their personalities. I guess one could call it a "pack" mentality, where people would do things to be "part of the group" that they would not do alone—such as drinking all night long, being critical and obnoxious to those who were "different" or who were overly studious, performing devious pranks and practical jokes, and ignoring their neighbors by blasting music at 200 decibels well into the early morning hours.

I stayed in this environment most of my freshman year, and, initially succumbing to peer pressure, even joined one of the local fraternities—although I never became fully active in fraternity life and eventually only marginally participated in its activities. In reflection, I think that the only reason I thought about joining was that everyone else around me was going through the process of being recruited by fraternities. Although the fraternity and sorority system had a positive side in that it provided some sense of camaraderie for many students, it also brought to the surface the worst aspects of student life. Blatant abuse of alcohol, rude and inappropriate behavior, and fostering the "us" versus "them" attitude was common in the fraternity system. Fortunately, the fraternity I joined was less along these lines than some others. However, that proved to be its ultimate doom as well. People were attracted to other, more traditional houses, and the population of our fraternity house continued to decline over time. It seemed sad to me to realize that in order to attract active members, some of the brothers were drawn into more destructive and outrageous behavior to fit in with the frat image. That trend was what ultimately turned me off, and over time I stopped going to meetings and eventually drifted away. In the end, the strategy of being more "fraternity-like" did not save that house, and it has recently been sold to a new sorority.

The fraternity that I joined was one of the few that actually had some Indian members. The fraternity system's undying support of the unofficial "Indian symbol" mascot turned the stomachs of most Indian students, who did not want to be associated with the part of the student body that supported the Indian symbol. As a result, few Indian students were fraternity members—at least of the more popular fraternities that sought the return of the Indian as the school mascot and bemoaned the loss of all of the associated cheers, outfits, and related offensive sporting paraphernalia. The use of "the Indian" as a mascot for the College was officially discouraged by the administration, but its return was the rallying cry for those rebels without a cause and for some of the more aged alumni who tenaciously clung to memories of the different and now bygone era when they were in school.

The Indian symbol, or simply "the symbol" as we knew it, was the source of most of my negative experiences while in college. The use of the symbol was opposed by most Native American students because we did not appreciate having the cheerleaders lead the crowd in "war whoops," fake scalpings, and hatchet throwing during the football halftimes as they had done in the past. I remember looking at some of the photos and memorabilia from the "good old" days, including such items as fake tom-toms, "Indian chief" headdresses, souvenirs, diaper pants with an Indian head insignia, and huge drums that were pounded by wild green, bare-chested Dartmouth "braves" with Mohawk wigs at the football games.

I was always very puzzled when people would attempt to change my mind to support the Indian symbol, telling me, "You should be proud that we are honoring Indians in this fashion." I would doubt very seriously if any other minority group would tolerate being treated in such a way. For example, running out on the football field in blackface with a watermelon and doing a tap dance at halftime would hardly be considered to be "honoring" African American culture. In any event, few of the older, non-Indian Dartmouth alumni wanted to hear that, and instead became incensed when the real Indians did not similarly embrace the college's unofficial symbol. In their minds, I guess we were the living incarnations of their mascot, and they simply could not understand why we did not run out on the field ourselves or appreciate being held up as the school's mascot. We clearly did not choose or want that role. I presume that they wanted us to act appreciative—for what, I still don't know. In return, we objected to any use of the symbol and were consequently attacked, criticized, and labeled "too sensitive."

I remember one traditional Indian song that was sung at one of the Dartmouth Pow Wows which clearly embodied the students' sentiment. That song, called a '49 song, is sung along with a drum at night after a pow wow. The lyrics were a variation of a popular, traditional Kiowa '49 song, "I'm from Oklahoma." Our version instead began "I'm from Dartmouth College" and concluded with the phrase, "We are not *your* Indians, we are not *your* symbols anymore." That's how the students felt—we were not the symbols of the majority population—we refused to be *their* Indians. We were who we were, not who the alumni wanted us to be—not the drunken, bare-chested, green Indians who pounded on the big drum in feathers at football games in the '50s. None of that was real.

While the Indian symbol was a blatant example of tensions between racial groups, other well-intentioned and supposedly knowledgeable persons committed less obvious faux pas. Like many other Indian students, I was constantly bombarded with myriad questions and statements from peers on every topic from the innocuous "Does your mother wear leather dresses?" to the often-repeated "Did you know *my* great-grandmother was an Indian princess?" I remember vividly one incident when someone asked an Eskimo friend of mine whether he and his family lived in an igloo. I thought to myself, "and these are supposed to be educated people." After about three years of effort, I eventually became tired of continually fighting and trying to educate the entire campus about the Indian symbol. Although it was a challenge and the Indian students appreciated those individuals who wanted to learn more, after countless seminars, rallies, and classes where one's consciousness was raised through the roof, I eventually became tired of functioning as the ambassador and expert for every tribe from the Bering Strait to Tierra Del Fuego—especially when I had my normal class schedule and other academic assignments to keep up with. Like many Native American students, I eventually became worn out by the effort of trying to educate my peers about Indians and why one group of people should not be forced to be the mascots of another.

About the same time that I realized I did not feel totally comfortable with the dorm and fraternity life, I began to become more interested in participating in the Native American Program on campus. Since I did not come from a classic "reservation" background, at first I felt a little reluctant to become involved with the Indian student organization. After my initial contact, however, I felt that the Indian students were more friendly and supportive and that I had much more in common with them than with any other students at Dartmouth, particularly those students in my dorm and fraternity. Although most of my contact with other Indians had been with Indians from Oklahoma, I felt a common bond with other Indian students even though they came from places like Alaska, New York, New Mexico, and Arizona.

When the student group Native Americans at Dartmouth (a.k.a. NAD) chose an Indian design I had drawn as a freshman as the official logo of the organization, I felt as though I was officially "accepted" by my peers. My close association with the Native American students for the next three years gave me much of the incentive to continue on with school despite the academic pressure and the rigorous class schedule. Being from a public high school, as opposed to a prep school, I did not feel as adequately prepared for the academic assignments as some of my classmates. I felt, at times, like I had to spend twice as much time as my classmates to get things done. For all I know, I was spending no more time on my classwork than anyone else, but I guess because I came from a public school, I thought my preparation must have been inferior.

My close association with the Native American students ultimately provided me with the motivation to go on to law school and, in a real sense, gave me some purpose for my education. The other event triggering my interest in Indian law was a class that I took in Native American studies during my freshman year. In particular, there was one final lecture in an introductory course taught by Professor Michael Dorris that in some sense changed my whole outlook on how Indians fared in and fit into American society.

This course had explored the rich culture of the Pueblo tribes, the unique and complicated Maya cosmology, the intricate Natchez system of marriage and class mobility, and the balance and stability

of the Iroquois system of government. For the first time, I learned in an academic setting about all of the fascinating and unique characteristics of American Indian peoples in the western hemisphere.
The class covered a vast period of time and had taken us all the way from 40,000 B.C. to 1492 and contact with the Europeans.

With this background, Professor Dorris summarized the class by describing the modern, post-contact history of one tribe, the Cherokee Nation. Unlike many other tribes, the Cherokee ultimately accepted many aspects of the non-Indian culture and did not strongly resist the adoption of European systems of government and social organization. Unlike the Kiowa and Comanche, who were classic horse-mounted Plains Indian tribes that were described in most books as "warlike and tenacious," the Cherokee were, for the most part, a peaceful people who cooperated with the U.S. government. As I sat there in class, I wondered to myself, "What was their history? How did their story end? Was it any better than that of the other tribes? Since they cooperated with the United States, are they in a better position today? Were they an example for other Indian tribes to emulate?" Not knowing their history and not being Cherokee, I really had no idea.

It was during this lecture that I hoped the culmination of the class and the history of Indian-white relations would end on a positive note. Unfortunately, as I guess I should have expected, it did not. Instead, the feeling I was left with was shock bordering on genuine outrage about the treatment of the Cherokee people. Although the Cherokee had repeatedly done everything that had been requested of them, including giving up huge parcels of land, removing their entire population thousands of miles to west of the Mississippi, adopting Western constitutions and court systems, wearing European-style dress, and adopting many "American" customs, in the end they fared no better than any of the other tribes. In fact, they ultimately were much *worse* off because they were so powerful, educated, and influential. In an ironic twist of fate, they were, through various Congressional acts, legally stripped of their tribal property, power, and authority because they were too successful as a separate nation. In order to cripple their power and influence at the turn of the century, their courts were shut down and their power to tax and raise funds for continued operation of the tribal government was abolished. Their lands were opened to non-Indian land settlement and their towns and villages were overrun, despite the fact that such actions violated numerous promises guaranteed by treaties. In the end, they lost almost ninety-five percent of their reservation to the "boomers" and "sooners" who claimed and grabbed their land. Many Cherokee ceremonies and religious practices were outlawed, as were traditional customs and languages. I wondered to myself, "Where was the justice in what was done? How could the American system of laws authorize such a complete destruction and utter dispossession of a people?"

I still remember sitting there in my seat with my head spinning and stepping outside the lecture hall into the sunshine thinking, "My God, why didn't someone do something? How could this have happened?" At that point, I felt the need to learn as much as I could so that I could understand what had happened. I felt that Indian people in general were vulnerable because there was no one to understand their desires or to speak for them. I hoped that at least I could learn more about the law and maybe someday, in some fashion, do something to have an impact on the recognition and development of tribal sovereignty.

Several Dartmouth students had participated in internships with various Indian organizations and I, too, wanted to find some work connected with Indian law that would bring me back home where my relatives lived in Oklahoma. I had always enjoyed talking to my grandfather about treaties and various agreements that the United States government had made with the Kiowas and Comanches. I recall when I spoke to him at times, his normally calm exterior would give way to a quiet excitement of sorts. I knew that he had served as an elected tribal leader and as a commissioner for the tribal housing authority. He had also been one of the original drafters of our tribal constitution. Although he never said it, I subtly felt that he had always wanted to be a lawyer or at least gain some background in law.

He often spoke to me about his older brother, Guy Quoetone, who had been instrumental in testifying for and implementing various pieces of legislation dealing with the Kiowa-Comanche-Apache land claims with the United States government. If ever there was a modern-day delegate and spokesperson for the Kiowa Nation in Washington, D.C., he was it. My relatives used to call him "Senator Guy" since he had made so many trips to the nation's capital to work on various issues of importance for the Kiowas.

Sometimes my grandfather would close his eyes, lean back, and tell me about various legal questions that had bothered him, or recount how various parcels of tribal land had mysteriously ended up being sold or claimed by businessmen or the nearby Army base. Often, he would pull out a big, tattered old expandable leather briefcase that was about to burst because it was stuffed so full of papers, newspaper articles, and documents. My grandfather used to call it his archives. From his own memory and those of other tribal members, he recounted different stories of certain fence boundaries that had been changed, certain laws that had been passed, and certain promises that were made but not fulfilled. By the way he spoke to me, in some instances I got the impression that he felt a little anxious, but hopeful that the legal questions that he had always wondered about could perhaps now be answered. At other times, I felt like he wanted to tell me everything he could remember about various concerns that he had so at least there would be someone who would be able to research and uncover what had happened years ago. Because of my courses in Native American policy, I, too, began to ask questions. I wondered to myself, "Why hasn't anyone done anything to protect tribal sovereignty? Why haven't any Indian lawyers been involved? Can't someone do something?"

In late 1980, while I was visiting relatives, this growing interest in Indian law led me to visit a local Bureau of Indian Affairs office in Anadarko, Oklahoma. After speaking with several employees, I met a friendly paralegal who was a fellow tribal member and who indicated that the newly established tribal court system was interested in an intern to assist in the tribal prosecutor's office.

The Court of Indian Offenses, located in Anadarko, Oklahoma, served as a tribal court for seven tribes in the area, including the Kiowas and Comanches. It had been set up only a year before, when a federal court case had upheld the tribes' continuing rights to exercise authority over several hundreds of thousands of acres of land in the original reservation boundaries. In Oklahoma, for decades the Indian tribes had been told that they did not have the right to function as separate governments or that they had no land under their jurisdiction. The status of tribal jurisdiction had been in limbo since statehood in 1907, and for the first time in modern history in Oklahoma, the tribes' rights to self-government were reaffirmed.

When I began working with the tribal court, I realized the practical importance of tribal jurisdiction and was influenced by the support of fellow tribal members in the legal field such as Frances Oheltoint and George Tah-Bone, Jr. For the first time, I recognized not only the cultural and historical elements that a tribe possesses, but also the powers that a tribe has as a government. I was fascinated with this concept of a nation existing within a nation, having its own laws, police, court systems, and authority over designated lands. It was during this internship with the court system, arranged through Dartmouth's Native American studies department, that I first set foot in a courtroom. I so thoroughly enjoyed working with the tribal court system that I returned to Dartmouth with a new goal and understanding that the law, particularly Indian law, would play a part in my future. Little did I know that not even a decade after graduation, I would be serving as the chief judge for ten tribes in the very same court system that I had served as an intern.

About the time of my internship in the tribal court, I had abandoned my idea of going into television production and changed my major to government, with certification in Native American studies. The government major was viewed as a rigorous undertaking. Nevertheless, I wanted to have a proper foundation and background for law school. After my internship, the Native American Studies Program continued to give me some direction in focusing my energies, since I felt that I now had at least some sense of purpose for my education.

I later went on to take several classes from Professor Dorris, who opened an entire world of understanding to me about Native Americans from all over the United States and Canada. I thought I knew about Indians before going to college, but I came to realize that many different tribes had vastly different histories, traditions, and cultures. I found that Navajos, Eskimos, and Mohawks were almost as different from Kiowas and Comanches, and from one another, as people from different nations. Of course, as I now understand, we *are* from different nations.

After graduation from Dartmouth, I went on to Yale Law School and received my law degree. While in law school, I worked one summer for the Kiowa Tribe, and another summer for the Native American Rights Fund, a nationwide public interest law firm located in Boulder, Colorado. With this background, I came to appreciate the intricacies of Indian law more fully. I also realized that I wanted to return to the traditional homelands of my own tribes and be involved in some fashion in the legal field.

I am thankful that my education led me back to Oklahoma and drew me into Indian law because I feel as though my legal education has had a positive effect on others in understanding the unique status that tribes hold. After my graduation from Yale, I spent a year working for a federal judge on Indian law cases at the United States Claims Court in Washington, D.C., and then spent another year working for a federal judge in a United States District Court in east Texas. After working for these judges, I returned to Oklahoma permanently and accepted employment with a private law firm in Oklahoma City, to litigate cases and assist tribes in legal problems. Fortunately, the law firm permitted me to pursue my interests by developing this practice and allowed me to continue to serve as a tribal judge for over a dozen tribes and also to work as an adjunct professor in Oklahoma City University Law School's Native American Legal Assistance Clinic. The clinic helps law students acquire practical experience working with Indians and other poor people who need legal services through local legal aid offices.

In 1994, I accepted a position as an Assistant United States Attorney with the United States Department of Justice for the Western District of Oklahoma. As the first person to hold the position of Special Assistant for Tribal Relations, I have primary responsibility for handling all Indian affairs, bringing suits to protect tribal assets and properties, and prosecuting crimes committed on Indian lands. As the first Kiowa tribal member and one of the first Indian persons ever to hold such a position in the state, I am thankful to be given this opportunity by the local United States Attorney. In a sense, appointment to this position has fulfilled a dream for me, permitting me to return to Oklahoma, to practice law, and to be directly involved in legal matters affecting the tribes.

I recall an essay entitled "Coming Home" that I wrote for a Native American studies class at Dartmouth. It chronicled my trek up a small creek to get some spring water requested by some Kiowa elders for an upcoming meeting. In a larger sense, the essay described my return to Oklahoma and my Indian roots. I had traveled back to Oklahoma during one of my breaks from Dartmouth to a place north of the Wichita Mountains in the southwestern part of Oklahoma, where my ancestors had lived and where my maternal great-grandfather Jimmy Quoetone raised his family:

The creek winds like a snake down through the Wichitas, in a twisting and winding path and all the green is drawn to it like some great magnet. From Mount Scott's summit you can see the trees that surround it, that draw life from it. In the driest of seasons, when every river and lake dries up to reveal their muddy bottoms and smooth flat rocks, this creek still flows. These waters nourish, even in the scalding rays of the summer; the ice-cold currents give life to the land. This is Jimmy Creek, this is where it all began.

The old Kiowas wanted some spring water for their next get-together so they asked me to get some for them. We began our journey on foot, to follow the waters that bear my great-grandfather's name—Jimmy Quoetone, whose last name means "wolf tail."

On we walked up the stream, its cool waters forming deep pools along the curves of the bank. Water spiders zipped across the glassy surface like ice skaters as small fish broke the surface trying to catch them.

From the creek, we could see where the old house used to be. It was Jimmy's house, the one he built himself. There was the climbing tree and over there was the swimming hole. My mother grew up here and she can still remember. They always had a big arbor up to shade themselves from the hot August sun. Jimmy was always there, telling stories of how it used to be. There always seemed to be someone stopping by to visit, to share the fry bread, corn soup, and boiled meat. They would stay and talk, and Jimmy would sit under his medicine bundle.

In his later years, he would wait, wait for the return of Kiowas who came back from Wyoming with water from the springs. They got the water near the place where a great rock formation came out of the ground; it was called Devil's Tower. My mother was but a young girl, but she remembers. He would take the water and sprinkle it all over his body. He said it revitalized him and made him stronger. It must have worked, for Jimmy Quoetone lived to be 101 years old.

We continued to walk on, just beyond where the house once stood, following the bend of the stream as it carved its way through twisted roots and trees that had fallen. We finally reached the end of the creek. It was a circular pool of deep blue water, a kind of oasis on the prairie. The reflections of the sun streaming through the trees danced on its surface as it trickled over the cool stones into the creek. The pool seemed bottomless, and its underwater form merged with the shadows. This was it, the source of Jimmy Creek, where it all began—the flow of water, the flow of time, and the point of origin. I had come nearly 2,000 miles to this spot, a place that I had always heard about and imagined in my mind. This is where Quo-yoit, my great-great-grandfather, had first settled, where Jimmy Quoetone built his house, where my grandparents brought up all of their kids, where my parents came after they were married, and where I now stood.

This place symbolized the beginning of my family. In the same way we drew strength, power, and the will to survive from my great-grandfather, so too does this land from the waters which bear his name. As I looked down into the waters I could almost imagine looking into time. I wondered if Quoetone ever looked into these same waters and reflected on his own past, and also hoped for the future of his people, in the only place that they could truly call home.

For me, this place is significant not only because it is where we hold our family reunions and where I swam as a child on countless occasions, but also because it's where my mother and father first went after they were married, and is near the spot where I was married to my wife Tracey on the top of one of the Wichita Mountains.

Like the journey I described in the essay, that pulled me back to a little stream named after my great-grandfather in Oklahoma, my education has had a lot to do with where I find myself today. It is curious to think that the experiences I had at a small college on the border of Vermont and New Hampshire could have led me to become an Indian attorney, professor, and judge in Oklahoma. These experiences helped me "come home" to the traditional tribal homeland of the Kiowas and Comanches, and appreciate that much more the value of family while also giving me the opportunity to use my education to positively affect the future of Indian people. I sometimes wonder where I would be today had I not made that journey. Now, I'm just glad that I did.

Arvo Quoetone Mikkanen, a Kiowa/Comanche attorney, is a Phi Beta Kappa honors graduate of Dartmouth College, where he obtained a bachelor of arts degree in government and certification in Native American studies in 1983. He received his juris doctor degree from Yale Law School in 1986. In 1988, Arvo returned to Oklahoma as an attorney practicing in litigation and Indian affairs with the Andrews Davis law firm. He is active in Indian legal matters, and serves as an adjunct professor of law and Associate Director of the Native American Legal Assistance Clinic at the Oklahoma City University School of Law.

On August 8, 1994, Arvo was sworn in as an Assistant United States Attorney and the Special Assistant for Tribal Relations with the United States Attorney's Office. He handles both civil and criminal matters involving the twenty federally recognized tribes located within the Western District of Oklahoma, and serves as liaison to those tribes.

Arvo is a member of the Kiowa Gourd Clan Warrior Society and is also a southern plains style straight dancer. He lives with his wife, Tracey, son, Brandon, and daughter, Julia. His interests include Indian art, beadworking, fishing, graphics, model rocketry, and computers.

▼▼▼▼▼▼▼▼▼▼▼

● SIOBHAN WESCOTT

Machiavelli and Me

        Spending my senior year engrossed in the study of Niccolò Machiavelli definitely soured my view of human nature. If a crowd disliked you in Machiavelli's Florence, you might have gotten burned at the stake. Carrying this vivid image on graduation day, I feared that by opting to wear my Native regalia instead of the traditional cap and gown I would feel the burn of rejection from my peers.

    The volatile spring weather greeted me that morning as a bad omen. Ominous dark clouds loomed above, threatening sudden thundershowers. I risked the potential damage to my buckskin in hopes that nature was bluffing. At the government department morning gathering, my professors and friends offered approving smiles and comments. This litmus test assured me that at least no one would yell "wah-hoo-wah" at me. This battle cry is paired with the lingering Indian symbol, the unofficial and controversial mascot of our college's athletic teams.

That secure feeling vanished when a classmate nervously passed me wearing a tie featuring the Indian symbol. With physical proof of the tenacity of the symbol, my resolve began to waiver. I reminded myself that the reason I chose this particular outfit was Stacey Coverdale. The previous year, Stacey had organized Indian graduates to wear regalia on graduation day with great success. Moments after her family started the drive back to their reservation in New York, an undergraduate driver tried to pass on a double yellow line, causing a terrible accident. The impact to the Coverdale station wagon killed Stacey and left her parents and a small cousin in critical condition. I could not convince any of the other Indian graduates to dress in regalia, so I was the only one in 1989.

During the ceremony, though, an unsettling feeling swept over me. I was the lone break in a uniform sea of 898 mortarboards. Stacey had displayed her Indian heritage proudly; I detested the possibility of ridicule, especially on an occasion as significant as graduation. Stacey had been a skillful leader and a strong individual; I preferred the comfort of blending in with the crowd.

The name Wescott put me near the end of the graduation ceremonies. By the time I approached the platform, the crowd had endured several hours packed with speakers, honorary presentations, and an endless stream of students. The sun's periodic appearances had the intensity of laser beams, sizzling everything in their path. Did anyone even care when I came around, or was I simply another graduate keeping them seated for a little longer?

My thesis advisor gave me a supportive nod from the bleachers. As I heard my name called, the applause rose to a slightly higher level. I shook President Freedman's hand with a broad smile plastered on my face, a useful nervous habit. I walked around the stage to the spot where the now-official graduate turns the tassel from one side to the other.

I had planned for this moment by placing an eagle feather in my hair, which my shaking hand barely managed to switch over. I then heard the sweetest music to my ears: a swell of laughter from the crowd. One official on the platform almost fell over backward, chair and all! That my classmates and their families felt comfortable enough to react lightheartedly filled me with relief and complete contentment.

This is one of the rare moments that I could share a Native quality, like my sense of humor, with a large group of non-Native people. Most of the time, I must demystify the misconceptions that others have about Indians; I feel like a broken record in doing so. No matter how far-fetched the misconception (such as that Alaska Natives still travel exclusively by dogsled), losing long-held ideas about Indians somehow disappoints many people. At Dartmouth, I often chose to educate myself rather than others.

I was only nominally involved with the Native American Program, dancing at the annual Pow Wow and attending meetings now and then. This is largely a reflection of the way I was raised. My childhood was spent nestled in university settings from Cambridge, Massachusetts, to Palo Alto, California, and Fairbanks, Alaska. I remember having only one good friend who was Native when I was growing up. Children of other academic parents were my playmates, although not always with a good outcome. When I was four, the children in Harvard's preschool beat me up on the first day because they thought that was what you did with an Indian.

In high school, I spent three awkward weeks with my mom's family in an Alaskan village of 300 people. I didn't feel comfortable with them and they didn't really know what to do with me. One of my relatives was having trouble with an abusive spouse. The unsettling nature of the trip closed the book on my exploration of rural Native life.

My parents were raised with strong Indian role models. Both have Ph.D.s and teach at universities. The university pow wows were a way for my parents to revisit Indian traditions; but they made up my primary exposure to Native cultures. The rest of the time, I buried myself in books to try to keep up with the bright students around me.

The obscure nature of my name, Siobhan (pronounced sha-von), does not help in my efforts to be understood by others. The odd spelling, coupled with my dark skin, leads some people to guess that I am Pakistani, Puerto Rican, or Filipino. The name is Irish. People usually cock their heads to the side and inquisitively remark, "You don't look Irish." So I must launch into the explanation of my unique Alaska Native and Native American heritage. My mom is half Athabascan, from interior Alaska. Her other half is French and Norwegian. My Irish/English dad is an honorary Mohawk, who was taken under the wing of a movie Indian while growing up in North Hollywood.

The explanation usually never gets past Alaska and Native. People connect these two and conclude "Eskimo!" I have been asked "Do you live in an igloo?" more times than the number of igloos built in Alaska—which is none. Only some Native Canadians made temporary shelters out of ice. Contrary to popular belief, the rest of us do not go into culture shock when we see buildings stay up all year round. Furthermore, confusing Athabascans and Eskimos is like asking the English how they like being French. Some people do know of my heritage or my name, and I feel an instant sense of relief around them. One person in Alaska knew about Athabascans, cited the etiology of my first name, and then correctly guessed the heritage of my last name. He will always hold a special place in my heart.

Except for the occasional brush with the Indian symbol, though, being Native was not a stumbling block to enjoying college. Everyone felt a little out of place at first; we were all homesick and most of us felt a little different for some reason or another. During my freshman year, I cured homesickness by having the *Fairbanks Daily News Miner* sent to me. I slogged along academically by studying a little bit more than other students, maintaining a B+ average. I joined a sorority and went to France for a term. The first two years of college were very typical. The last two were extraordinary.

The most significant turning points in my life occurred in my junior and senior years. The first was an internship in Manila, the Philippines, during which just about everything that could go wrong did go wrong. During my junior fall, I naively set off on a Peace Corps internship. I left the United States for Manila thinking that I would contribute in some small way to the saving of the world.

Since then, a few years in the "real world" have taught me that no one wants to be saved, and that if they claim to, then they probably have a dependency disorder. You can offer people information and an occasional insight, but to try to overcome other people's problems is a quick and sure way to alienate them. Many of the Peace Corps volunteers had a rude awakening when they met with initial lack of interest in what they had to say. I never got that far though, because I didn't directly deal with Filipinos at work. All I did was start a write-up of the administrative procedures at the main office. The Filipinos sure seemed to punish me for thinking I could help save them, though; they thought I was a prostitute.

Unwritten social rules combined with my own ignorance left that unfortunate impression. Anywhere outside of Manila, the only time a Filipina will walk with a white man is when she is married to him. In Manila, if a Filipina walks with a white man, she is either married to him or she is a prostitute hired by him. Everyone, including Americans, thought I was Filipina. So every time I walked with a Peace Corps volunteer or staff person, "knowing" looks chilled me to the bone.

To make matters worse, the Peace Corps lodged me in a hotel for foreigners that had not been thoroughly investigated beforehand. The Tropicana caters to Johns from all over the world. Hotel brochures even touted "sex tours." Naturally, these scums-of-the-earth believed me to be available for a price. This was hard to fathom for a Catholic girl used to a sheltered, ivory-tower life.

The indiscriminate character assassination forced me to seek shelter. I sought out the company of Peace Corps volunteers. Around them, I could continue to be an intelligent person with a future. A cluster of Peace Corps volunteers in the countryside, including two Dartmouth graduates, exchanged visits with me. Except for work, only these brief interludes of comforting friends could pull me out of my hotel room. I hid there like a hibernating bear waiting for the harsh winter to blow over.

When I left for the Philippines, I had gone hoping to save the world. I returned barely able to save myself. Paradoxically, one of the most valuable opportunities Dartmouth offered was this glimpse of what I might be without an education. That experience frightened me to the core and forced me to reflect on what skills I needed to make it outside of academia.

Writing was hands-down my most painful sore spot. Papers came back to me with so many red marks on them that I felt the pen must have died of massive ink loss. At every level of schooling, from cursive writing to college courses, I disappointed teachers with my substandard performances. Even when I spent weeks on a paper, I was never able to weave sentences together in a completely cohesive manner. To add salt to the wound, many of my Dartmouth classmates could write eloquently with hardly any effort.

A senior honors thesis is the toughest test of writing at Dartmouth, especially one on something as esoteric as Niccolò Machiavelli's political thought. I set my sights on writing a thesis, come hell or high water. This involved being chosen for the government department's honors program. The twelve other people selected for the program were as intimidating as any group of students I have ever encountered. These smart, articulate scholars thrived on heated debates. I rarely tried to get a word in edgewise.

Perhaps even more intimidating was my thesis advisor. Roger Masters is a quickwitted, disgustingly articulate, tough critic of student work. He bucks the trend toward grade inflation, shocking some students used to coasting by with Cs. With his beard, scholarly wire-frame glasses, herringbone jackets, and impressive list of credentials, he personifies the brilliant professor. You can imagine my horror when the four-page thesis proposal I submitted to him turned out to be littered with spelling errors.

Instead of a reprimand, Professor Masters gave me a possible diagnosis: he recognized that my errors were in a pattern consistent with learning disabilities. Dysnomia and dysgraphia emerged as my diagnosed learning disabilities. Dysnomia involves a tip-of-the-tongue syndrome where retrieving the correct names for things is hampered. No wonder I do not like the public eye or having to explain things like my name and heritage. Dysgraphia involves difficulty with writing, such as organizing coherent sentences and paragraphs around a related thesis statement. An utter inability to spell (for instance, it never seems clear to me when to use "a" or "e") is also commonplace among the learning disabled.

The tragedy is that I spent fifteen years of schooling letting silly errors weigh me down into mediocrity. Among learning disabled people, some describe receiving their diagnosis as feeling like "a Volvo has been lifted off your chest." During the academic term in which I received my diagnosis, my grade point average jumped from a 3.3 (B+) to a 4.0 (A). I was perfectly poised to stretch my newfound intelligence: a year's worth of thesis work. This became the second major turning point in my life and made my entire senior year the richest year of my life. I awoke each day with purpose and determination, instead of my usual grogginess. I discov-

ered more about myself and my abilities in that year than I had
before or have since.

Professor Masters could only afford to give me a small amount
of his time each week. His office was a corner room with gigantic
windows that reached to the top of the high ceiling. The combination of natural light and wall-to-wall books made me feel
strangely at home. I would scribble notes madly as he fired off a
series of astute observations about the philosophy of power. He was
constantly ten steps ahead of me. I would spend a week mulling
over what he had said, painstakingly taking every one of those steps
until I could say "aha!" and understand his point. I slowly began
exploring avenues on my own, including a few where Professor
Masters could not help me. The challenge of studying Machiavelli
made me feel like I had come into my own. I pushed the outer
limits of my abilities, including trying to retranslate English from
Italian, Latin, and Greek. The only foreign language I know is
French. I would sit in the reference room hour after hour thumbing
through four or five colossal dictionaries until I could accomplish
the task.

I had three homes that year: my dorm room, the stacks of the
main library, and the English library. I had my own cramped cubicle in the stacks with barely enough room for a desk, a bookshelf,
and a tiny window to keep reality close by. My cubicle was one of
a long row of little offices accessible only by a bleak steel corridor
illuminated by bare lightbulbs. Despite the sparse nature, I love so
many things about the stacks. The main pleasure is being surrounded by the successful end products of so many authors' efforts.
I also like the idea that others before me have browsed through the
same copies of books also in search of understanding.

The English library, Sanborn, is an opulent room one could
easily picture as belonging in a huge English mansion. Big, over-
stuffed chairs tucked away in book-laden alcoves welcomed me
every afternoon. The English thesis writers also called Sanborn their
second home, and a group of loyal friends took shape early in the
year. We became known as the Sanborn Tea Crowd, named after
the weekday tradition of tea and cookies served every afternoon in
the library at 4:00 P.M.

Much like the Peace Corps volunteers who kept my sanity from
slipping away in the Philippines, the Tea Crowd saw me through

the considerable ups and downs of writing a thesis. They also served as a good distraction, with enough group dynamics and personal chemistry to fill up a book's worth of anecdotes. What held us together the tightest, though, was that one of our crowd, Katie, had a potentially fatal disease. Each time she had a relapse or had to have surgery, we rallied behind her. Her ordeal helped us keep perspective on our own lives as well.

Only one non–Tea Crowd friend, Dennis, told me he envied the satisfaction I would gain from the experience of writing a thesis. Almost everyone else questioned my sanity for taking on so much work during our last year of college. The friends I had come to hold dear during my first three years faded away; their eyes glazed over at the mere mention of Machiavelli, and I only saw them when they came to the library.

The goal I set at the start of my thesis was simply to pass, which requires a B+. The final grade for my thesis, however, was "A with a citation," meaning I had performed above and beyond what was required for the course. The government department also awarded me high honors, which only a couple of the other twelve thesis writers received. Professor Masters called my chapter on Machiavelli's view of human nature "one of the clearest and most insightful things I've ever read on Machiavelli." The undergraduate academic journal eventually published it. I had finally reached my potential after years of wallowing in an academic rut.

The compliment I cherish most came near the end of my thesis work. When I handed in a 110-page draft, Professor Masters's return comments included: "You have come to a deeper understanding of Machiavelli than most of the scholars in the field of political theory. (I don't say that idly.)" My senior year could not have ended on a happier note.

The attempt to prepare myself for the real world had backfired, however. Writing a thesis served only to push me deeper into the ivory tower mentality. Studying Machiavelli's work made me weary of human nature and unsure of my place in the world. The Tea Crowd, too, had a cynical view of life common among academics. For instance, though we all counted each other as friends, we divided ourselves into the "Sisters of Sorrow" (women looking forward to a fulfilling spinsterhood) and the "Brothers of Bitterness" (a group of he-men woman haters). As graduation drew closer, I still had no idea what to do with myself, and I was not feeling optimistic about my possibilities.

Six years have passed since those tenuous last days as a Dartmouth student when I did not want to leave college. As much as I appreciate the wonderful gifts of Dartmouth, I look forward now to getting older. In the past six years, I have explored many career paths, searching for ways to channel my energy and ability into important issues where I could possibly make a difference. In the process, I have come to a deeper understanding of the Native respect for elders. So much of life is adjusting to subtleties, guided by having been through the same or similar experiences previously. Classroom experiences help you learn to think, but do not necessarily help you develop the savvy you need to make a life.

I find it ironic that the predominant image of Indians is that of a lone warrior. The Indian friends I have are some of the most prolific networkers I know, especially my mom. Family friends helped me get almost every single job I have held since graduating, either directly or indirectly. Karen Perdue, for instance, helped me get internships or jobs with the Alaska Bureau of Vital Statistics, the U.S. Senate Select Committee on Indian Affairs, U.S. Senator Tom Daschle (now Senate minority leader), my local Native health corporation, and the Alaska Division of Public Health.

The policy level is where most of my jobs have been focused. I even earned a master's in Public Health, concentrating on policy issues at the population level. I see this as having gone about things backwards, since I now feel I need a grounding in dealing one-on-one with people before trying to affect system-wide change. The reason I have managed to have a semblance of success is the same reason my thesis was a triumph: having a close-knit group to lean on for support.

Professor Masters spent fifteen minutes of my hour-long defense discussing how the Sanborn Tea Crowd had helped me soar above his previous Machiavelli advisees. For me, the void left by the inevitable disbanding of the Tea Crowd was filled by the parents and professionals in the field of Fetal Alcohol Syndrome (FAS), the cluster of birth defects caused by drinking during pregnancy. Desperate for new voices to herald the warning, these kind people quickly accepted me. I devoured the literature on FAS, writing a few articles of my own for *Winds of Change*, a Native American magazine. I co-edited a book on the subject, *Fantastic Antone Succeeds! Experiences in Educating Children with Fetal Alcohol Syndrome* (University of Alaska Press, 1993).

It makes me feel proud to know that I not only overcame my own learning disabilities but that I also used my newfound confidence in my writing skills to make a difference in such an important problem area. When Senator Murkowski, R–Alaska, and Senator Daschle, D–South Dakota, held a reception for the publication of *Fantastic Antone Succeeds!*, I was especially pleased that two of my closest friends from college attended. Having Dennis, my only non–Tea Crowd friend who admired my thesis efforts, and Sandy, a strong-willed and talented black woman who was my favorite roommate, attend the ceremony made it a truly unforgettable experience.

Yet I know that I have reached a limit with what I can do in the field of FAS. When I returned to Alaska with a degree in public health, I could not find a job working on FAS issues. Most of the programs are struggling under significant budget cuts. My efforts to find grants to fund prevention projects have failed so far. I have to take another hard look inside to decide where to go from here.

On a drive from Anchorage to Fairbanks one year ago, I felt uncomfortable as I mused over the issue. I turned a corner, and suddenly Mt. McKinley appeared with only one wispy cloud over the summit. This is a rare event, but being the jaded Alaskan I am, I take such scenes for granted. I realized that some people wait all their lives for a chance to catch even a glimpse of this particular sight. What opportunity is that important to me? The answer surprised me: a medical education.

As I continued that drive, reasons to pursue medicine began popping into my mind. I love being in school, and this would guarantee ten more years of it. I will be thirty-eight by the time I can actually practice medicine, but that's just about the time I thought I would be hitting my stride anyway. I enjoy the hard sciences—my Dad is a geophysicist—which require a sharp mind and a disciplined approach to succeed. I can work with people one-on-one or administratively, or some combination of both.

My husband, Ken, is not thrilled with the idea of more student debt (oddly enough, I married a Ph.D. student in political science). The long hours are another significant sacrifice. Some family members have racked their brains searching for any possible reason that

I should not pursue this latest goal. Nevertheless, medicine draws out more of my good qualities than anything else I can think of.

The need for a Tea Crowd–like group will probably always be a constant in my life. An analogy I used in the dedication to *Fantastic Antone Succeeds!* applies here: a lone cyclist must bear the full brunt of the wind on his shoulders. At that time I was referring to Michael Dorris, the first director of the Native American Program at Dartmouth, who raised a son with FAS. But it also pertains to me during times like graduation, when I felt utterly alone. In contrast, a pack of cyclists can spread the burden of adversity across all of its members. So much more can be accomplished together than the sum of the individuals working alone.

While Siobhan Wescott has moved around the country, true to her semi-nomadic Athabascan roots, she has always called Fairbanks, Alaska, her home. When she was growing up, Siobhan's family stressed Native ways and education equally, with spring pow wows as much a tradition as taking advanced classes in school. After graduating from Dartmouth in 1989 with a degree in government, she obtained a master's degree in public health from UCLA in 1994.

Siobhan applied her degree through work in the field of Fetal Alcohol Syndrome, the cluster of birth defects caused by drinking during pregnancy. She worked at several levels, including developing policy and enacting prevention and intervention strategies for affected children, before deciding to become a physician. Siobhan is married to Ken Osterkamp, Ph.D., and the couple currently resides in Fairbanks, Alaska, where Siobhan is completing the basic science prerequisites for medical school.

▼ ▼ ▼ ▼ ▼ ▼ ▼ ▼ ▼

VIVIAN JOHNSON

My Grub Box

A grub box, or, in Yup'ik, *Taqurvik*, is the container in which we pack food and other items when going on hunting, camping, and other trips. A grub box can be a discarded cardboard egg box or a simple wooden box.

My grandmother, Pearly, told me that she made her own grub box out of canvas. She used it when she checked her trap line. She said she carried string in it to "tie around the foxes' necks to pull them across the snow and slide the foxes home." Grandma said she wasn't born early enough to see the old-style grub boxes made out of grass or seal skins. She told me that Grandpa, when walking on his long trips, would use a seal poke for his grub box, which carried his clothes, seal oil, dried salmon, and matches. "Just in case of emergency, you know."

My parents' grub box sits in the living room of our home when it's not being used by one of the family. My mom and dad are experts at preparing a grub box because they are always going on camping and hunting trips. Their grub box contains a standard list of items, including sugar, salt, tea, coffee, matches, a knife, a knife sharpener, bathroom tissue, snuff, and candy. Other items are added as needed.

Some of the items in grub boxes are intangible things that are passed on from parents to children, such as a sense of who you are and how to survive. They are things that are basic to living, things a person relies on when she is taken out of her environment. My Dartmouth experience is basically a story of being out of my environment and how I survived by relying on my grub box and the things I learned from my childhood.

When my brothers and sisters and I were growing up, we would go with my parents on hunting trips. During the summer and into the fall, we would go on berry picking trips for several days at a time. Hunting trips would take us out into the Bering Sea for whales and seals. Fall was the most active time of the year, because birds and fish were migrating, animals were done rearing their young, and the berries were ripe to pick. Life was based upon the seasons, and we were always looking forward to camping with either my parents or one of our relatives.

Before I left for Dartmouth College, my dad told me that because I used to go on these trips to Black River to pick salmon-berries or out into the Bering Sea to hunt seals and whales, I would be different from others at the college. He said, "You are going to stick out like a sore thumb." He was right.

College expanded my way of thinking about things. I developed a "global" perspective by being exposed to people, places, and ideas that were different from what I had known. I saw places like Boston and New York from bus stations and windows. Before this, I had only read about such places. I had never seen a person steal from others until I watched a pickpocket in Boston's South Station. Basically, what happened to me was that I went beyond the physical and figurative boundaries expected of a young Eskimo girl from rural Alaska. It has taken a long time for me to make sense of these experiences. Writing this story has helped.

During my freshman year, my grandpa sent me a grub box. He sent me a care package prepared by my Aunt Babe. It contained dried salmon, tundra (Labrador) tea, Sailor Boy crackers, Royal Cream Boy crackers, tuna, peanut butter, butter, jam, and chicken sandwich spread. My favorite food is seal meat smothered in onions; looking back, I don't think it would have been possible to send that to me. Aunt Babe told me later that my grandmother sent similar care packages to my aunts and uncles when they were away at Mt. Edgecumbe High School, a Bureau of Indian Affairs boarding school in Sitka, Alaska.

If it weren't for my grub box, I would probably have starved at college, simply because I was not used to the food. I will never forget eating tacos with hot sauce with my academic advisor. I don't like hot food, but I forced myself to eat the tacos because I thought it would be rude not to finish my food while he was talking to me. I had beads of sweat on my nose by the time he was finished. My college experience wasn't a simple trip. It was a hard, long, and sometimes lonely adventure. Lucky for me, there was more in my grub box than food. Looking back, I believe that my strength to meet the challenges at Dartmouth came from my family and the contents of my grub box.

I grew up in my home town of Emmonak, a rural village of 800 Yup'ik Eskimo located on the Yukon-Kuskokwim River Delta in Alaska. Emmonak is situated at the mouth of the Yukon River, where the river empties out into the Bering Sea. The landscape is a relatively flat, tundra river delta with many lakes and streams, much like the Mississippi River Delta.

I was born at the Indian Health Service Hospital in Bethel on the Kuskokwim River, which is about 200 air miles southeast of Emmonak. This is the same hospital for which I currently work as an administrator. I am the oldest of seven children. I have four brothers—Joe, Jake, Don, and Howie. My sisters, Dar and Bev, are the youngest. My family's log house was right next door to my grandparents' house. I remember celebrating Christmas at their house as a young girl. Grandpa would play his mandolin while I tried to get him to open the present I had given him. He said that he would wait until Russian Christmas, which was two weeks after December 25th, and he kept on playing. Grandpa was Russian Orthodox and we were Catholic.

I remember spending time chewing Bazooka bubble gum in

Grandpa's room, which was filled with all of his stuff. Hanging from the ceiling in a fishnet were Japanese clear glass buoys he had found along the Bering seacoast. Stacked neatly in a corner were reel-to-reel tapes that held stories from the elders. Some of the stories were from elders who had lived up north in St. Michael when it used to be a Russian fort, in the late 1800s. Framed awards and certificates from the Alaska Territorial Guard and the Alaska Territorial State Legislature checkered the wall. A set of encyclopedias lined the first three shelves of a bookcase. Copies of *Reader's Digest* and *National Geographic* filled the remaining shelves. A shortwave radio, a record player, and a safe deposit box completed the room.

I used to chew the Bazooka bubble gum and stick the wrappers in a hole in the wall. I would line the gum up, and however long it took me to chew through the lineup was the amount of time I would spend looking through all his things. I practiced blowing bubbles while I looked at old letters and pictures of our family or of Grandpa's work. Sometimes I would run out into the living room and ask him who the people in the photographs were. Most of the time I would start looking at pictures in his books or magazines and make up stories about the pictures. When I finished my gum, I would kiss my grandparents, put on my parka, and run back home.

My grandpa's room represented to me all that was out there in the world. The books were filled with pictures from around the world, and I loved looking at them. I knew as a child that my family was not full Yup'ik Eskimo, and that some of my ancestors had come from someplace else. I wanted to find out more about my ancestors and where they were from.

Growing up in the village was sometimes hard, because I used to get teased by my peers about my race and my academic skills. I was not a full-blooded Yup'ik Eskimo—both of my parents are mixed Alaska Native and white—and I did well in school. I would be called *Ka'ssaq*, or white person, by some of my classmates. It was a lesson in tolerance for me, because over the years, I had to learn when and where to open my mouth and to watch what I said.

When I was young, my father would bring home workbooks for me from his business trips. I would erase the pencil markings and do the work over and over again. Mr. Curren, in the fifth grade, showed me my national test scores and explained to me that they were in the ninety-eighth percentile. I didn't know what that meant

at the time; I just loved learning.

My brothers, sisters, and I went to grade school at the BIA Elementary School in Emmonak and then to Mt. Edgecumbe High School, just as our parents did. My parents, Jake and Eunice, met at Mt. Edgecumbe High School. Instead of accepting a scholarship to attend college after graduating in 1963, my mom married my dad. Mt. Edgecumbe is like a second family to many Alaska Natives. It has created a huge network of family and friends in Alaska who share the common bond of having lived away from home while going to school. Over the years it has evolved into an excellent school operated by the state of Alaska.

My experiences accompanying my dad on his business trips made many of the strongest impressions on me as I was growing up. My dad would take my brothers and sisters and me to Anchorage to expose us to the city. I remember accompanying my dad to a luncheon meeting with the company attorney, who was a white man, and a fish broker, who was a Japanese man. I remember thinking as I sat at the table listening to their conversation, "Why does my dad have to negotiate with these men, when there should be someone like him doing the work as an attorney and broker?" I made up my mind I would learn and do whatever it took in order to be in control—like those men who were doing business with my Dad. I didn't know how I was going to do it, but I knew that it would take a college education.

In May 1982, I graduated as valedictorian from Mt. Edgecumbe High School. During my senior year, I applied to four colleges, including Dartmouth College. I don't think I ever doubted that I would go to college. In my mind, it was a given, not because my mom didn't go, but because I knew that formal education would get me the qualifications that I knew I needed to have. I felt that I would limit myself if I stayed in Alaska because there was so much to see and experience in the "Lower 48," but I also knew that I would return to Alaska when I was done.

During my senior year, a representative from Dartmouth College had visited Mt. Edgecumbe to give a presentation to interested seniors. By the end of the presentation, the recruiter had talked me into applying. I had nothing to lose at the time, because I didn't think I had anything to offer. I was not under any kind of pressure from my family or friends to get into a prestigious college.

All through my senior year, I filled out the college and scholarship applications that my school counselor, Mary Hilficker, gave me. At the time I thought, "Why is she picking on me?" But I didn't realize that she was actually helping me live up to my academic potential. Mt. Edgecumbe High School had about 300 Alaska Native students; there were no non-Native students. All except one of the teachers were white.

The day I found out I was accepted to Dartmouth, I was on kitchen detail in the school cafeteria. I was serving lunch when the guidance counselor came running into the crowded cafeteria hollering and screaming, waving the piece of paper that listed who got into Dartmouth College from Alaska.

The Native American Program at Dartmouth invited me to visit the campus to help me decide if I should attend. I spent one week at Dartmouth to find out if I liked it. That was when I became acutely aware that I was entering a different world. I flew from Sitka to Seattle to Washington, D.C., to Boston. From Boston I flew to Lebanon, New Hampshire, and then drove to Hanover. I remember an instant attraction to the campus because it was in a rural area and I didn't want to attend college in the city. But even the taxi ride was a foreign experience—there were no cars in my village, only motorcycles.

My first impressions of Dartmouth College during that week began with trying to understand the environment. I first dealt with opening and closing the huge hardwood doors that were about twenty feet high at the Admissions Building. I barely managed to move them. I timed my entering and exiting the Admissions Building with other people who were either coming in or going out. If I had to leave the building by myself, I found that the key to opening those doors was not to rely on strength in my arms but to push with my legs planted firmly on the ground. Otherwise I would be stuck on either side of the door.

One night, as I was walking across the campus, I happened to look up at the sky. Without thinking, I started laughing uncontrollably at what I saw because it did not make sense to me. The big dipper was in the wrong position. It was upside down. The big dipper was supposed to hold water in, but in this case all the water was gone. In retrospect, I realize that it was only by chance that I saw the dipper upside down. I could have looked at it right side up, but at that moment, it was all messed up.

Another thing I noticed about the surroundings that was different was the smell of the trees. The scent of the willow trees at home was not as strong as the smell of the trees in New Hampshire. I could not place their smell. There were many trees that I'd never even seen before: some of them looked like broccoli. I was familiar with the Sitka spruce in southeast Alaska, but these trees seemed larger. I was not used to all the squirrels and pigeons all year round—I had only seen them in books and movies. I was used to seeing seagulls and swallows in the summertime and ravens in the winter. I was completely out of my environment.

Ultimately, what sold me was the academic challenge that I felt Dartmouth College offered me. Someone asked me if I was scared when I left for college. I was more curious than scared. If there was anyone on earth who did not have a clue about what she was getting into, it was me. When I think of what I experienced when I arrived, I smile. I smile because if I had not maintained a positive attitude, I would have dropped out and gone back home.

In the fall of 1982, I said goodbye to my family and left for college. I arrived at my dorm feeling tired after fourteen hours of flying from one end of North America to the other. Students were running up and down, and I remember thinking that they were real loud. It was the middle of the night, and the whole dorm was awake, with all kinds of music filling the air. No one listened to each other—they were too busy talking all at once.

As I made my way to the fourth floor, a guy, who I found out later was my undergraduate advisor, came flying toward me with a beer in his hand and said to me, "Where in the hell have you been, you dirty 'shmen?" I looked at him and did not answer. I was shocked. I remember thinking, "This is crazy!"

I found my room, but my roommates were not there. I put my things down and sat in a chair. As I made my way from the chair to my desk I looked up to the ceiling to establish my bearings. While I did so, my two roommates came screaming into the room with a whole bunch of other students. They were asking me all kinds of questions all at once like, "Why are you one week late?" and "What's it like in Alaska?" I told them I had been on a hunting trip. I sat back down in the chair and smiled the whole time they were talking to me. I remained in the chair until I told them that I needed to go to the bathroom.

Drained of energy, sleepy and exhausted, I eventually called my parents in Alaska to let them know that I had arrived at Dartmouth in one piece. Although my sleeping bag had not made it, I went to sleep that first night thinking, "What have I gotten myself into?" Since I had attended a government boarding school, I was used to dorm life, but not like this!

In the first term at Dartmouth, I had trouble with my classes. My government professor referred me to the Dean of Freshmen's office because I was failing his class. I did not understand anything he said in class. The way he talked and carried on, I didn't think anyone could have understood him. He was too philosophical; I had not been exposed to that kind of education yet.

The Dean's office sent me to a counselor, who asked me, "What are you?" I told her that I was Eskimo—Yup'ik. She didn't know what to do with me. She sent me back to the Dean's office, and I was placed in a Personal Writing Seminar.

My seminar professor, Priscilla Sears, helped me understand what was happening to me through my writings in her class. At first it was confusing to me, but eventually it made sense. She helped me by having me describe in my journal my home, my family, and basically how I saw the world. Through my personal writing journal, I walked through my experiences and came to an awareness of how I fit into Dartmouth College. Or should I say, how I didn't fit into Dartmouth College.

I tried to explain to my peers, for example, why there were no fences where I lived. The concepts of land, subsistence hunting, and fishing were even more complicated to discuss in a conversation simply because, like my Dad said, I used to go on trips to Black River to pick salmon-berries or out into the Bering Sea to hunt seals. My way of life was different. I learned how to describe concepts and started to anticipate questions related to my "sticking out like a sore thumb."

My peers in the dorm talked about prep schools, vacations, and other experiences I couldn't even picture, because I had never seen these things. It was helpful when my roommate took me to visit her parents outside of Boston. She and I would talk about our differences—like why I liked walking on the lawns, and she liked walking on the sidewalks, or why I wore a T-shirt in the winter, when everyone else wore sweaters, or why I never went home for breaks. That one was simple; it cost too much money, so I stayed in the dorm or went home with a friend.

I looked forward to learning things from the people around me, but living at Dartmouth was like living on the moon. I had no orientation or preparation for a trip like that. I did not have a legacy to claim, nor did I come from a socially advantaged family. I had no pearls, no fancy clothes, no car, and no prep school class ring. I was more than 5,000 miles away from my home, and I did not want to become a sister in a sorority. I was not versed in Shakespeare or acquainted with using a computer. I had never skied, nor did I know how to swim. I didn't even feel comfortable in church because the church was filled with the same people who filled the classroom.

It was critical that I gained an understanding of what was happening to me when I first went to Dartmouth College. If not for Professor Sears, I probably would have failed my freshman year. I learned from her the importance of a person's perspective. I had my own angle on everything, and she helped me describe what that was through my writing. Slowly, I learned to apply this technique to my other classes. For example, for an oceanography class project, I put together a portfolio on the variety of animals we hunted for food on the Bering Sea.

I enrolled in the environmental studies program at Dartmouth College and truly enjoyed the classes, discussions, field trips, and exchanges with both professors and students. I was also fascinated with the history and circumstances of the Native Americans in the Lower 48. I enrolled in Native American studies classes and gained an understanding of the context in which Alaska Native history developed in the United States, specifically with regard to the Alaska Native Land Claims Act. I didn't know what a reservation was, and I didn't know I belonged to a tribe. I learned that I was not only a minority at Dartmouth College, but in the Native American community in America, and in the general American population as a whole. In addition to learning new terminology, I gained an understanding of different perspectives.

Native American studies was particularly interesting to me because of my family tree—Russians on my father's side and Americans on my mother's side. Both intermarried with Alaska Natives. My interest was in Japanese history, specifically the Native Japanese, the Ainu, so I majored in history. This fascination grew out of my father's dealings as a businessman with the Japanese, selling Alaskan salmon. In the context of my undergraduate experience, I became acutely aware of the sense of difference and similarity among people.

The student organization, Native Americans at Dartmouth (NAD), also had a great impact on me. I personally don't think I would have gotten my diploma if NAD had not existed. My closest friends and sources of support at college were American Indians from the Lower 48. There were about ten of us that stuck together. We would gather every Thursday night to watch "Hill Street Blues," or to make the trek through the snow to steal firewood from some poor professor's back porch so that we could spend the evening cooking, studying, or partying together. I felt that I was a Native American like they were, even if I was not an Indian, and I appreciated the fact that they accepted me for who I was. It was a comfortable feeling to be welcomed in NAD; they wanted to help not only with academics but with housing, food, mail, and all the little things that make it easier to settle into a new place.

Graduation day in 1987 was a bittersweet experience for me; I had finally finished college, but my parents, brothers, and sisters were not there to share my success. I remember sitting on the green with thousands of people around me, watching a classmate I had never seen before paint her fingernails. I don't regret not branching out more to meet these people just for the sake of meeting them, because I knew I probably would not see them when I returned to Alaska. I don't remember who the guest speaker was or what was said during any part of the ceremony.

As I look back on my Dartmouth experience, I realize that my exit from Dartmouth College was just as perplexing as my entrance. When I first went to college, I was alone and bewildered. I felt the same way at graduation. I looked forward to going back home.

After graduation, I continued my education at the University of Alaska-Fairbanks in a master's program in cross-cultural education, and I received my Alaska state teaching certification. I taught junior high school in Bethel for a year, then took a job with the local hospital.

I am currently the support services administrative officer at the Yukon-Kuskokwim Delta Regional Hospital in Bethel, Alaska, which serves fifty-seven tribes on the Yukon-Kuskokwim Delta. I find it both challenging and extremely rewarding to be working in the health field. I constantly use my training in cross-cultural education in my daily activities, especially when I interact with health professionals who travel to Alaska from the Lower 48. I use the exposure I gained at Dartmouth College to establish some shared reference points with these individuals. For example, a common point could be a place we have both visited, a book we have both read, or a person we both know. More important, my direct tie to my family and community makes my job rewarding. It works for me to be tied to both.

My mom sometimes reminds me of what I did to a Canadian professor who went with my family on a camping trip when I was young. She says that after I finished eating my dried salmon, I wanted the skin burned. This man said he would help me, and not understanding that I wanted to eat it, he threw the fish skin into the fire. I looked at him and said, "You're so dumb!" He felt bad, but got educated. At Dartmouth, in much the same fashion, I had the chance to share my world with other students.

My advice to other students is to use those things that your parents and family taught you—the things in your "grub box"— because they are your strengths. It's good to have the academic drive, but what got me through college was common sense and the ability to figure things out when they were not that obvious. When I received the grub box from my grandpa, I set it up on the floor in my room, just like we would set it up at camp. Whenever someone came in, I would offer to share what I had with them. Some students liked dried salmon, crackers, and tea, and some didn't. What I learned at college and have come to value in the subsequent years is the knowledge that I can create opportunities for myself and others in my life, with a little help from my grub box.

A Yup'ik Eskimo originally from Emmonak, Alaska, Vivian Johnson graduated from Dartmouth College in 1986. At Dartmouth, she majored in history and minored in both Native American studies and environmental studies. Vivian obtained her Alaska teaching certification in 1989 and received a master's degree in cross-cultural education from the University of Alaska–Fairbanks in 1995.

After teaching social studies at the Bethel Regional High School, Vivian took a job with the Yukon-Kuskokwim Health Corporation in Bethel, Alaska, which serves an area the size of Oregon and represents fifty-seven tribes in the region. She now works as the Yukon-Kuskowim Delta Regional Hospital's support services administrator, par-

ticipating on the national, state, and local levels as an ambassador for the people of the region in the fast-changing field of health care.

Vivian is an advocate for education, small business, and cultural interests in the Yukon-Kuskokwim Region. She plans to open the Lower Yukon River Museum in Emmonak, Alaska, a project she has been pursuing for ten years.

▼ ▼ ▼ ▼ ▼ ▼ ▼ ▼ ▼ ▼

LORI ARVISO ALVORD

Full Circle

"Dr. Alvord, Dr. Alvord, please call the hospital,"
my beeper goes off with a voice message. I am sitting at the kitchen
table in my home in Gallup, New Mexico, just fifty miles from
my childhood home of Crownpoint, a tiny town on the eastern
border of the Navajo reservation. I am a surgeon, in my fifth year
of practice at the Gallup Indian Medical Center. Three decades
ago, I played on the mesas surrounding Crownpoint, never dream-
ing that my life path would turn down the most unexpected of
"canyons," leading me back full circle to my home and my people.

As a child, I never dreamed of becoming a doctor, much less a
surgeon. We didn't have Navajo doctors, lawyers, or other profes-

sionals. I grew up in a poor community of working-class families. Even poorer families, who lacked running water and electricity, lived nearby on the reservation. When I reach back in my mind to my childhood, my past would not have been a predictor of future successes. My own family had a precarious existence; my father was Navajo—charming, intelligent, and handsome—but subject to alcoholic binges. My mother was blonde, blue-eyed, and very attractive, but she married my father before she finished high school. He brought her to the reservation to work with him at a trading post when she was two weeks shy of her sixteenth birthday. She had been raised in Belen, a little town along the Rio Grande. They began married life in a remote part of the reservation, a little settlement called Whitehorse Lake. My two younger sisters and I grew up in a fragile world. I remember childhood as a succession of never-ending worries: Would my dad lose his job? Freeze from exposure during one of his binges? Get involved in a car accident that hurt him or someone else? Fear and uncertainty were a part of my everyday life, but our family seemed to respond with an abundance of love for one another, as though that would shelter us if everything else collapsed. During the times when Dad was drinking, though, all bets were off. As a young child, I listened many nights to my parents fighting—the shouting, slurred words, doors slamming, and cars roaring off into the darkness. I remember the craziness of those nights, the despair, the rides in the backseat of an erratic, fast-moving car. When I grew older, Dad woke me up at night to discuss things far too philosophical for a child. I would listen quietly, and talk with him, hoping he would fall asleep, hoping he wouldn't get up and walk out the door into the night . . .

I sought refuge deep in the pages of books, escaping to Russia with Dr. Zhivago, or to Alaska with Jack London's characters. My mother and grandfather had taught me to read before I entered school, and I preferred reading to almost any other pastime. In grade school, I did so well academically that I was accelerated from third to fifth grade, a move which pleased me, but which almost led to my social downfall. Younger and smaller than the other children in my class, I found it hard to fit in, and I began to retreat into solitude. When I emerged from my books, however, the real world was still waiting for me.

Crownpoint was a very small town on the western side of New

Mexico. Though there was a significant Native population, all the merchants, teachers, doctors, and engineers were white. I found myself between two worlds: living inside the Navajo world, but sometimes feeling very distant from it; being half-white, but never referring to myself as white.

My father and grandmother had been punished for speaking Navajo in school. Navajos were told that, in order to be successful, they would need to forget their language and culture and adopt American ways. They were warned that if they taught their children Navajo, the children would have a harder time learning in school, and would therefore be at a disadvantage. This pressure to assimilate—along with the complete subjugation of the tribes following the Indian wars of the 1800s, the poverty due to poor grazing lands, forced stock reduction, and lack of jobs—all combined to bring the Navajo people to their knees, and a sense of deep shame prevailed.

My father suffered terribly from this; he had been a straight-A student, sent away to one of the best prep schools in the state. My father wanted to be like the rich, white children who surrounded him, but the differences were too apparent. At home on the reservation, he enjoyed his Navajo lifestyle—hunting deer, fishing, and cherishing the outdoor world. Later, he would bring these loves to our family life; we spent many happy times camping and fishing on mountain lakes in the summer, and hunting deer in the winter. We learned how to track animals, and how to appreciate and respect wildlife. Though hunting is usually a "male" activity, he seemed not to notice that his three children lacked a Y chromosome.

Outside the reservation, however, the world was not so friendly. In his mind, my father rebelled against the limitations of being Navajo in the 1940s and '50s. He went to the University of New Mexico, majoring in pre-med and Latin, until he married my mother and took a job to support her. He began to hate himself for not being able to fit into the white world and for not fulfilling his dreams. He flooded his grief with alcohol. Later in his life, his drinking episodes became much less frequent as he sought to control the disease, but he didn't escape its ultimate outcome. My father's life ended in 1993 in an alcohol-related automobile accident.

As a child, I saw the darkness of this subjugation over our lives, but I did not understand the roots of his anguish until I was a teenager, when I began to read Native American history and absorbed the reality that the all-American hero, Kit Carson, was in fact an arsonist who waged his campaign against the Navajo by burning settlements of men, women, and children to the ground. I read the history of tribe after tribe: the broken treaties, the massacres, the battles that were won not by wits and skill, but by superior weapons technology. I was heartbroken and very angry. With like-minded friends, I watched the takeover of Wounded Knee, South Dakota, and the rise of the American Indian movement. Although I didn't agree with all the principles of the movement, I too wanted to strike out against the America that had done this to my people. It took me years before I understood that this kind of anger was more destructive than beneficial.

Meanwhile, I added courses in Navajo language to my studies. The struggle to become fluent in Navajo began as a teenager and continues to this day, for Navajo is a very complex language, described by linguists as one of the hardest in the world to master. Though I cherished both sides of my heritage, I often felt that I didn't completely belong in either world. I would find, in the non-Indian world, that respect for elders was not present: people talked too much, laughed too loud, asked too many questions, had no respect for privacy, were overly competitive, and put a higher value on material wealth. Navajos, on the other hand, place much more emphasis on a person's relations to family, clan, tribe, and the other inhabitants of the earth, human and nonhuman. In the Navajo world, there are also codes of behavior that were sometimes hard for me to follow as a child. We were taught to be humble and not to draw attention to ourselves, to favor cooperation over competition (so as not to make ourselves "look better" at another's expense, or hurt the feelings of someone else), to avoid prolonged eye contact, to be quiet and reserved, to respect those who were older than us, and to reserve opinions until they were asked for.

This was hardest for me in the classroom, where peer pressure against attracting attention to oneself prevents Navajo children from raising their hands to answer a question in class even though they might know the answer. I enjoyed school and loved learning, so I felt like a racehorse locked in a barn. While I often felt more competitive than my classmates, when it came to college, I found that I wasn't nearly competitive enough.

I made good grades in high school, but I was receiving a marginal education; good teachers were very difficult to recruit, and funding for our little school was often inadequate. I spent many hours in classrooms where nothing was being taught. Nevertheless, my parents always assumed that all their children would go to college. I don't remember any lectures from them on the importance of higher education, just the quiet assurance that they believed in us. My college plans were modest; I assumed I would attend a nearby state school, until I happened to meet another Navajo student who was attending Princeton. I had heard of Princeton, but had no idea where it was. I asked how many Indians were there, and he replied, "Five." I couldn't even imagine a place with only five Indians, since our town was ninety-eight percent Indian! Then he mentioned Dartmouth, which had about fifty Indians on campus at that time, and I felt a little better. "Ivy League" was a term I had heard before, but I had no concept of its meaning. No one from my high school had ever attended an Ivy League college. I learned you had to be "smart" to go to schools like these, and I didn't feel all that smart. I was fourth in my class, not even valedictorian or salutatorian. I decided to apply to Dartmouth anyway—it was so far away and different, like a place out of one of the books I had read. I was flown to visit the college, and it seemed like another reality: the beautiful buildings, the trees, the lush grass. Back at home, I waited anxiously, and one day the letter came: I was accepted, early decision! The year following my acceptance, a student at Crownpoint was given an appointment to West Point, and following that, my younger sister was accepted at Stanford. The trend continues today, and I'm very proud of the role I was able to play, but I must admit that my applying to Dartmouth was more due to chance and destiny than to any well-designed plan.

Dartmouth College was founded in 1769 by a charter from the king of England to provide an "education for Indians." By 1970, that commitment had gone largely unfulfilled and only a handful of Native Americans had actually graduated from the school. In 1970, the college renewed its commitment and developed, in my opinion, the strongest college program for Native Americans as well as a Native American studies program which has also been called the finest in the country.

I came to Dartmouth at the age of sixteen and entered a world so different from my home that I could hardly believe both places existed on the same continent! What a contrast to Crownpoint, my tiny, dusty, reservation bordertown. I felt very lucky to be there, but I was in culture shock. Having come 2,500 miles from home, I was soon very lonely. I had always considered myself to be very independent (and I've been told I'm pretty strongwilled), so I was determined not to give up, even though the obstacles were often enormous.

Academically, I held my own in classes like literature and social sciences due to my strong reading background, but I was totally unprepared for the sciences. I had worked in the hospital pharmacy in high school and loved learning about different medications. I was planning to become a pharmacist, but found myself in a liberal arts college that didn't offer a degree in pharmacy. I decided to prepare for a health career by taking pre-med courses, and tried several science courses my first year. After receiving the first D of my entire life, I retreated. At the time, I assumed that I just wasn't smart enough to handle the sciences. It took me years to realize that my problems with science courses in college stemmed from my previous high school training. I was inadequately prepared to compete with the Ivy Leaguers. After sampling a number of other courses, I finally decided on a double major: a full major in psychology, and a sociology major modified with Native American studies. I received honors in my freshman seminar as well as in two Native American studies courses that stressed writing. As a result, I found myself thinking of teaching Native American studies as a career, and perhaps also becoming a writer.

Academics and loneliness were not my only struggles; I had trouble connecting with the non-Indian students. At Crownpoint, I was often "gabby" compared to the other students. At Dartmouth, I talked far too little. I blamed my own natural shyness, fear of people, and preference for solitude. It never occurred to me that this was related to my background, that my upbringing was so radically different from my non-Indian classmates that we shared little common ground. I think I realized this problem years later when I returned home as a surgeon. Though I began encouraging other Navajo students to go to college, I knew that many Navajos would have a much harder time than I did. In fact, many of the other Indian students at Dartmouth, especially those from reservations, were experiencing similar problems, and many ended up leaving school. Navajos, and many other Indians, retreat and with-

draw when alone in the midst of predominantly white populations.
Very few of the students from traditional communities were able
to make the transition; most never wanted to, and many never
tried.

Understanding the culture of Dartmouth was like a course in
itself. I didn't comprehend the meaning of places like fraternities,
or the value systems of students from upper-class families. Had
their parents taught them survival skills through camping, tracking,
and hunting? Did I have any interest in making four-story-high
sculptures out of ice for Winter Carnival? Did they respect their
elders, their parents? Did I know which fork to use at a formal
dinner? What sort of ceremonies did their "tribes" practice? We
had so little in common. While they pondered such burning questions as when the opening day of ski season would be, I was struggling just to stay warm in the frozen New Hampshire winters and
not slip on the ice! I was very homesick, wishing I didn't have to
miss so many familiar events: the Navajo Tribal Fair, the Zuni
Shalako, Laguna feast days, Santa Fe Indian Market, Gallup Cer-
emonials, and on and on. Everyone at home was having a great
time (or so I imagined), eating wonderful food—roasted corn from
the Shiprock market, posole, red chile stew, and venison jerky, and
I was stuck in the library! I missed the beauty of watching the
Apache Devil Dancers or the Pueblo Buffalo Dancers. I missed the
splendor of Navajo traditional clothing, showered with silver and
turquoise. I missed the pink and purple sunsets of New Mexico.
Despite these differences, and my sadness, I took heart in the quality of the education I was receiving. This benefit, along with my
own stubbornness and inability to accept failure in myself, was
probably what kept me at Dartmouth.

But there was another significant influence in my decision to
remain at Dartmouth: the Native American Program. The Native
American Program had a tough job: recruiting students like us,
who were very high risk—we frequently had only marginal high
school preparation, many were reluctant to come to school so far
from home, and, like skittish wild horses, some would turn tail and
run back home at the least provocation. We were a group of students who found great comfort in one another, for though we came
from many different tribes, our experiences at Dartmouth were
similar: we came from very different worlds, and we all felt discon-
nected from the mainstream student body. For minority women,

it was even worse. At the time I arrived on the scene, Dartmouth had only recently changed from an all-male to a co-ed student body, and the presence of women was resented by many of the men on campus. Referred to as "co-hogs" instead of co-eds, we were shunned for dates as girls were bused in from nearby women's colleges on weekends. Social activities were dominated by the fraternities, and if we went to their parties at all, we were often ignored. At home I had never had a problem attracting men, so I began questioning myself. Maybe I really wasn't very pretty after all, since these men barely noted my existence. For all these reasons, the small group of Native American students at Dartmouth coalesced into a solid community of students that did almost everything together. We went on many trips: to Native American basketball tournaments in Maine, on Long Island, or at Harvard; to pow wows all over the Northeast; to New York to visit the Indians at the New York City Community House; to Washington, D.C.; even across Canada to attend a wedding in Michigan. Our group was made up of Paiutes, Sioux, Cherokees, Chippewas, Navajos, Pueblos, and many other tribes. We were friends, lovers, rivals, enemies; we felt many things about each other, but in general, whatever we felt, we felt it deeply because we were so close. I have been many places since then and have been a part of other student groups at other colleges—nothing compared to the intensity of the experience of being a member of the Native American student group at Dartmouth.

Through this group, I met another Navajo, Lloyd Brown, who came from a little town about eighty miles north of Crownpoint, and I was instantly attracted to him. Lloyd had shoulder-length thick brown hair and large, expressive brown eyes. I admired Lloyd because he was everything I was not. He was full-blooded Navajo and spoke Navajo fluently, but at the same time, Lloyd was more sophisticated and (I thought) smarter than I was. He had attended high school in Hartford, Vermont, through a program called "A Better Chance," which was administered by a volunteer organization at Dartmouth. This program provided Indian students with the kind of high quality academic preparation at the high school level they would need in order to excel in college. Lloyd had spent three years in high school in Vermont. He had been a starter on their basketball team, and he was much better adjusted to white people than I was. He did better in classes with less effort than I did. We spent several years at Dartmouth together as a couple, before going our separate ways. Lloyd remains a good friend. He is now married and is working to develop businesses on the Navajo reservation.

There was, however, a dark side to Dartmouth: the Indian symbol. For many years, the unofficial mascot of the college had been the "Dartmouth Indian." Native Americans objected strenuously to this symbol, and the college officially discouraged students and alumni from using it, but it was everywhere on campus when I was a student. Imagine, if you can, a young Navajo girl coming to live in a non-Navajo community for the first time, seeing her people portrayed by members of the community as caricatures with paint on their faces, watching them jump around with toy tomahawks, and cheer, "Wah-hoo-wah," supposedly the "sounds that Indians make," at athletic contests. Imagine that she is told that this is meant to convey honor, pride, and respect to "Indians." It didn't make sense, and I was shocked and hurt. If my classmates wanted to respect and honor Indians, I would have brought Navajo code-talkers to Dartmouth, men who fought in World War II and used a special code in the Navajo language to communicate by radio secret military information in the Pacific; it was a "code" the Japanese were never able to break.

The Indian symbol was represented by silly images of Indians with feathers and loincloths. This symbol was widely adopted by many fraternities on campus, and any objection to such use was certain to cause hostility. As Native students, we held protests, we got into fights with fraternity members (yes, some fistfights), and sometimes we cried at night. The college that was chartered to provide education to Indians was doing just that, but it wasn't the education I expected. Dartmouth was built for us, but the welcome mat was often pulled out from under us. This contributed to the sense of isolation I felt while at Dartmouth. I didn't really absorb this until years later, and I began to ask myself, "Do they really want us here?" Despite all I experienced, I think the answer is yes. Dartmouth has made many favorable changes since then.

This year, I was invited by Dartmouth's president, James Freedman, to serve on the college's Native American Visiting Committee. This committee advises the president on matters relating to the Native American Program, a student support program, and Native American studies, an academic program. One of my first recommendations will be to develop programs to build bridges between Native Americans and the rest of the Dartmouth community, possibly by creating "host families" among the faculty, or by developing liaisons between the Native American students and the other organizations on campus. We have much to learn in breaking down the barriers of misunderstanding that separate us.

After graduating from Dartmouth with a double major in psychology and sociology and certification in Native American studies, I decided to take a break before going on to grad school. Once home in New Mexico, I began looking for work in Albuquerque, and my life took a decidedly different turn, much like a car on the freeway veering onto an exit ramp at the very last minute! I had always thought of myself as a "right brain" person. As a child in Crownpoint, I had received an unlikely education in classical piano. In an effort to keep my mind occupied, my mother found a series of piano teachers: the English high school teacher, the Mormon preacher's wife, then finally, a true piano teacher. I took classes all through junior high and high school. I also wrote poetry occasionally, and later embarked on a self-taught education in Impressionist art. I had no plans for a "left brain" career, but a psychology course in neuroanatomy had opened a small door to the world of medicine, and I was fascinated with what I learned about how the brain was "hard wired." While job hunting, I found a job as a research assistant in a neurobiology research lab. I didn't expect to be hired, because of my limited science background, so I was a little surprised when I got the job. My supervisor, Dr. Gary Rosenberg, later told me he thought he could train me to do what I needed to do; since I had a Dartmouth education, I probably had enough innate intelligence to be trainable. I did prove to be trainable—I learned how to run experiments and process and analyze data with statistical packages on computers. Soon Dr. Rosenberg was asking me if I had ever thought about going to medical school. I remember blushing and shaking my head no. "Well, maybe you should think about it," he told me. I smiled. My mind swept back to my years at Dartmouth. With a touch of shame, I remembered my initial failures in chemistry and calculus. What was I thinking? My mind reminded me that I really wasn't smart enough to be considering this. But the thought wouldn't go away. Medicine! Wow! There are some things that seem so far out of reach that you don't dare even dream about them. This was one of them. In high school, I had worked part time at the hospital, in the pharmacy. I loved the rows of medicine bottles, the pretty little pills, each uniquely different, and I would count them very carefully when assigned to help fill a prescription. I thought it would be a very admirable goal to be a pharmacist, but I was so naive as a teenager that I didn't even check to see if Dartmouth had a pharmacy program when I applied. Of course, they didn't! It had been many years since I had thought about studying anything in medicine, even pharmacy. Now, I couldn't let go of the thought. How wonderful it would be to be a doctor, to be able to heal people. It would be a very special gift, a wonderful treasure, and the more I thought about it, the more I thought it might be perfect for me, but was I perfect for it? I had never even met a Navajo physician. I knew of one, Dr. Taylor McKenzie, but no others. What made me think I could do this? I thought about the commitment: four years of medical school, and then a residency which would be three to six years more. This didn't include getting ready for medical school—a year of pre-med science courses I would have to take and pass.

Nevertheless, I decided to consider it, and tested the waters by taking a biology course at night. I did well, but this was a "softer" science. I tried to think of which course intimidated me most, and decided it was physics. I took a physics course on my lunch break, and finished with a B. I was ecstatic! It was the end of the summer of 1980. I went back to Dr. Rosenberg and told him I was quitting. I wanted to go back to college full time to finish my pre-med requirements. Next, I went looking for funding. The scholarships from the college and my tribe had always been there before; now they were nowhere in sight. In order to qualify for these funds, I had to be in a degree-granting college program, yet I was taking a bunch of courses that didn't qualify for any specific degree. The news worsened. I couldn't even qualify for loans! I took a deep breath and thought about it. I was so excited about the chance to go to medical school, I decided to keep trying. Luckily, tuition at UNM was fairly reasonable, so I decided to use my savings. I quit my job and went back to school full time. I took a minimum-wage work-study job for twenty hours a week and hoped I would have enough money. I applied for food stamps, ate a lot of beans and rice that year, and somehow made it. I needed eight more science courses, and took four per semester. Rather than wait out another year, I applied to medical schools that same fall and took the Medical College Admissions Test in October. It was a gamble, because I had taken less than half of the science courses I needed for the test. I told myself that this year's application was really just a "dry run," and I didn't really expect to get in that year.

My scores came back in the 7-9 range, on a 1-15 scale, with an 11 in reading. I knew most students needed 10 or better to qualify, but I pointed out in my application that I had yet to take most of my science courses. I applied to four medical schools: University of New Mexico, Stanford, U.C. San Francisco, and U.C. San Diego. At the time, San Francisco was the highest-ranked medical school in the country. Stanford was not far behind.

My first interview was at UNM. I remember it distinctly as a turning point in my life. My interviewer and I sat down. He looked at my application and said, "I see you've applied to Stanford." I expected to hear him say, "What makes you think you can get into Stanford?" Instead, he said, "I think Stanford will probably accept you. What can we do to get you to come to UNM?" I was completely speechless for a few moments, taking it all in. I thought to myself, "I have a spot in a medical school! I'm going to medical school! The only question now is where?" I thanked him and said I would definitely consider UNM. I was accepted at all four medical schools, and while common sense told me to go to UCSF, I chose Stanford instead for a number of reasons—primarily because my sister Karen was there as an undergraduate and was incredibly lonely. Also, however, I was intimidated by San Francisco—I was afraid of the city. I had never lived in an urban environment. Stanford was much more rural and it had a beautiful campus. In addition, the curriculum was more flexible.

I realized that medicine seemed to be a perfect choice; I had always wanted to help people, and this was a direct and powerful way to do it. But I was fueled by another strong drive: I wanted to be able to provide for my family if anything happened to my father. I had a strong need to protect the people I loved and to eliminate some of the insecurity our family continually experienced.

Medical school was extremely challenging. I studied like I had never studied before—long hours every night, often into the morning. I knew I wasn't as naturally brilliant as everyone else, so I would have to work overtime to make up for it. The biggest stress of medical school was convincing myself I could do it. I had a very real fear of failure that persisted all the way through my training, well past medical school, into residency, and beyond. There was just no way of knowing whether I was capable of all this. Competition was keen; there were over five thousand applications for eighty-six class slots per year. I feared the other students and felt like a poor relation invited to the ball, because I had no connection to places like these. No family or community members had been here before and I came from a very poor part of the world—a world so vastly different from what I was experiencing that I often could hardly believe I was really there. Though I did have a Dartmouth degree behind me, this was a whole new echelon. Until very recently, I battled with this inferiority complex, which finally left me only after I became board certified in general surgery.

While classroom demands were tough, clinical medicine was even tougher. I spent long hours in the hospital, up all night every third night, trying to absorb everything I was experiencing without falling asleep from exhaustion. In addition to my sleep deprivation, a more subtle problem occurred. I didn't fully comprehend it, though, until much later, when I began caring for Indian patients. As a medical student, we were learning to interview patients and perform physical examinations, and I was having a real problem with it. I disliked asking the questions and I hated doing the examinations. I was very uncomfortable with the whole process and I began to question whether I was really meant to be a physician. I finally realized that I was facing a cultural barrier, an impasse; in the Navajo world, it is considered improper to ask a personal question unless the subject is first brought up by the other person. It is improper to even hold hands or touch in public, and traditional clothing covers a person from head to toe. I found I was breaking rule after rule by asking intimate, probing questions, and touching total strangers in every place imaginable. Yet I knew these were not Navajos, these were Californians, and they expected this treatment as part of their visit. Once my mind was able to capture the reasons for my extreme discomfort, I was able to do what was expected of me with much greater ease. I tried to make sure that everything was done in a respectful manner, and I told myself that I learned what I needed from the interview and exam in order to give the patients good medical care. Later, for my Indian patients, I developed techniques of asking questions without being overly probing or invading their privacy, sometimes gathering the information I needed over several interviews, rather than in one lengthy interview on my first visit with a patient. I kept all of their bodies covered except for the small part I was examining and tried to make them feel as comfortable as possible in an uncomfortable situation.

In my third year of medical school, I did a summer assignment at a hospital very close to my home: Acoma-Canyoncito-Laguna Hospital. I met a Native American physician working there named Ron Lujan. I had met other Native physicians before, but Dr. Lujan was different—he was a surgeon. Full-blooded Taos, he had a style of interacting with Indian patients that was deeply caring and respectful, accented with a touch of humor. His patients were crazy about him, and I was astonished. Here, thirty miles from my parents' doorstep, was the man I would learn the most from, for not only did he know how to relate to his patients, he was a surgeon! At first, I could not get over it; I didn't know Native surgeons existed. I took my first steps into the world of the operating room with him. It was a strange and beautiful experience: it was like walking into a place I had known all my life, and into a place I knew I was supposed to be. As he taught me the initial steps to an operation, how to hold and use the tools, and how to gently enter the world inside the human body, I watched, listened, and sometimes held my breath, for the experiences had a spiritual component that I had not expected. Entrusted with the lives of these patients, Dr. Lujan made it clear that this was nothing that could be undertaken lightly. He did his best to try to dissuade me from considering surgery as a career. "The hours are longer and harder than for any other medical profession, the years of training are the longest, and once you're done, your lifestyle will still be very hard," he warned me.

But I was not to be deterred. "I can't help it, there is nothing else I would rather do, there is nothing else I want to do. I love this and I feel this is what I am supposed to do."

"Okay," he replied, "but don't say I didn't warn you." Once he was sure of my decision, the training began in earnest. "You will be questioned because you are Indian. They will think you don't know what you're doing." He was referring to affirmative action and the backlash that led to an assumption that minorities hadn't rightfully attained their place in professional society. He continued, "Therefore you must be better than everyone else: you will have to study longer, work harder, to rise above this. You will have to prove yourself." He was right, of course. And I could sometimes feel it—when a nurse questioned an order I wrote or when doctors sent patients to me for surgical evaluations, and then questioned my decisions. I made sure I made the right decisions, that my arguments were correct, and yet part of me became very angry. I am rarely questioned these days, for I have worked with the same people in my hospital for many years, and I don't have to prove myself on a daily basis, but I remember the past—this type of discrimination is so subtle one can barely point a finger at it. Yet it exists.

I returned many times to work with Dr. Lujan, learning more with each visit. I began to understand the naturalness of Native physicians working with Native patients, a harmony that is most certainly the way things are meant to be. These patients deserve doctors who understand their culture, lifestyle, and ways of thinking: doctors who have respect for them. At times in this hospital, we realized a dream—an O.R. team completely composed of Indians. Our nurse anaesthetist is Laguna and the O.R. nurses are also Indian, so when Lujan and I face one another across the operating table, a dream comes to life. I see a visual example of a primary goal of our people: that of creating our own professionals, who will lead our communities, in order to control our own destiny as a people.

When I returned to Stanford to do my regular hospital rotations, I had a clear advantage in general surgery, for I had seen much of it already. My professors thought that I had been planning to train in surgery for many years. My evaluations were rated as excellent. This helped my decision to apply for a residency in general surgery. While most students had ten to twenty programs they applied to, I chose only three: University of New Mexico, Stanford, and a program in Phoenix. UNM was at the top of the list this time; after four years in California, I wanted very badly to come home. Phoenix didn't receive all my letters of recommendation in time, and this application was forfeited. I interviewed with a woman pediatric surgeon at UNM who wrote me a letter saying she was very impressed with my interview, and could I please come back and interview with the chairman of the department. I went back immediately. Then I relaxed—UNM liked me. I was a Stanford graduate and a resident of New Mexico, what more could they want? The applications are processed by computer match; the applicant ranks the surgery programs from the most desired to least desired, the surgery programs do the same with the list of applicants. Each list goes into a computer and the computer matches the applicant with a surgery program. Finally, on an anxious day called Match Day, the results are announced, and your fate is determined. Some students don't match at all, which is very frightening; you are faced with a choice of trying to get a spot in a program that didn't completely fill, choosing another specialty, or waiting a year.

The night before Match Day, I had a dream. In the dream, I opened my letter and found that I had matched in general surgery at Stanford Hospital. I cried and cried because it meant I wouldn't be going home. I woke up, realized it was just a dream, sighed with relief, and went back to sleep. The next day, I went to Match Day, opened the letter and found I had indeed matched at Stanford. I laughed at myself, my dream, and the fact that I had already cried, so there was no need to do that again. I knew also that I was one of a privileged few; there were hundreds of applications for only four positions in the surgery program at Stanford. I realized that my mind had not dared to hope for this, and instead had focused on UNM. In fact, I soon found that destiny, always the best navigator, had made the right choice. I learned that UNM was spoken of as a "good ole boys" program; they had not matched a woman there in many years, and the residents weren't very happy there. Stanford, on the other hand, was training more women and more minorities than any comparable program. The hours, while rigorous, were more humane than those of most programs, and the training was excellent. I trained for six years, spending my last year there as a chief resident. I owed three years of service to the Indian Health Service for scholarships while in medical school, and so returned home to work in Gallup, deciding to stay on after my obligation was finished.

My life as a surgeon is hard, as Dr. Lujan said it would be, but extremely rewarding. It is like anything of great value—difficult to achieve, and once obtained, treasured beyond measure. It is a beautiful discipline, in that part of it is an art form, because performing surgery well requires a precise choreography of the hands, eyes, and mind. Beyond that, however, is the part which is hardest for me— the fact that patients place their lives in our hands, and an error during an operation, or in the management of a patient afterward, can cause serious damage or death. This level of responsibility, this weight, can be very hard to shoulder. It comes with the trauma patient who is wheeled through the doors after a gunshot wound or a car accident, losing blood rapidly, and facing certain death

without intervention; it lies in the patient who is crashing in the Intensive Care Unit from a severe infection, and is so ill that an operation is risky. These cases and others come to you in dreams, keep you up all night, and never really leave your side. It is like riding a spirited stallion—it can be the ride of your life, but it is so fast and dangerous that you never want to ride again.

Because medicine is so competitive and because the surgical profession requires so much effort and discipline, it commands its own respect. For me, a young Indian girl who came from the reservation, from a family without money or power and with little education, it sometimes feels like I'm basking in the sun—though the clouds might roll in at any minute. I fear I may wake up one day to find it has all been a dream. This immense difference between my childhood, my culture, and my profession, has often been hard to reconcile. It is as though I am living in two parallel words that exist side by side but only rarely intersect. Native American friends who see me in action at the hospital or hear me speaking "medicalese" on the phone often have a hard time integrating that doctor with the woman they know. Surgeons and others I work with rarely see the woman who goes to a medicine man for advice during her pregnancy. My roles are complicated and even I get lost in them sometimes. Yet I have found a unique place in my culture as a role model for young people and as a human cultural "bridge" for Navajo people. I have given countless commencement addresses and speeches to groups at the request of Navajo communities. What I tell them often involves my passion for their success as individuals and as communities. I encourage them to learn who they are, respect themselves, and believe in themselves and in each other. These attributes are linked to and enriched by appreciating and preserving their culture—and will help them to be successful. My hopes and dreams are wrapped up in theirs: it is a dream for healthy, strong Navajo families and communities.

I entered medicine as a way to help my people, and, at the time, I thought that meant help in the most literal form, to fight disease. Now I find that my career is helping my people in ways I never imagined, for as they see my success, they are better able to realize their own potential.

A few years after I arrived at Gallup, I met my husband-to-be,

Jon Alvord. Jon was training with the Army in a Special Forces medic group that used our hospital for part of its training program. He arrived with others to help us in the operating room and to get
hands-on training. Though I was used to these soldiers coming and going, I found Jon in my operating room more often than not. He was quiet but friendly, with blonde hair and hazel-blue eyes looking over his mask. I was stunned when he asked me out, and I accepted, hoping this was not improper, for he was over ten years younger than I! I later found out that it had taken him two weeks to get up the nerve to ask me out. We hit it off from the very start, though I refused to take the relationship too seriously. Two months later, however, he proposed to me, and I realized his intentions were quite serious! Cautiously accepting, I nevertheless made him agree to an engagement time of at least a year before we tied the knot. In the first year of our marriage, I became pregnant and we were both delighted. On August 18, 1995, I gave birth to a beautiful baby boy; we named him Christopher Kodiak Alvord, and he goes by Kodi, or Kodi-bear. He is a good, even-tempered baby, with golden brown skin and dark brown eyes. I love him so much, I can hardly remember what life was like before him. We plan to stay in Gallup for now, raising our family. Jon takes care of Kodi and attends classes at the community college, while I try to balance my duties as surgeon and mom. In addition, in the past year, I have been working on a book, called *The Scalpel and the Silver Bear*, about my life and my work with Indian patients, which I hope will be completed shortly.

Well, the beeper's going off again, so it's time to run to the hospital. A kiss for Kodi, and one for Jon, and then I'm out the door and back to work.

Lori Arviso Alvord is a member of the Navajo Tribe. She was raised in Crownpoint, New Mexico, and graduated from Crownpoint High School. She attended Dartmouth College as an undergraduate, double majoring in psychology and sociology modified with Native American studies, and graduated in 1979. Two years later, she went on to Stanford Medical School, receiving her M.D. in 1985. Dr. Alvord stayed on at Stanford University Hospital, completing a six-year residency training program in general surgery in 1991. After finishing her training, Dr. Alvord returned to New Mexico to serve the needs of the Navajo people; she works at the Gallup Indian Medical Center in Gallup, New Mexico. She is married to Jonathan Alvord, and they have an infant son, Christopher Kodiak (Kodi) Alvord.

▼ ▼ ▼ ▼ ▼ ▼ ▼ ▼ ▼

N. BRUCE DUTHU

The Good Ol' Days
When Times Were Bad

It was 1965 and I was six when Hurricane Betsy
struck the Louisiana coast and all communities south of New Orleans were evacuated. We lived in Dulac, a small town seventy miles
southwest of New Orleans, about as coastal a community as you
can find in this part of Louisiana. It hugs the bayou and is virtually
surrounded by small lakes and wetlands, flooding easily—and Betsy
was no ordinary storm. People spoke in somber, almost reverential
tones about this hurricane. Everybody said it was the kind of storm
that changes lives forever.

The hurricane taught me my first lessons in justice—real, true,
bitter justice. Storms like Betsy did not discriminate against any-

one—Indian, white, or black; rich or poor; fisherman or professional. Betsy was an equal-opportunity destroyer. I recall a perverse sense of satisfaction returning to Dulac after Betsy and seeing the flooded homes of well-to-do white families, their drenched and ruined furnishings piled high on the roadside for the trash haulers. Indian families like ours hadn't suffered less, but neither had we suffered more. To me, that was significant.

I also saw the strength and love of my mother. Mom, my older brother Chuck, and I had moved in with my maternal grandfather after Mom's divorce from my father. The four of us made up what I knew as my immediate family. Since we didn't have our own car, we relied on the evacuation buses to get us out of Dulac. Our grandpa, or "pe-pere," had helped us secure the house and then gone to help other family members. By early evening, the brooding gray skies had turned fierce and deeply black. And the wind! It howled and pressed us from all directions. The three of us waited in the front room, listening for sounds of the bus. Mom clutched us tightly. She must have been terrified. I should have been but I don't think I was. She made me feel secure and protected. She spoke to us but I don't remember her words. What I do remember is her calm and her resolve. I never doubted we would make it through, because my mother had already willed it so.

The bus arrived just as Hurricane Betsy began to re-landscape our front yard. While the storm was occupied uprooting a large tree, my mother walked us from the front porch onto the bus. The whole ground around that old tree moved up and down. It was, as my own ten-year-old son would say, "awesome"—and terrifying.

My mother calls those "the good ol' days when times were bad." Pe-pere and Mom had wonderful stories about those days, the hardships and the good times of life in Dulac. Most were about being Indian. Our people belong to the Houma Indian Tribe, one of two tribes indigenous to the land now called Louisiana. The tribe occupied two village sites near present-day Baton Rouge when they encountered French explorers in the late seventeenth century. There followed a pattern of southerly migration, sometimes voluntary, sometimes not. Our oral tradition establishes that the tribe settled in present-day Terrebonne and Lafourche Parishes (counties) in the early nineteenth century. The seat of government in Terrebonne Parish is the city of Houma, some seventeen miles north of Dulac. Many of Houma's 40,000 residents have no knowledge of the existence, let alone the history, of the tribe for which the city is named.

Settlement patterns of the tribe tended to be kinship-based, and large family clusters lived along the banks of the many bayous that meander toward the Gulf of Mexico. Leadership was informal, relying on a local patriarch to advise or help resolve disputes. The traditional language slipped away in the nineteenth century and was replaced with an archaic French, known in the vernacular as "Cajun French." Most tribal members also converted to Christianity, primarily Roman Catholicism. But the sense of identity as Indian people, as Houma, didn't erode. Despite the adaptations, the necessary taking on of a new culture, the idea of being Houma Indian persisted.

Relations between Indians and whites were never easy in Dulac, and they became more strained during the mid-twentieth century, when tribal members began aggressively campaigning for basic civil rights, including public education. The first all-Indian public school in Terrebonne Parish opened in the mid-fifties at about the same time the U.S. Supreme Court declared "separate but equal" school systems unconstitutional.

My mother did not have access to this "separate and not-so-equal" education. Her formal education occurred in mission schools operated by various Christian churches. She attended the Catholic church school through the fourth grade, when she had to quit her studies and help support the family. I don't know if she would have chosen to go further. Her recollections of these mission schools are not happy ones. Religious dogma was used regularly to underscore Indian children's "unacceptability" in the sight of the Almighty. She told me how, in receiving the Eucharist, Indians had to wait until all white communicants had received the sacred Body of Christ. Seating in churches was segregated, with the "Indian section" in the back. I remember the marks left on the pews by the removal of the dividing railings. One elder Houma woman once told me that a priest tried to make her promise to withdraw her kids from the Baptist school and send them to the Catholic school as the "price" for her confessions to be heard. She punched him square in the jaw and never set foot in the Catholic church again.

Such experiences are not unusual in the history of missionization among the various tribes. From the time of first contact, religious doctrine has played an enormous role in the subjugation of Indian people. Now a law professor, I teach the evolution of Federal Indian law; students read United States Supreme Court opinions openly acknowledging, and even relying upon, oppression as the basis for decision. The high court's earliest major opinion on Indian land rights (Johnson *v.* McIntosh, 1923) describes how "the character and religion of [this continent's] inhabitants afforded an apology for considering them as a people over whom the superior genius of Europe might claim an ascendancy. The potentates of the old world found no difficulty in convincing themselves that they made ample compensation to the inhabitants of the new by bestowing on them civilization and Christianity, in exchange for unlimited independence."

Given such a history it would seem unlikely that a single Indian soul would still believe in the white man's god. And yet most of my relatives and other tribal members are Christian. Only recently have my mother and I asked ourselves why this is so. Part of it, we decided, is that we like the stories—not the ones interpreted by the priests, but the ones in the Bible, in the New Testament. For my mother, the lessons of loving your enemies and praying for those who despise you had immediate and personal significance.

These lessons became the hallmarks of a survival strategy that allowed us to go about life in a segregated community and a segregated church. They taught us how to profess love for white parishioners who visited our home to collect money and canned goods for the church fair—which we could not attend because we were Indian; how to overcome a narrow and racist interpretation of the Creator as one who would allow us into the eternal kingdom only after all the whites had safely and securely entered their glory. This was, to me, Christianity. Practicing it devoutly not only got us "soul protection" (in the event the "superior geniuses of Europe" were right about their moral and religious ascendancy), but it also helped expose the utter hypocrisy of the faith as practiced by many of those geniuses. I suppose one could say we engaged in civil disobedience by living in religious obedience.

These thoughts obviously did not preoccupy me while growing up in Dulac. As a kid, I felt wonderful and special being Indian when I was around Indian people. For my first five years of formal education, I went to the all-Indian school in Dulac. I was bright, precocious, polite, with a strong work ethic and light skin. I didn't work particularly hard at developing any of these traits—and I had no choice about skin coloring. My mixed ancestry—French and Houma Indian—is evident in my appearance, but in my community, last names and family connections tell the whole story. I identified myself and was identified as only one thing—Indian. Still, I know I received what favorable treatment could be expected. For example, my lapses into French, my first language, were typically forgiven, while other students got pretty bad whippings for the same offense.

Entering sixth grade was a big deal. It was 1969, and the elementary schools in our area were finally being integrated. Federal courts in Louisiana had ordered the public schools to desegregate in the early 1960s. In Terrebonne Parish, the high school was desegregated first, the elementary schools later. The all-Indian elementary school was dismantled and loaded by sections on large barges that were floated up the bayou six or eight miles to the site of the all-white school. There, the sections were unloaded and reassembled. For the first time, I attended school with white and black children. This was my first real opportunity to interact with non-Indians outside of the church, and I made friends easily, probably for the same reasons my teachers at the Indian school had liked me. I heard that some white kids were pulled out of the school and sent into mainly white parochial schools in Houma.

Until this point I did not value formal education either for its own sake or for what it could offer in terms of a future. Education was so closely linked with religion in the minds and hearts of some families that it left bitter memories, and young Indian kids dropped out in large numbers and at an early age, often before sixteen. For other families it was difficult to imagine that education would make any difference in their children's lives. As one young friend, a distant cousin, used to tell me, "My parents ask me why I need a high school diploma to work on a shrimp boat." We expected simply to follow in the footsteps of our parents. To think or want otherwise was unrealistic; worse, it might be perceived as a rejection of the traditional way of life. "What's the matter?" a parent would demand, "being a shrimper isn't good enough for you?"

My mother, however, pushed education. She must have thought it would give my brother and me options she had never had. Perhaps she pushed education because she knew it was valued in the white culture and, like religion, if you practiced it well, even the white people would have to acknowledge you. In any event, now that we were at an integrated school, we knew we were supposed to bring home good grades. Dropping out, for us, was no longer an option.

My brother and I did well in school. Many people called us the "Duthu twins." Chuck is older by nearly a year, but we looked very much alike and even dressed alike until fourth grade. But Chuck and I have very different personalities. He's much more introverted than I am. I was more vocal in class than he was. I asked questions of everybody, while Chuck preferred to work out answers on his own. After school, he often went into our bedroom and quietly played his guitar. I usually tore out of the house looking for the nearest cousin or friend to play sports with. Chuck chose a vocational-technical curriculum with emphasis in marine and nautical science, and I followed the standard college preparatory track. He seemed quite confident that his future, like most of our friends' futures, lay in working in the maritime industry. Despite our different aspirations, we were very close as brothers and as friends. I admired him for his resolve, for I still had absolutely no clue as to what I wanted to do.

I knew I wanted something different in life, even though I couldn't say exactly what it was or how I was going to go about achieving it. Much of my decision to pursue the nontraditional route of college preparatory work stemmed from negative experiences. I remember once playing with my cousins alongside the bayou in front of our house. I must have been ten years old or so, and a white man sped by in a truck and yelled, "Get out of the way, you goddamn sabines!" "Sabines" was a derogatory term for members of our tribe. I had seen fights break out when that word got tossed around. I was angry and hurt because his comment had nothing to do with what we were doing, but with who we were. No matter what we did, in his eyes we were unalterably "sabines." The prejudice came indirectly as well. The parents of some of my Anglo girlfriends opposed our relationships because I was Indian. In one particular case, my friend was punished when her parents learned she was dating an Indian.

But my encounters with racism did not approach those experienced by older relatives. Pe-pere had a brother who had been tarred and nearly drowned by some white men because he had entered a "whites only" bar. I suppose it was a mark of some progress in race relations that we had moved from blatant and physically threatening expressions to more subtle forms of racism which only scarred emotionally. But I was angry and frustrated and impatient with this glacial pace of change. I wanted to do something different, if only to demonstrate that it could be done, and could be done by an Indian.

The more positive encouragement to go to college came from my mother and other family members. Aunt Belle, one of my mom's older sisters, used to say, "An education is something no one can ever take away from you; once you've got it, it's yours for life." This was usually followed with an admonition that all the education in the world was worthless if it was not put to good use. "Never forget what was done in the past!" Aunt Belle also taught me. "That will remind you of what people are capable of doing to each other." She'd also say, "You can get angry; that's okay. But don't *just* get angry, do something about it." Aunt Belle was uncommonly blunt, and I loved that about her.

In the early '70s, I had the good fortune of meeting people who had good educations and were putting them, as Aunt Belle would say, to good use. These people were transplanted Northerners, mostly white and politically and socially very liberal. Among them was James Bopp, who directed the community center in Dulac for several years. This center served tribal and non-tribal families and provided a whole range of services—daycare, after-school programs, a medical clinic, adult education, youth programs, etc. When I became an office aide at the center, I got to know Jim. I was inspired by his ideas for strengthening community leadership among tribal members, particularly through the tribal council. He had thoughts on economic development, on forming associations with other tribes in the state and the region, on getting young kids to stay in school and even to think about college. Some of his ideas were terrific; others were probably unrealistic. Jim had his share of critics, but in the eyes of those who mattered to me—my family—he was seen as a voice for positive change. "He's not just another white man coming in here to show us how to live our lives," said Aunt Belle.

Jim had gone to Dartmouth College, a school originally founded to educate American Indians. I'd never heard of the place, but it sounded interesting. He encouraged me to consider applying there. Jim left Dulac before I finished high school, but he stayed in contact with me and had the college send me materials and application forms. He even sent me a check made payable to Dartmouth College for the application fee, along with a glowing letter of recommendation. Eventually I did apply to Dartmouth, but more out of a sense of gratitude to Jim than any genuine interest in the college.

Once I had applied to Dartmouth, I was bombarded with information about its various academic and support programs. I was particularly excited about the college's Native American Program, the rich diversity of tribal backgrounds represented by the students there, and the opportunity to pursue academic study in tribal history, culture, and literature. All these impressions were confirmed when I had the opportunity to visit the college as part of a recruitment program. By now I was also familiar with the general profile of Dartmouth's student body; I knew that in more ways than one, I would not be a typical Dartmouth student.

With a high class standing, a 3.99 grade point average, and strong recommendations from two high school teachers, I knew I could at least hope to gain admission. The only negative influence in all this came from one of the high school guidance counselors. "Perhaps," he advised me, "you should readjust your goals, your expectations of yourself." I interpreted him to mean that maybe Dartmouth wasn't the place for someone like me, from the South, from a poor background, from an Indian background. Perhaps he was simply being a realist and saying, "Don't get your hopes up too much." Maybe. The man may have been saying "Please be realistic, for your own good," but the attitude in which it was delivered said, "Who do you think you're kidding?" I took it as a challenge to prove him wrong.

I was accepted into Dartmouth and matriculated in the fall of 1976. The local paper actually ran a front-page story, "Duthu's Journey—from Dulac to Dartmouth." The hoopla was somewhat embarrassing but also gratifying. It provided me with fifteen minutes of fame, and it also informed the entire community that an Indian person from Dulac had done something just a little bit different.

My new success was difficult for my brother Chuck. We had graduated the same year, both with academic honors. He had gone to work on a tugboat running barges up the Mississippi River to Illinois; I was in school in Hanover, New Hampshire. We wrote frequently and shared all our new adventures. He'd always remember to list the friends who had asked about me. What I didn't know was that some of these same friends, and even some family members, had unintentionally bruised Chuck's feelings by inquiring only about me. They didn't intend to diminish what Chuck was doing, but the effect was exactly that. Yet Chuck made no mention of this in his letters.

I stayed in touch with other family members and many friends. I phoned home every weekend. Pe-pere always asked about the weather. When I saw my first snowfall on October 18, 1976, I phoned home immediately to tell him. Mom told me that after my calls, he made the rounds in the neighborhood to let the family know how I was doing. When asked exactly where it was I was attending college, he'd answer, "It's pretty far up the bayou." This was a humorous take on how most people give and understand directions in our community; everything is either "up the bayou" (north), "down the bayou" (south) or "across the bayou" (east or west). The bayou, at least until recently, was the main avenue of transportation and commerce, the lifeblood of the community.

Most of my friends at Dartmouth were Native American or black. I had spent the summer between high school and college in Dartmouth's "bridge program," which was designed for students who came from disadvantaged backgrounds and who might, in the judgment of admissions officers, benefit from a chance to sample Dartmouth's social and academic rigors before the fall term. All the students in this particular program were either black or Native American, and our friendships lasted throughout our time at Dartmouth. I also felt I had more in common with other students of color.

I credit these particular friendships and the support of the Native American Program with helping me survive my first year at Dartmouth. Without them, I would have had no outlet for expressing how I truly felt and would probably never have known that others felt exactly as I did. I could tell these friends that I felt intimidated in class and rarely spoke, fearing that I would say something stupid. The other students seemed so well-read. In an English class, it seemed that everyone had already read most of the books assigned for the class and had well-formed opinions about an author's major influences or another author's personal life. How did they know all this? Even when they were clearly wrong, according to the teacher, they sounded like they knew what they were talking about. I took an astronomy course fall term for a required science credit. It had the reputation as an easy class, but on the first day, the professor announced that the course would be different and would not likely live up to its reputation. On the second day, it seemed half the class had dropped. I should have taken the cue. The course was a monster, emphasizing aspects of physics that I had never studied before. I scraped by with a D, my lowest grade at Dartmouth. It was quite a blow to my ego and not the kind of grade I had hoped to send home in my first quarter. But I did get B's in my other courses, so all was not lost.

The social life at Dartmouth was more difficult to manage than the academics. First, Dartmouth seemed to have traditions for everything. One particularly unfortunate tradition was the use of Indians as the school's mascot. Explanations as to why Indians were chosen for this honor were as varied as the fall colors, though hardly as brilliant. To some, this tradition commemorated Dartmouth's historic commitment to the education of Indian students. As a freshman, I was often put on the spot by students who wanted my opinion on the Indian symbol—specifically, why I found it offensive. One student wanted to know if there was a portrayal of Indian people that would be acceptable to us. In other words, "How can I still play Indian and not hurt your feelings?"

Chants of "wah-hoo-wah," "Indians on the warpath," or "Dartmouth—Indians—scalp 'em!" were accompanied by face paint and mock Indian ceremonies at athletic events to capitalize on Dartmouth's so-called Indian heritage. All the while, we real Indians were assured by students and alumni that all their displays were done to honor Native people and that we shouldn't take offense at any of it.

I, and others, did take offense. Years before I came to Hanover, Indian students recruited by Dartmouth lodged protests against the college mascot. The college administration responded in 1972 by declaring that any continued use of the Indian symbol was "inconsistent" with Dartmouth's educational and moral aspirations. By the time I arrived, the Indian symbol had become the touchstone for general debate about institutional capitulation to minority student interests. "First, they took away our Indian symbol . . . then they created all those 'victim's studies' programs . . . now there's the gay problem." The sentiments were voiced by students, alumni, and even some faculty members. In this "us versus them" atmosphere, I was made to feel responsible for all of the divisiveness on campus because I was part of the Native American population that had "started the trouble."

The tradition of wealth at Dartmouth also had an impact on me. Many of my classmates came from some of America's, and the world's, wealthiest families. In itself, this was not a problem, but it did accentuate the differences between me and them. These kids used "vacation" as a verb. "We vacation in the Swiss Alps," they would say, and sometimes the differences between our lives were so vast the wealthy kids found them funny. And many times, so did I. The guy across the hall from me couldn't remember how many bathrooms were in his Tudor-style Scarsdale home. When he learned that our family had installed indoor plumbing facilities, complete with one working toilet, during my junior year in high school, he couldn't get over it. "Hey," he would say introducing me to his friends, "this is Bruce. Did you know that his family didn't have indoor plumbing until he was in high school?"

In contrast to feeling so apart from traditional Dartmouth, I felt a special closeness to nontraditional students—mostly Indian or black—with whom I forged tight bonds. They never asked about symbols or for help in de-mythologizing U.S.-Indian history. I was particularly comfortable at the Native American House, a small building that housed a few Indian students and served as a cultural center. It was an oasis on campus, where I could refresh my spirit, my mental health, my sense of humor. A couple of Native American teachers also encouraged and supported me. Professor Michael Dorris (Modoc), now a well-known novelist, headed the Native American studies program and was mentor, friend, and advocate to many of us. Professor Inez Talamantez (Mescalero Apache) taught a course in oral traditions my freshman year that allowed me to celebrate and share my culture with other students in the classroom.

My freshman winter term in 1977 was difficult. The Christmas break had allowed me to return to Louisiana to be with family and friends. That was alternately fun and scary. My close friends were now talking about work on the oil rigs or on boats. They had nice new cars and fairly serious girlfriends. I had no job, no car, and no girlfriend; I had a D in astronomy, had discovered how much I didn't know about Milton and Shakespeare, and had warred over symbols. High school was ancient history, and these guys were making a living. My decision to go one way while the others went another began to seem illogical. I was odd man out, and I didn't like it. Other classmates had gone on to college, but neither my closest friends nor Chuck had, and I wanted desperately to fit in. My stories of all-nighters, endless reading, and campus crises didn't compare with theirs about life out on the Gulf of Mexico or the Mississippi River. Their work was real work; it seemed like I was wasting time in la-la land.

Returning to Dartmouth—a world very different from the one I had just left—complicated things even more. I felt caught somewhere in between. I again struggled with a supposedly easy course, Psychology 1. I drew an even tighter web around the Native American House, where I spent more time than in my own dorm. I must have been scared. Feeling and thinking that I belonged nowhere, I called home, hoping that someone—Mom, my brother, or Pe-pere—would say, "come home." I told my sad tale to each of them, but it was Pe-pere who offered the most succinct, and the most unnerving, advice: "If it gets too rough," he told me, "you'll know what to do."

That's exactly what I didn't want to hear. It already felt too rough and I didn't know what to do. Moreover, I didn't want the responsibility of figuring it out. I wanted an easy, quick, painless order to return home, where all would be forgotten, even if it meant my disparaging high school counselor would have the last laugh. I stayed up all night trying to decipher Pe-pere's message. A man of few words, he was as difficult to figure out as my professors.

I concluded, somehow, that Pe-pere's message was actually very simple: Whether I stayed or returned was up to me. It wasn't a matter of succeeding or failing, but of assuming responsibility for my decisions. I chose to stay. My "journey," as the local paper in Houma had called it, was really beginning; now I was in charge.

Soon after, in August 1977, Hilde Ojibway came to Hanover to visit her sister Therese, one of my best friends. I knew from Therese that Hilde was the fifth child of eleven and that their father was an enrolled member of the Sault Sainte Marie Band of Chippewa Indians. Like me, she had been raised Catholic, but no longer practiced.

An undergraduate at Michigan State University, Hilde was returning to the United States from a language program in Spain. The trip to Europe, I learned later, was a declaration of independence for her, an opportunity to do something just for herself. Since I was leaving for Europe myself in a few weeks, I was a good audience for her stories from overseas, and by the end of her one week in Hanover, we loved each other. I even suggested marriage. But I was only eighteen, Hilde was twenty, and we had no idea if and when we'd ever see each other again. I spent the next six months in Europe, while Hilde continued to study and work in Lansing, Michigan. We wrote constantly and ignored all the well-intentioned advice from friends and family to get on with our lives. When we began making plans for a rendezvous in London, both family and friends felt we had gone off the deep end. But it happened. Hilde met me in London and we traveled throughout Europe. We were engaged in Paris, in the spring, in front of the Arc de Triomphe.

Eventually, we decided that the best and only way for us to finish college was to do it as a married couple. We married in March 1979 during Hilde's spring break. I worked in Lansing as a high school counselor to American Indian students while Hilde completed her studies at MSU. In the summer, we returned to Hanover and switched roles; I resumed the student life while Hilde worked in the area as a community organizer.

Neither of us knew what would happen after that. I had always felt that I wanted to return to Louisiana in some position of authority. I had once seriously considered the priesthood and had corresponded with the local Louisiana bishop while I was in Hanover. My motivations were hardly heavenly ones; priests and the church were powerful figures in my community, and several promoted social change. It was a Louisiana Catholic priest who had helped our tribal leaders pressure the local school board into opening the all-Indian school in Dulac. But a friend, who was a priest in Hanover, pointed out the limitations of pursuing the priesthood as a means of achieving my goal, and by the time I met Hilde, I had abandoned that idea. The story I usually tell is that love forced me to choose between God and the person I loved. It's not true, but even so, I'm glad I finished college with a degree in religion. Just in case.

I half-jokingly told Hilde that when she married me, she married Louisiana. I don't think I ever mentioned attending law school to her, because the thought never seriously entered my mind. Hilde recalls first hearing about law school at a fancy dinner party for

Dartmouth alumni being feted by the college as part of the fundraising seduction process. Selected undergraduates were invited to these events to share their observations about current life at Dartmouth to help remind the alums of their own glory years. We sat at a table with several alumni, most of whom seemed to be lawyers or the spouses of lawyers. The inevitable question for graduating seniors came my way: "Bruce, my good man—what will *you* be doing after Dartmouth?" "I'll be going to law school," I said without a moment's hesitation. The approving smiles with some audible "ah's" mixed in for effect told me I had answered appropriately. Only Hilde wasn't smiling. She was too busy dislodging her spoon from her throat. The ride back to our married student apartment was very quiet. "So," Hilde said later, "if we had been sitting at the next table, with all the doctors, you'd be considering medical school?" Perhaps.

But getting into law school wasn't a sure thing. My grade point average was a B, but my LSAT scores were barely average. An admissions officer at Loyola University's law school in New Orleans told me my application was not promising. But I did get accepted there and at Louisiana State University's law center. Tulane waitlisted me and eventually denied me admission. I decided to attend Loyola, in part because living in New Orleans seemed attractive at the time. And because Loyola was run by Jesuits.

Hilde got a job at Loyola, which meant we were able to spend a good deal of time together. Every few weekends, we stole away to visit with my family in Dulac. Pe-pere died in 1979. My loss was doubly painful because he had been the only father I ever knew. The house was so different without him. Chuck married and moved to Houma, where his wife Sandra bore the first of their three sons. With many relatives living nearby, Mom wasn't totally alone. On Sunday mornings, Hilde slept in while Mom and I lost ourselves in stories. We talked mostly about family, about people getting married or divorced, about babies being born, and about older people dying. We talked about the community, about how things were changing so fast. Families didn't seem as close anymore; more people were moving away. There were still plenty of stories about discrimination; the old hatred was barely covered by a mask of civility.

In the early '80s, the petroleum industry suffered a downturn, which meant people in southern Louisiana had problems finding and keeping jobs. Many close friends from high school were being partly or wholly laid off. Hard times hit many of the families back in Dulac and Houma, and Hilde and I wished so often we could help, but we were still living on student loans, grants, and small incomes. Talking about law school made me uncomfortable, because it seemed like an indulgence in light of the hardships other family members were experiencing. I think now my discomfort wasn't necessary. When I graduated from law school, with honors, literally hundreds of family and friends showed up at my graduation party in Dulac. It was a community celebration. Family members had cooked and baked all kinds of food. Old friends of mine provided music. The most memorable moment came when an Indian man in his late thirties shook my hand and, with tears in his eyes, told me how proud he was. I cried, too, knowing how my opportunities had come through the coincidence of time and history. What might have been for all those like this generous man, I can scarcely imagine.

Also on hand was Tom Foutz, a Tulane Law School graduate who had been a mentor to me and one of my best friends during my time in law school. I had had the chance to work as a summer law clerk in Tom's firm, and we spent hours talking about some of his cases, about the law and legal strategies. It was a free class in trial practice, but Tom's mentoring went beyond academics and trial practice. After my first year, I called Tom for advice on how to interview for summer clerkships. He came over, and at some point during the evening he asked what I planned to wear. I hadn't given it much thought. I owned only two suits, the one I got married in and an old polyester number from college days. Tom politely suggested that I consider upgrading and updating my wardrobe, but given the late hour, and the interview in the morning, he let me borrow some of his clothes. The next morning, I walked into my interview looking quite lawyerly. It must have helped, because I got the job.

After I graduated, my first job was in downtown New Orleans with a firm that defended corporations, mostly insurance companies. Its lawsuits involved medical malpractice, admiralty, and products liability, among others. I hadn't thought I would be doing defense work. I had somehow assumed I'd be representing injured workers, the "little guys." In fact, my clerking experience had been with firms doing just that, but these firms were not offering jobs when I graduated. Despite not being on the side I would have preferred, I liked this firm, which took training and supporting new associates seriously. The salary was nice and grew quickly. Hilde and I could now afford to splurge a little.

We continued making periodic trips to Dulac, but now the visits were different. Now that I had a law degree, lots of people, mostly family, had legal problems to talk about. My mom usually got the calls: "When is Bruce coming down the bayou? Well, when he comes, tell him I need to talk to him about a case." The calls annoyed my mom. It bothered her that so many people expected me to provide them with free legal help. The time spent counseling people about their legal issues was also time spent away from her. Given the nature of my firm's practice, I couldn't take many cases anyway and referred most people to other lawyers. Some folks felt a little betrayed when I tried to explain why I couldn't take their cases. How, they thought, could there be a potential conflict of interest when we were all from the same community?

The most surprising call came from my father. He came to our firm's offices in New Orleans, like a regular client. I introduced him to my boss and showed him around the place. Except for Christmas and Easter and an occasional birthday, Chuck and I had not had much contact with our father after the divorce. He continued to live in Dulac, remarried, and had another son. His wife was always kind and generous to us—more comfortable with us during our short visits than he was. I suppose I understand why, since we were also pretty uncomfortable. He had attended our high school graduation and my law school graduation, and now here he was seeking my legal help. Only later did I realize how hard this must have been for him. I knew what a proud man he was. Despite our lack of intimate knowledge about each other, he came to me. I was sad that I couldn't do very much to help him on this occasion, but things did eventually work out for him.

By the summer of 1986, Hilde had completed a master's degree in public administration and was directing a large, private nonprofit agency serving mildly retarded adults. I switched to a law firm representing plaintiffs, doing the kind of law I'd always hoped to do. We had finalized the adoption of our six-year-old niece, Lisa, and Hilde was pregnant with our second child, expected in October. Neither of us intended to make any moves professionally or geographically.

We had maintained ties to Dartmouth through the Native American Program's Visiting Committee. As a member, I returned to Hanover twice a year to evaluate and make recommendations to the college regarding Native American student support services. I learned on one of those visits that the current director of the NAP was stepping down to pursue his own legal education. When I had expressed interest in the position, the dean of the college had not dismissed the suggestion out of hand. Hilde and I discussed my applying for the position. I had no formal training in student counseling or college administration, but I applied for the job. I had a background like that of many of today's Native American students, and I knew personally how difficult Dartmouth could be. I could also attest to the value of a Dartmouth education. I convinced myself and Hilde that this was a sound career move. My law partners advised otherwise, and so did some family members. Wasn't this a waste of all those years of legal training and experience?

But I needed to make my own personal contribution to the program that had supported me and had helped open so many doors. I never doubted that I had something of value to offer to-day's Native students, but I did worry that I might, indeed, be throwing away my legal training and experience. The prospect of developing and teaching a course in Native American law was an added incentive, but I was going to be paid much less to be an administrator than I was earning as an attorney.

Then an older gentleman in our firm, who had had a successful career as a trial attorney, warned me that his success had come at a stiff price. Like so many lawyers we both knew, he had been consumed by his practice and its material rewards. His family life had suffered. His marriage had broken up, and a teenage daughter had been tragically killed in an auto accident. He told me how he had lost the chance to spend time with his family, how he could not turn back the clock and get to know the daughter who was now gone from this world. It had to do with choices, he said. "If I had your youth and your choices, the answer would be very clear." The law degree, he reminded me, would always be mine. No one could take that away. But I wouldn't always have these choices. There was a familiar ring to this. Some of Aunt Belle's pragmatism and Pe-pere's wisdom was echoing.

I was offered the Dartmouth job and took it. Hilde, Lisa, and I established our new home in White River Junction, Vermont, about five minutes from the campus. Our son Joseph was born two months later. One of the hardest things about leaving Louisiana this time was knowing that our children would not grow up with family nearby. Long-distance phone calls, an occasional visit, and exchanged photos would be the primary ties to our home. But the decision felt right, difficult as it was.

I had no particular mission or agenda when I became director of Dartmouth's Native American Program. I knew that one-on-one work with students was indispensable, but beyond that, I devoted my attention to programs to educate the larger community about the Native student population. I hoped that greater understanding might lead to greater sensitivity. It was frustrating to watch students fight the same battles I had fought as a student, among them, still, the symbol issue. The greatest joys were to see students setting and attaining high goals for themselves and being happy being Indian. I rekindled many friendships with Native alumni now living and working throughout the country, mostly in service to their own or another tribal community.

I am still very close to my family, despite the distance. My mother visits us every year, and we've been to Louisiana a few times as a family. Once my brother visited, shortly after Christmas. Several feet of snow fell just before he arrived, and he felt he had stepped into a winter wonderland. He and I drove up to Montreal to visit a good friend of mine, another of the many good voices who have come into my life. Our time together gave us the opportunity, at last, to talk as men, as husbands, as fathers, and as brothers. We saw that though we had taken different directions, we still shared so much—respect for one another and love.

In 1991, I left Dartmouth to join the law faculty at Vermont Law School in South Royalton, Vermont. I teach first-year law courses in torts and criminal law and an upper level seminar in federal Indian law. I also teach federal Indian law at Dartmouth as a visiting professor in Native American studies. Hilde directs a large, nonprofit agency in New Hampshire. We have a third child, a daughter named Alanna, born in January 1993.

When I think of my children and my brother's children, I think of the wonderful stories of our youth—the good ol' days when times were bad. I hope the children will all hear these stories. And I hope they will also have the good voices to teach and guide them. And I hope they will listen.

N. Bruce Duthu is enrolled with the United Houma Nation of Louisiana. He was born in Houma, Louisiana, and raised in Dulac, one of the oldest Houma Indian settlements in southeastern Louisiana. He attended an all-Indian elementary school until 1969, when local schools were integrated. After graduating fourth in a high school class of several hundred, Bruce entered Dartmouth College, graduating in 1980 with a degree in religion and Native American studies. He received a law degree from Loyola University in New Orleans and was in private practice for several years before returning to Dartmouth to direct the Native American Program. Now a tenured faculty member at Vermont Law School, Bruce specializes in federal Indian law, a course he also teaches annually at Dartmouth. He is married to Hilde Ojibway. The couple lives in Vermont with their three children.

Andrew Garrod is associate professor of education and chair of the department at Dartmouth College, where he teaches courses in adolescence, moral development, and educational psychology. As an assistant professor at the University of Victoria, he worked in a teacher preparation program for Gitksan and Carrier Natives in northern British Columbia, and at Dartmouth he acts as an academic advisor to Native American freshmen. His recent publications include a casebook, *Adolescent Portraits: Identity, Relationships, and Challenges* (co-edited with Lisa Smulyan, Sally Powers, and Robert Kilkenny), a book, *Preparing for Citizenship: Teaching Youth to Live Democratically* (written with Ralph Mosher and Robert A. Kenny), and the edited volume *Approaches to Moral Development: New Research and Emerging Themes*. For the last two years, he has spent time conducting moral development research in India, the country of his birth. In 1991, he was awarded Dartmouth College's Distinguished Teaching Award.

Colleen Larimore is a 1985 graduate of Dartmouth College, where she majored in sociology, and a 1990 graduate of Harvard's Graduate School of Education, where she received a master's degree in administration, policy, and social planning. Ms. Larimore is the youngest of her family's four college graduates, and is of mixed Comanche and Japanese descent. She has held several positions in higher education administration, including assistant director of undergraduate admissions at Dartmouth College, director of Dartmouth's Native American Program, and assistant director of graduate studies at Stanford University's School of Humanities and Sciences, where her major responsibility was increasing the presence of minority graduate students at the university.

She is at present a doctoral student in sociology at the University of California at Berkeley. Her current research focuses on urban Indian elementary school students, cultural styles of learning, and children's adaptability and resistance to varying instructional styles and learning environments.

Louise Erdrich was born in 1954 and grew up in Wahpeton, North Dakota. She is the oldest of seven children, and two of her sisters, Heid Erdrich and Angela Erdrich, are fellow alumnae of Dartmouth College. Louise's mother, Rita Gourneau Erdrich, Turtle Mountain Ojibwa, encouraged her pursuit of an education outside of the Midwest, and her father, Ralph Erdrich, wrote to her every week of the four years she was in college.

In 1981, she married Professor Michael Dorris, director of Native American Studies at Dartmouth College, and started to write in earnest. She finished *Jacklight* (poems), *Love Medicine* (winner of the National Book Critics Circle

Award), *Beet Queen*, and *Tracks*, both *New York Times* best sellers, and with Michael Dorris, *The Crown of Columbus*. She has most recently published the novels *Bingo Palace* and *Tales of Burning Love*, as well as a children's book, *Grandmother's Pigeon*. Her next book, *Gakahbekong*, will appear in 1997.

23   Bill Bray, Class of 1989. Creek/Choctaw. Photo by Sandra Heath.

43   Davina Ruth Begaye Two Bears, Class of 1990. Navajo.
        Photo by Dawn Kish.

64   Ricardo Worl, Class of 1984. Tlingit. Photo by L. Melissa Worl.

80   Gemma Lockhart, Class of 1979. Rosebud Sioux.
        Photo by Theodore Brockish.

93   Nicole Adams, Class of 1995. Colville.
        Photo by Expressly Portraits, Foster City, Calif.

115 Elizabeth Carey, Class of 1993. Hawaiian. She is pictured with her
        mother, Lehua Carey, and her grandmother, Christine Canda. Photo
        by Linda M. F. Welch.

136 Robert Bennett, Class of 1994. Lakota Sioux.
        Photo by Robin Conn/ *The Huntsville Times*.

154 Marianne Chamberlain, Class of 1994. Assiniboin. She is pictured with
        her sister, Ashlee R. Packineau. Photo by Linda M. F. Welch.

171 Arvo Quoetone Mikkanen, Class of 1983. Kiowa/Comanche.
        Photo by Jerry Stewart.

189 Siobhan Wescott, Class of 1989. Athabascan. She is shown receiving her
        degree from President James O. Freedman. Photo courtesy of Special
        Collections, Dartmouth College Archives/Stuart Bratesman.

200 Vivian Johnson, Class of 1986. Yup'ik Eskimo.
        Photo copyright Michael Faubion. Used by permission.

212 Lori Arviso Alvord, Class of 1979. Navajo.
        Photo © Hulleah J. Tsinhnahjinnie.

230 N. Bruce Duthu, Class of 1980. Houma.
        Photo copyright 1996 by Charlton A. Duthu.